WITH
GOD
IN
AMERICA

Other Books by Walter J. Ciszek, S.J.

With God in Russia

He Leadeth Me

WITH

GOD

IN

AMERICA

the SPIRITUAL LEGACY of an
UNLIKELY JESUIT

WALTER J. CISZEK, S.J.

Compiled and edited by
John M. DeJak and Marc Lindeijer, S.J.

LOYOLA PRESS.
A JESUIT MINISTRY
Chicago

LOYOLA PRESS.
A JESUIT MINISTRY

3441 N. Ashland Avenue
Chicago, Illinois 60657
(800) 621-1008
www.loyolapress.com

Chapter 1, "Jesuit Returns from Exile behind Iron Curtain," first appeared in English as an article in *Catholic Light*. Bill Genello, editor of *Catholic Light*, gave permission to reprint the interview in this book.

Chapter 3, "Return from Russia," reprinted from *America* (March 28, 1964) with permission of America Press, Inc., 1964. All rights reserved. For subscription information, call 1-800-627-9533, or visit www.americamagazine.org

Chapter 32, "Father Ciszek Dies—Russian Missionary," was published in *National Jesuit News* (March 1985). Reprinted with permission.

Cover art credit: kapitanyphotos/iStock/ThinkStock, prapann/iStock/ThinkStock, davidcreacion/iStock/ThinkStock
Back cover author photo, Father Walter Ciszek Prayer League.

ISBN-13: 978-0-8294-4454-4
ISBN-10: 0-8294-4454-8
Library of Congress Control Number: 2016943246

Printed in the United States of America.
    17 18 19 20 21 22 Versa 10 9 8 7 6 5 4 3 2

Contents

Foreword

At the beginning of the gripping account of his years in Soviet captivity, *With God in Russia*, Fr. Walter Ciszek notes that one of the most common questions he received after returning to the United States was, "How did you survive?" His answer, which is so evident throughout his memoir of some very difficult years, is that Divine Providence—the working of God in his life—is the only explanation.

This new collection of Fr. Ciszek's writings, drawn from roughly the last twenty years of his life after he returned from Russia, demonstrates just as clearly his reliance on God in all circumstances. When I first read *With God in Russia*, I was moved by Fr. Ciszek's deep faith and his ability to find ways to live out his priestly vocation while in Soviet prison camps. Not long after that, he published a second book, *He Leadeth Me*, which contained additional reflections on his imprisonment with an emphasis on the spiritual lessons he had learned and greatly wished to share with others. You see, Fr. Ciszek was convinced that God was working through all the events in his life, that God had brought him safely home from the prison camps, and now it was his responsibility to share with others the great lesson he had learned of relying on Divine Providence. It was a message he never tired of preaching.

It is precisely this laser-like focus on the importance of trusting in God's will for us that comes across so powerfully in this collection of writings. After his return to the United States, Fr. Ciszek was tireless in exercising his priestly ministry—whether offering Mass, hearing confessions, spending time teaching God's Word in Sacred Scripture to others, giving retreats to Jesuit novices, or offering counsel and support to countless people with whom he crossed paths. Fr. Ciszek knew that God loved him and was leading his life, and he wanted others to see how God was working in their lives as well.

I am pleased that this collection of retreat talks, personal correspondences, and spiritual conferences is available, and am certain it will provide spiritual enrichment to its readers—thus continuing the impact of Fr. Ciszek's ministry. His deep love of Scripture, his fidelity to the Church, and his profound trust in God's loving plan are lessons from Fr. Ciszek's life that I hope we all take to heart.

June 21, 2016
Timothy Cardinal Dolan
Archbishop of New York

Editors' Note

When Walter Ciszek came back from Russia in 1963, he had not spoken English for twenty-five years, nor had he much experience in writing. The letters, conferences, reflections, and other writings published here have been carefully edited, both preserving as much as possible Father Ciszek's unique style and vocabulary, and correcting grammar and spelling where necessary. In those instances when the original wording made it difficult to discern what Fr. Ciszek meant to say, the editors have made slight alterations in an attempt to make that meaning clearer—always being careful, however, not to take too many liberties with the original text. Square brackets indicate those passages where three or more words were deleted or added.

Part One

THE PRISONER COMES HOME

1

"Jesuit Returns from Exile behind Iron Curtain"

On[1] October 2, [1963] a sleek airliner touched down its landing gear at Idlewild Airport. Among its passengers was one who was to re-discover America on this prophetic day—Rev. Walter J. Ciszek, S.J., released after 23 years in Soviet prison camps in Moscow and Siberia.

The scene was quite different from the one he remembered of his native land, which he had left so many years ago as a young priest. After disembarking from the plane he was greeted by scores of newsmen who later reported that he had been away for so long that he had forgotten how to speak his native tongue. Actually, he was so choked up with emotion that he could find no words to express himself. On the taxi ride from the airport, the emotional block was shattered, and he carried on an animated conversation, punctuated by sobs, with his two sisters, Mother M. Evangeline, O.S.F., stationed at Mount Alvernia, Reading, and Mrs. Helen Gearhart, Washington, D.C., a registered nurse.

After a few stopovers, Father Ciszek, accompanied by a Jesuit confrere, Rev. Edward W. McCawley, professor at Gonzaga High School in Washington, D.C., arrived [on October 18] in his home town, Shenandoah, where he was accorded a hero's welcome. I had visited the town the day before his arrival to meet his family and was privileged to read his correspondence with them. [. . .]

The real story of his life in Russia is still secret, still hidden in his heart and mind—to reveal it would be damaging to others still held prisoners in the U.S.S.R. Publicity to him has become an irritant. "The veiling," he says, "destroys the spiritual value of the suffering." Major publishing firms have set before him lucrative prospects. But for the present he contemplates no published memoirs. He says, "I was born poor, I am poor by vocation, and have been happy till now. Why should I seek any other reward than the 'Providence of God,' Who has been so good to me?"

Father Ciszek was born 53 years ago in the mining community of Shenandoah, the seventh of thirteen children. His family, of Polish origin, were poor but deeply religious. Still living are three brothers and six sisters, including two who are serving as nuns in the Bernardine Order. His family best remembers him for his joviality and his sturdy physical stamina. After high school, he entered St. Mary's Seminary at Orchard Lake, Mich., where after several years he joined the Society of Jesus and began his novitiate in the Maryland province. "The two years at the novitiate," Father Walter says, "provided the cornerstone for my entire spiritual formation." A few days after his return from Russia, he was asked by the Master of Novices at the Wernersville novitiate to address the students, and it was in this lecture that he stressed the spiritual value of this important era in a seminarian's life. In the tundra when he felt he couldn't stand anymore; when the vast solitude of ice and snow assailed his soul and body, his memories of the novitiate were enough to give him the spiritual vigor, enthusiasm, and confidence to survive these ordeals.

After completing the novitiate, [Walter] answered an appeal from his superiors to dedicate his life to serving the eastern Church. He and a few other select volunteers were chosen. During his years in Rome [1934–1938] he became fluent in Italian, which he still speaks, Polish, German, French, and Russian. "One thing that always remained with me," he says, "that I could never forget were the languages." Ordained in 1937, he left the next year for Poland, where he was to become the pastor of a Polish parish near the Russian border—the last step on a long exile from the United States.

An article in the Jesuit *Mission* magazine written by Father McFarlane, S.J., (March 1949) describes events after the assignment of Father Ciszek to Poland. After his ordination, Father Ciszek was sent to a little Polish city near the Russian border, Father McFarlane reports. "I was just a young seminarian returning from Rome to America. The rector of my house permitted me to send one-half of the money sent to me to Father Ciszek. He used it to buy milk for the children and meat for the Sisters, commodities that for them were in short supply. One day, I received no letter from Father Walter. The Russians had entered the city and the missionaries were swallowed up. There were rumors that he had been sent to work in a factory in Moscow along with other priests. This was all the news we had on the matter until a few years later," writes Father McFarlane, "when some refugees brought to our attention some bits of information. One of them brought us the news that one priest was buried in a cave along with hundreds of refugees. The coincidence seemed to indicate that Father Walter was that priest who died with his flock."

The article concludes: "An American priest, completely innocent, died from hunger and suffering, unknown, unwanted and dishonoured under the open skies." Thus from 1940 to 1950, nothing was heard from Father Ciszek. He was presumed dead by his superiors, who sent letters to Jesuit communities to offer funeral Masses for his soul. His name was included on the roster of the dead. From what we could learn from Father Ciszek after the Russian occupation, his parishioners were put on trains and sent to labor camps in the interior. In order to remain with his flock, he offered himself voluntarily as a worker in order to share the lot of these poor unfortunate Poles, many of whom were to die on the squalid Russian tundra.

For many months [March 1940—June 1941] Father Walter worked at [Teplaya Gora and] Chusovoy in the Ural range where he could at least, once in a while, care for the spiritual welfare of his people and he could also, after taking many precautions, celebrate Mass. He managed to hear confessions and to celebrate Mass clandestinely. [For] a chalice he used a common metal drinking cup, and the wine was extracted by himself from grapes. [In August 1941 he was imprisoned in the Lubianka prison in Moscow and five years later, in June 1946 sent to the labor camps in Siberia.] The life was hard and bitter, and only after Stalin's death [on March 5, 1953] did he come to know better conditions.

In 1955, the term of his penalty expired, and the most terrible period of the Jesuit's life began—a period he doesn't like to discuss. Only his superiors know at least in part the secrets of Father Ciszek and so too does Atty. General Robert Kennedy, with whom he had a long conversation. Rumors and conjectures are rife in this regard, one more dramatic than the other. The true story will be revealed in time. It is enough for us to know that from my observations which were confirmed by Father McCawley and that is—the more difficult the trial, the stronger was the faith of the martyr.

During the five years in which he lived in solitary confinement without books, newspapers, or news of any sort, he told me that the five fingers of his hand were enough to say the rosary and preserve his faith. To this day he looks back on that period with true Christian humility, without bitterness or rancor. "The Russian people around me were good," he says. After the end of his term, Father Ciszek had some degree of liberty but was not entirely rehabilitated. He went to live [in Norilsk, till April 1958, and then] in Krasnoyarsk in Siberia. He asked on several occasions to be repatriated to the U.S. but was rejected each time. In the meantime, whenever possible he tried to carry on his spiritual duties. Next [in July 1958] he was sent to Abakan where he earned his living as a mechanic and locksmith.

In 1955, he resumed correspondence with his family. His first letter was addressed to his sister Mrs. Helen Gearhart in Washington. He could write but three letters a year, and these contained little of news value because of the fear of censorship. However, we can read between the lines. The letters reveal his spiritual vigor and his humanity. One thing is clear; the many years of martyrdom did not leave him a living relic. The virile fibre is still intact, even stronger, and his spirit remarkably serene. [. . .]

For reading, Father Ciszek could peruse *Pravda*, *Izvestia*, and some of the Communist magazines. Now at least he could receive some news of the free world though in a filtered version. He was aware of the election of the new pontiff, Pope John, but not about the visit of Khrushchev's son-in-law to the Vatican. The letters from his relatives were mostly about family affairs, in order not to arouse the suspicion of the authorities. In some letters home, he asked for medicines, but his family was afraid to send anything for fear that they would fall into other hands.

In the meantime, his relatives in the U.S. started to pressure the State Department to obtain his release. The results of these efforts reached a culmination in the decision of Mrs. Gearhart and Sister Evangeline, O.S.F., mother provincial of the Bernardines, to visit Moscow in order to meet their brother. The Sister was to travel in civilian clothes after receiving a visa from the Russian Embassy. Father Walter was anxiously awaiting his transfer to Moscow after so many interminable years to meet his two dearest sisters. Suddenly the State Department and Moscow suspended the proceedings. Father Walter was stunned. But his family had the definite impression that something good was in the stars.

Two weeks before his liberation, the secret police came to Abakan in Outer Mongolia to visit him. For three days he was subjected to intensive interrogation. Though he did not reveal the nature of the questioning, it is enough to say that he feared a new trial, perhaps worse than the previous one in which he was sentenced to 15 years in prison and eight in exile. After the inquisition, they ordered him to pack and they bundled him into a plane to Moscow. During which time he did nothing but pray and confide his trust in God.

Finally someone came to pick him up, and he was taken to the airport and a waiting plane. Here he was awaited by three officials, who gave him a booklet and told him to sign it. Father Ciszek asked, "What's this all about?" They replied: "This is your passport, Father, you are an American citizen—sign." Overjoyed, the jovial Jesuit took three rubles out of his pocket and said to the American and Russians surrounding him, "Let's celebrate. Come over to the bar and I'll buy you a tea! It's the best I can do."

Shortly thereafter, he winged away from Russia aboard a BOAC plane headed for the United States. He returned without bitterness and with no pride in the fact that he had been a champion of the faith, a defender of the Church, and an invulnerable hero. He took with him only a lot of charity and affection for the Russian people and the memories of a long exile. We have said before that he re-discovered America on Columbus Day, but the comparison may be more rhetorical than factual in that his return coincided with the feast of the Maternity of the Blessed Virgin Mary—a minor thing for the secular reader—but for Father Ciszek it was a moving moment. He had prayed to the Virgin Mary for 23 years with his ten-finger rosary to release him from his Calvary.

He made an interesting observation that in all of Russia bibles are in short supply. He had searched for many years to find one. One day an American in a cultural exchange program came to the city where he was living and on visiting the local library noted that they had no copies of the bible and complained. Almost in embarrassment, the Russian authorities hastily gave the order for the printing of 60,000 copies of the New Testament, which were sold out in a few days. Father Ciszek purchased one and read it with the thirst of a man approaching an oasis after many years in a desert.

As he prepared for a spiritual retreat, he informed me that "I need it, to meditate upon myself and the wonder that God had worked on me. And to thank all those through prayer who sustained me with their own petitions to heaven. In the whole adventure," he said, "I am only an insignificant part, important only because behind me there was an array of praying saints."

This is the story of Father Ciszek, who saw the sunset of Stalin. Perhaps he will remain to us as the living symbol of a man who stood steadfast before tyrants who attempted to extinguish the flame of his faith, which instead grew to heroic proportions and ultimately triumphed.

2

The Transition Home

"One doesn't often have the opportunity to be there when a man comes back from the dead."[2] That was the remarkable, shared feeling of Father Walter Ciszek's Jesuit confreres and family on October 12, 1963, as he returned from twenty-three years of captivity in the Soviet Union. One can only imagine what he felt at that moment of return, having been away so long, having endured so much suffering, and having witnessed so much pain. He was returning from the mission for which he had prayed and prepared from his earliest days in the Society of Jesus: to minister to the suffering people of the Soviet Union. The Russian people he had encountered there were his little flock. Now he had been taken from them, and, although he was once again free, a year after his return, Ciszek sadly observed:

> Now that I have returned to America, I can no longer work even among those few. Yet I continue to work and pray and live for them daily. Here, among friends and fellow priests and religious, near again to my family, in a certain sense I am still lonely—for I know the needs of "my people" in Siberia, the work I was not allowed to do. It is good to be "home" again, but in my heart there is still an ache.[3]

Father Walter's own words were corroborated by the observations of many others who became aware of his first impressions and experiences following his return to the United States. One of Walter Ciszek's friends who had an intimate understanding of his sufferings was Dr. Marvin Makinen, who returned from Russia on the same flight as Father Ciszek. Makinen, then a twenty-four-year-old student, had been imprisoned in Soviet labor camps for two years prior to his release back to the United States. He and Father Ciszek first met at the airport in Moscow in October 1963. They became friends from that very moment until Father Ciszek's death in 1984. Reflecting upon his friendship with Father Walter many years later, Dr. Makinen remarked, "In my limited experience of the world, and its human inhabitants, he was the closest of anyone I knew who could be considered a saint."[4]

Dr. Makinen recounts his own experience of having been freed from the Soviet Union and returning to the United States with Father Walter in October 1963. It is a small but important part of the story of Walter Ciszek told here for the first time:

> I was brought to the Moscow airport by automobile. Because the automobile was parked adjacent to another car, I could see that there was a short man in the back seat of the car. To me he did not seem Russian, and it turned out to be Father Ciszek. At some point we were both taken into the terminal building and brought to a place where we sat at a table in the departure lounge. There were representatives of the American Embassy and of the Soviet Ministry of Foreign Affairs accompanying us.
>
> This was the first time I was introduced to Father Ciszek. I had not known of him prior to that time. (Father Ciszek did tell me at a later time that when he saw me from the other car, he knew I was an American.) The officials told us that we were being sent home. They did not state specifically that we were being traded for Soviet spies, but we were told that the agreement was that we were not to speak to anyone *en route* about what was happening. (I mention this because of a humorous incident that later came up.)
>
> Our first flight was on British European Airlines from Moscow to London. Because of our appearance and our being placed in the rear of the plane, some people were (I would say) suspicious of who we might be. Once on the plane, I noticed that there was a person who came and tried to sit near us to catch any conversation. I'm not sure whether he may have been a journalist—journalists are always out with their ears to hear and see what's going on.
>
> Father Ciszek and I just spoke to each other in rather low tones. We exchanged experiences of where we had been and what prisons we had been in. One thing that struck me immediately about Father Ciszek was that it was obvious that he was a good person. I never heard him speak badly of anyone, even in talking about his experiences. And as far as I recall, he was in a labor camp where a mutiny by prisoners had taken place, indicative of how wretched conditions must have been. He was lucky to have come out of that alive because the Soviet way of handling those situations was just to execute the leaders and many of the prisoners. Control in the Soviet Union was through fear—that was the basis for controlling the whole society. But Ciszek didn't complain, he didn't criticize, he didn't swear about them; he just stated

matter-of-factly how things were and what he did in response. Consequently, it was a very even-tempered discussion at the time.

Having spent twenty-three years in exile and in prison—surviving the austere conditions of Soviet society and Norilsk, a city above the Arctic Circle—Father Ciszek was very taken with the luxury of the aircraft. The quality of the covers of the chairs on the airplane and the seats fascinated him. Later on that flight, we were brought a meal. I saw it as a reasonable kind of airplane meal at the time. Having been out of society for only slightly more than two and a half years, I thought it was an appropriate meal that one would expect on a plane, but nothing really special. Father Ciszek, on the other hand, was very much taken by it. After he had finished it, he said, "This is much better than I would have expected," or something to that effect.

When we arrived in London, we were kept isolated from other travelers. A representative from the American Embassy and his wife came to accompany us, and it was then that we learned that we were being traded for Soviet spies. But the officials still wanted to keep this quiet. The agreement was apparently that we—Ciszek and I and the two Soviets leaving from Idlewild Airport—could speak publicly only after we reached our respective, final destinations. I must say that I am thankful for the fact that the Soviets for whom we were being traded, Mr. and Mrs. (Ivan and Alexandra) Egorov, who worked at the Soviet Embassy at the United Nations, did not have diplomatic immunity and that is why they were in court after having been apprehended and presumably interrogated.

What was rather interesting was that on the way from London to New York—as many flights had to—we stopped in Shannon, Ireland, to refuel. We were able to get off the aircraft and walk around the tax-free shop. I forgot how much time we had, maybe an hour or an hour and a half. I had heard of the tax-free shop earlier as being special at that time although I was not planning on buying anything—I didn't have any money to begin with! But as we walked around, I could see that Father Ciszek was just totally taken aback by the apparent luxury of the items for sale: cameras, Scottish blankets and sweaters, books of all types, chocolates, liquor, and wine—and that all of these items were for sale for anyone who wanted to buy them. He did not say anything, but I could just see it in his eyes. And I realized that I had to guide him a bit. I, at least, had not been out of free society as long as he had been.

An interesting point while walking around the tax-free shop in Shannon was that there was a request over the PA system "for Mr. Makinen and Mr. Ciszek to come to the information desk." I thought that we had misestimated the time for walking around the tax-free shop and that we had to get on board the airplane. Taken as he was with the sights, Father Ciszek actually did not even notice the announcement. I told him that we better get over to the information desk because of the announcement requesting us to go there. As we approached the information desk, the person said, "There's a reporter from New York who wants to talk to you." I just refused to make any statement because of the agreement that was explained to us in London. This incident upset me somewhat because my understanding was that there was to be no announcement of our trade until we arrived at our destination.

When we got back on board, I told the stewardess that I would like to speak with the captain. The stewardesses knew who we were; they had been informed. And so the captain came over to see me, and I quietly explained to him about the public address announcement in the tax-free shop. I told him that I was concerned about this because our instructions were not to talk to anyone and that I did not understand why there was already a reporter from New York calling us. I told him that I just wanted to be sure that when we arrived there would not be any further problems. The captain told me that he would check into the matter. How he did it and how he informed us was most interesting; it was the best type of British cleverness that one could imagine. After about a half hour—we were already in flight—the captain came down the aisle. He stopped at our row, and, as if talking to everyone but really to me, he said, "The weather report in New York is excellent; the weather is fine, and everything is cleared for landing." It was so clever of him because he could not really bend over and speak just to us, it would have brought notice to us immediately. Father Ciszek did not realize why he said that, so I explained it to him. But he was still so taken with where he was—re-entry into the free world again. I could see the state he was in. I felt that my job was to make sure that I guided him and that this was the best thing I could do and to help him wherever possible.

The way we were situated on the plane was that there were three seats on our side of the plane: Father Ciszek sat in the window seat, I was next to him in the middle, and there was a woman sitting on the other side of me. I remember a humorous situation with this woman. I began talking with her a bit. I asked her why she was going to New York, and I remember that she told me that she was answering an ad to be an *au pair*. She asked me (referring to Father Ciszek and myself): "Have you been long in Europe?" I said, "Oh, we've just been traveling a bit." Father didn't actually hear that. But I think it would have been rather startling to her if I said that we had been just released from prison. That situation was humorous.

I suppose that everyone realized at the end of the flight that we were somewhat special because, when we landed in New York, before any of the passengers could disembark, a person came onto the plane and said: "Would Mr.

Ciszek and Mr. Makinen, please, come to the front of the plane." And so we got out and onto the tarmac. Everyone on the plane could see that there were reporters taking our pictures. We were both inoculated for smallpox, according to the Public Health requirement for re-entry to the United States at the time. We had our passports stamped, and we were interviewed together for a short time by the press. There was a person from the State Department who unobtrusively was able to talk to me, and I just let him know that I would like to talk to someone in the State Department about whom I had seen and about what I had experienced in prison—I had met certain prisoners whom I had wanted to try to help. Father Ciszek's sister was there at the airport along with other relatives I did not get to meet. I departed from the airport with my family after the press conference.

In his first public statement, published on October 26, 1963, in *America* magazine, Walter Ciszek described briefly and factually the story of his long years in the Soviet Union, denying the charge of having entered the U.S.S.R. as a "spy of the Vatican."[5] He concluded on a more personal note:

> I went into the interior of Russia of my own free will, spurred by my conscience and a desire to do good in the line of my vocation. In spite of seeming failures, I cherish no resentment or regrets for what has transpired in the past years. I have the highest regard for the Russian people, because they are good and hospitable folk who are very sincere and hearty in their relation with others who truly live and labor among them. Having lived so many years with the working class, as one of them, I have not experienced anything antagonistic on their part toward me.
>
> I must thank the many persons, in and out of the government, who so perseveringly made it possible for me to see my country and family again. I am also grateful to the Russian officials who showed me such considerate treatment in these last critical days.

After leaving the airport that Columbus Day 1963, Father Ciszek celebrated Mass with his sisters and fellow Jesuits at America House in New York City and had a breakfast of "pig and eggs" (as Father Walter then called it in his broken English). He was then assigned to the Jesuit novitiate at Wernersville, Pennsylvania. He spent his first months back in America there, as the location was close to family and he was able to rest and reintegrate back into American life. The Jesuits who were there when he arrived still have vivid memories of those days.[6]

Walter Ciszek had been among the novices that moved from the old novitiate at St. Andrew-on-Hudson, Poughkeepsie, New York, to Wernersville, Pennsylvania, in 1930. He had been appointed "senior-of-the-grounds" and, as such, he subsequently was placed in charge of building the cemetery. Now, in 1963, on his first day back at Wernersville, he wanted to visit it. One of the Jesuits drove him down to the cemetery, at the foot of the hill upon which the novitiate was located. When Father Ciszek started identifying the names of those buried there—the first one was a novice who had died in 1930—his fellow Jesuits who had doubted whether it was really him and not some Russian spy were reassured and said, "There is no way that the Russians could possibly have prepared someone to have this sort of information!" In the weeks that followed, the novices would see him every day walking around the grounds. They presumed that he spent this time reflecting and readjusting to the western world and the daily life of the Society of Jesus after having been isolated from it so many years. One of them was heard to say, "When I think of it, I see a similarity to Rip Van Winkle." In fact, when someone mentioned Pearl Harbor on December 7, Father Ciszek leaned over and asked, "What's Pearl Harbor mean?" He had completely missed the years of World War II.

It was in 1964 that his superiors assigned Walter Ciszek to Fordham University's John XXIII Center. In addition to the work he would be doing at the Center, he was to be engaged in pastoral work in parishes. Bishop Timothy McDonnell—at the time a young Father McDonnell, ordained a priest on June 1, 1963—recalls Father Ciszek's early experiences of pastoral work in American parishes:[7]

I was a young curate at Our Lady of Perpetual Help Parish in Ardsley, New York, where priests studying religious education at Fordham would reside during the year. While they went to classes they would help out by serving in the parish. During that time, we were asked by the head of the Russian Institute at Fordham if Father Walter Ciszek could come and stay at the parish to experience American pastoral life following his return from the Soviet Union. That was the summer of 1964, his first summer back in the United States.

Father Ciszek was a very simple, gentle priest who lived in the room next to mine. He was still somewhat uncomfortable speaking English because he had to relearn his native tongue after so many years overseas.

We had an "open door" policy—we could kind of walk in and out casually. At first he would only attend Mass; then, with help, he was able to say

Mass privately. He did not want to speak publicly or say Mass publicly in Latin (English had not yet been introduced). He was more comfortable with the Byzantine rite. By the end of the summer, he was saying weekday Masses but not yet preaching.

I remember in the initial days how he showed wonder at things we took for granted, such as the electric coffeemaker; so many things had changed in the United States since he had been living here that everyday items that had come into common use were wondrous to him. I had to remember he had left the United States in the midst of the Great Depression, when times were very tight for almost all families. He once commented on the size of American homes—so much room compared to the space allocated for families in Russia, where everyone was cramped.

Father Ciszek would not speak about specific Russian conditions or situations that he experienced, I believe out of concern for people he had left behind. I think he didn't want to talk about anything that he feared could have repercussions or cause difficulty for people who had helped him. Occasionally, he would mention something about the prison camp in Siberia but never anything about the Lubianka prison. He did say that in the prison camp he would save some raisins from a little piece of cake, soak them and ferment them to make wine for the consecration, and save a piece of bread to celebrate Mass surreptitiously. In kidding around one day, he said he was starting to get a "pot belly" from the abundance of food he found back in the States. He was very abstemious at meals; he would not eat anything he thought was too rich for him.

Father Ciszek had not yet written his books at that time, we could only guess what he had been through, but his demeanor and his prayerfulness struck me the most. He would spend time with his rosary before the Blessed Sacrament and be lost in meditation. He told me once that the time flew when he could pray. When he left to return to the Russian Institute at the end of the summer, we promised to pray for each other using the Latin phrase "*Oremus pro invicem.*"

3

"Return from Russia"

When[8] Walter Ciszek moved to Our Lady of Perpetual Help Parish in the summer of 1964, he had actually already finished the manuscript of his first book, *With God in Russia*, but it needed heavy editing. The first thing the public would read from him was an article in *America* magazine, but it did not focus on his time in Russia. It was all about his new mission country, the United States of America, as mirrored in his experiences of the Soviet Union. He would repeat, "I am only recounting my impressions, not offering criticisms," but his questions were, nonetheless, still quite pertinent. The following text is reprinted from *America* magazine, March 28, 1964.

My plane landed at Idlewild International Airport, at 6:55 a.m. in the gray dawn of October 12, 1963. All during the long flight from Moscow, I had wondered what it would be like to see the United States again after 24 years in the Soviet Union, mostly in Siberia. Yet, as we taxied to the terminal, I forgot all about that; I could think only of my sisters and of the fellow Jesuits I saw waiting to meet me. My throat seemed somehow to grow suddenly tighter; I felt a nervous happiness in the expectancy of that first meeting. I hardly remember much about Idlewild, therefore, except flashing lights in the early dawn, the crowd of reporters, and that feeling of joy at being home. It was a long while before I could even begin to sift out my impressions of things here.

Cars, of course. Everybody asks about that, and it's true. You notice them immediately. Moscow streets are busy, but here the streets are crammed with cars—north, south, east and west—cars coming, cars going, and block after block of cars standing along the curbs. Not just in the cities, but along the country roads and in small towns, the main streets and the side streets and the alleys seem almost carpeted with cars.

And what cars! For five years I was a mechanic at ATK-50, the government garage in Abakan, working on the city's fleet of taxis. Those are really about the only cars there are, for few people can afford their own. The average workingman's salary is 90 rubles (roughly $90) a month; a really good salary is 150 rubles a month. But the little four-cylinder Moskvicz costs almost 3,000 rubles (nearly three years' salary!), and the bigger, six-cylinder Volga costs about 6,000. Those were the cars I worked with, and practically every American car I have seen looks like a battleship compared to them—especially after they had spent a month on the roads around Abakan.

Two other things connected with American cars amazed me. One was the very low cost of a secondhand car; even a dilapidated, rebuilt refugee from ATK-50 would cost a minimum of 2,000 rubles in Abakan. The other was the sight of a nun driving a car. When I stop to think about it, I suppose nuns are no better—or worse—drivers than anyone else, since most young people here seem to grow up behind the wheel. But I hadn't seen a nun in a religious habit for almost twenty-five years; the sight of one behind the wheel of a car struck me as incredible—and funny.

Housing, of course, impressed me tremendously. I don't mean the skyscraper skyline of New York and the block on block of soaring glass, steel, and aluminum towers that loom over you as you walk through the city. Everyone expects that of New York. What struck me, however, was the mile after mile of neat, well-painted and well-kept houses: the big, comfortable farmhouses in the countryside, the trim, sharp rows of "modern" brick and glass homes in every suburb, the solid, sturdy brick houses with their frame front porches in every little town.

Sometimes I still feel uneasy when I visit these homes. The idea that one family should occupy six, seven, or eight rooms! I can't shake the feeling that something is wrong. And every room has carpets, pictures, mirrors, lamps, chairs, even a radio. A house that had four rooms was a luxury in Siberia, and even then the "spare" room was generally rented out. I lived in such spare rooms all through my stay in Abakan, sleeping on a little iron bed with boards in place of springs. Frankly, you couldn't have fitted some of the "standard" American beds—with their oversized frames and mattresses a foot thick—into the room I had for the last two years in Abakan.

I can't get used to the notion, either, that hot water is available all day and all night, or that you can take a bath any time you want. In Siberia, houses that had hot water had it only twice a week, at best, during the winter. Central heating where I lived meant that the corners of the big, brick kitchen stove stuck into all four rooms of the house. Here even the poorest homes have central heating, and stoves are gas or electric, with the kitchens full of electric toasters, electric mixers, electric frying pans, electric roasters—electric everything, including can-openers. Everybody has a vacuum cleaner; I even saw teenagers walking around with portable hair-dryers. When people here buy a washing machine (and everybody does), they can choose between a dozen makes, all with special features and most of them with matching dryers. In Russia, there is only one type, the *Bielka*, with a hand wringer, no dryer—and you put the water in by hand! When you can get one, it costs 90 rubles, just about a man's whole wages for a month.

You don't just walk into the *Magazin* (department store) and buy a washing machine; you order one, and you put your name at the bottom of the list of those who have ordered before you. Then you go back every week and put a check beside your name to show that you still want and need that machine. If you fail to check your name for two weeks in a row, or if you miss about three times all told, your name drops off the list. There may be 500 or more names on the list, but only 35 or 40 machines will be delivered to the *Magazin* each month; so a wait of more than a year is not unusual. The same thing is true of rugs and refrigerators; it seemed incredible to see a kitchen with two refrigerators back home in Shenandoah, Pennsylvania.

The food in those refrigerators, or in the stores! You can't imagine what it means to see fruit in the middle of winter. Apples, melons, and grapes were about the only fruit we had in Abakan, and then only during harvest time. If you saw someone—even a stranger—with an apple, you'd go right up to him and ask where he got it—then go there right away. We did buy oranges a few times while I was there, but they were little Chinese oranges, and of course you never see them now. We never saw grapefruit, or such things as peaches, pears, plums, cherries, and pineapples. Bananas were so rare that some people honestly and literally didn't know what to do with them; they couldn't be sure whether they were fruit or vegetable, whether they should be cooked or eaten as they were. But here, store windows are full of every kind of fruit all winter long—and the people pass by without looking. Here you can go into any store on any street and buy meat, milk, butter, and every kind of vegetable, fresh, frozen, or canned. My sisters began to think the years in Siberia had affected my mind, when I went wandering for hours through a supermarket, staring wide-eyed and unbelieving at so much food. All the stores are that way. You never have to stand in line for anything, except the time it takes the girl to check out the baskets of food each person buys. In Abakan, you stood in line for everything; when there was a line in a store it meant they finally had something to sell. Before you went to work, on your way home from work, if you saw a line you automatically got into it. Whatever they were selling, it would be something you needed.

It isn't only the food in the stores that amazes me, it's the food an average family puts on the table for an average meal. The first few times I went to visit friends in Shenandoah, I felt guilty because they were going to such an expense for me. Several times I asked them how they could afford it. They'd look at me as if they didn't understand, then smile at me and wink at one another. In

Abakan, I used to cook myself a pot of soup from cabbage, onions and pota-
toes, with perhaps some beef or lamb bones I had saved—or a piece of meat if I
could get it—and that would be my breakfast and my supper for the next three
days. A handful of lard added to the soup, so that it would be covered with a
layer of grease as thick as your little finger, was the way I added fats to my diet.
A chunk of chewy, dark rye bread completed the meal.

I seldom had meat, except now and again a piece of boloney with another
piece of bread for lunch. Otherwise, my lunch at the garage consisted of a piece
of bread and an onion, or perhaps a piece of bread and fat. Here in America,
I've watched mothers in the kitchen after a meal throw away more food, and
better food, than I might eat in Russia in half a week. The dogs here eat more
meat in a week than I did in a month. And I simply can't help staring when
people leave their plates half full, as they do so often in restaurants.

The waste of paper here! Everything comes wrapped in paper, boxed in
paper, rolled in paper, packaged in paper. And if it isn't paper, it's plastic. Each
piece of fruit is individually wrapped, vegetables are bagged in cellophane,
and everything is boxed in brightly printed, attractive cartons. Then all this
is thrown away or burned! In Siberia, on the other hand, you bring your own
wrapping paper to the store. Most people found the best solution was to buy a
newspaper; it gave you something to do during those endless waits in line, too.

When I say things like this, of course, I am only recounting my impressions,
not offering criticisms. Somewhat like a Siberian Rip Van Winkle, I can't help
being struck by things in my own country that seem strange and new to me.
After all, as Wladimir Martinovich I lived the life of the people in Siberia, con-
formed to all the regulations, got used to all the customs, and came to take for
granted all the hardships. Abakan, Krasnoyarsk, Norilsk—the Siberian cities
where I was allowed to live as a free man after my release from the camps—are
not Moscow, Leningrad, Kiev, or Odessa. As a released "political" prisoner who
had been accused of "spying for the Vatican," I was not allowed to live in any
of those major, or "regime," cities. Neither am I a sociologist; so I don't pretend
to judge life in the Soviet Union as compared to life in the United States, or
vice versa. I am only recording my surface impressions, the things that struck
me when I first returned and that continue to startle me from time to time in
many little ways.

Just a few weeks ago, for instance, I was struck by the sight of a crucifix on
the classroom wall as I talked to the children in St. Ladislaus parish school in
Philadelphia. You never see that in Russia. Somehow I suddenly felt strange; I
almost felt out of place. I could see in the children's eyes an eagerness and a
respect for what I was (not who I was), a priest whom they called "Father." I
thought of the Russian children who used to come to me for help with their
English lessons. How cautious I had to be with them never to mention God!

Here in this classroom, beneath the crucifix, I could tell these children anything, speak to them of anything. In Abakan I felt restricted, and I had to be careful not to startle the children.

I remember a day I forgot and made some reference to God; I could see the surprise and the near-horror in their eyes. "Wladimir Martinovich," said one little girl, "is it possible that you believe in God, a smart man like you? How can you still let yourself be influenced by unscientific stories about God and religion?" She was perhaps in the seventh grade. I didn't want them to go away without an answer, so I told them they would come across the idea of God wherever they went; it was a serious problem that troubled many people, and they would make a serious mistake if they didn't consider it carefully and try to solve it for themselves. Under the circumstances, that was the best I could do. I had just been warned again by the KGB not to "agitate" the people about religion. If I had tried to tell these children about God, or to instruct them, it would have been considered "proselytizing immature minds." That's how it is in Russia.

Article 124 of the Constitution of the USSR states that "in order to ensure the citizen's freedom of conscience, the church in the USSR is separated from the state, and the school from the church. Freedom of religious worship and freedom of antireligious propaganda are recognized for all citizens." What that means in effect is that the right to propagate religion ends at the church door or at a mother's knee. In the churches that are open (generally only the Orthodox churches, except in the big cities like Moscow), services are held and people are free to attend—as long as they are not Party members or do not hold responsible jobs or positions they would hesitate to lose. That is "freedom of worship." But you cannot proselytize or talk about religion or try to make converts; whereas with the "freedom of antireligious propaganda" exercised by the schools, the Party, the labor unions, the press, radio, and television, atheism is actively and continuously preached.

Religion in Russia, therefore, is not suppressed or persecuted, as people here understand the words. Instead, it is talked about as something that retards the movement toward communism and impedes the education of the "new communistic man." In special courses, seminars, and lectures, Party members, school teachers, *komsomols* (members of the official youth organizations), and labor union members get a thorough grounding in atheism in order to help fight religion—not by government legislation, but by word of mouth and by example. In school, everything is "scientifically" explained to the children; ideas of God and of religion are treated as holdovers from the unscientific past. Children are told to humor their elders who still believe in such things and have never had the scientific and technical training that would show them how incompatible such notions are with modern science. The method can be devastatingly effective, up to a point.

Older people, however, still believe in God, and their influence is still noticeable in family life. As a result, the young people hear talks against religion in school but still can see examples of religious practices at home. It confuses them. Publicly, they do not believe; they will argue with anyone who suggests they should believe. Privately, however, they are not sure. I have had young married *komsomols* come to me to have their children baptized. When I asked about the possibility of religious education for the child, and why they wanted him baptized, they would tell me simply they had heard all sorts of things about God and against God, in school and in the Party organizations, but they were not convinced. They wanted to do for their children what their parents had done for them—just in case. When I asked, then, if they would teach their children what their parents had taught them, they were eager to agree. It was a strange and sad and yet, somehow, hopeful experience. The more I see here in America, the stranger it seems in a way. For the contrast between that hidden faith, fluttering as if it were always about to go out and yet somehow remaining alight, and the open, free, and almost proud profession of faith in this country is simply staggering.

Yet when I walked through St. Patrick's Cathedral in New York, do you know what impressed me most? The few people, out of all the crowds streaming by, who came in through those open doors to make a visit. I understand that my impression was not fair, that at noontime on a working day the church is jammed with office workers who take time out from their lunch hour to go to Mass and to Communion. At first glance religion here seems almost a formality, an obligation that can be dispensed with if you have been out late the night before.

In Siberia, when I said Mass, people risked arrest to come; here, they risk nothing, neither do they always come. In Krasnoyarsk and Norilsk, when people learned a priest was in town or was saying Mass at such and such a place, they came for miles, bringing their children to be baptized, going to confession before Mass and then Communion during Mass, asking to have their marriages blessed after Mass, begging me to come and bless their homes or sing the *panikida* (a requiem service) for members of the family who had died. They came to huts, to barracks rooms, to private homes, and they risked their jobs, their union membership, their chance for an apartment, or an education for their children. Having ministered to such faith, therefore, it was incredible to me to think that people here could look on Sunday Mass as an obligation, or the supporting of their parish and their school as a burden.

I should repeat again that these were my first reactions, my impressions, and are not meant in any way as criticisms. I am only reporting what struck me when I first looked at America again. As a priest who had worked very hard to help people who were so eager just to be able to go to Mass, I could not help being struck, thunderstruck, at this initial impression of indifference to religion in a country where there was nothing to restrain its open practice.

There is one topic about which people always ask me: the race question. Quite frankly, I was amazed to see Negroes eating in restaurants, working alongside white people (even in the government in Washington!), sitting beside them on trains and buses, talking with them freely and openly. I couldn't believe my eyes at first. I had read of riots in America, of Negroes being beaten. I had heard they couldn't go to school to get an education or eat with whites, and that they weren't allowed to hold certain jobs. I had seen pictures on television of several Black Muslim speakers in Harlem calling for a separate section of the country as their own, where they could be free and independent of the whites.

I tried to tell the Russians who asked me about this that such stories must be exaggerated. But what could I say about the TV pictures and the news photos, or the statements by prominent American leaders, both Negro and white, that were quoted so frequently in the Soviet press? What could I think? I had left America to study theology in Rome in 1934; I had no way of knowing what things were like in America after 30 years. I could say the news was exaggerated, but was I sure? You can imagine, then, how stunned I was to see Negroes walking freely everywhere, accepted by everyone. Again, this was my first impression, my spontaneous reaction in view of what I had been led to believe. I have begun to learn what problems still remain and how much is still to be done; but perhaps my impression will show how much the average Russian knows about America.

I am an American, happy to be home; but in many ways I am almost a stranger, as you can tell by these initial reactions to America. It may take me a while to feel at home, but I am happy to be back. What sort of picture, though, must others have of us who have no way of finding out the truth?

Part Two

THE JESUIT

4

Walter Ciszek, Jesuit Priest

Walter Ciszek came back to America in October 1963, a stranger to his fellow Jesuits. He had left the country in 1934, and they last heard of him in 1948, when his presumed death had been announced and they were reminded to pray for the repose of his soul. That is the recollection of Fr. Dominic Maruca, S.J.[9] He was there in October 1963, when Ciszek drove up to the novitiate at Wernersville, Pennsylvania. Father Maruca, then socius (assistant) to the novice master, recalled the event.

> I greeted him, and he asked, "Are all these young men lining up the road our novices?" I said, "Yes, they're making their thirty-day retreat." He asked, "Can I say something to them?" I said, "Sure." He then said to the novices, "I'm sure some of you think that you're wasting your time here; but it's what I prayed about here that gave me the strength to endure all the things I endured during my years afterwards." After that, I said to the novice master, "You can skip your afternoon talk; there is nothing you can say that would match what Father Ciszek just said." Then we went in to have lunch.

When the retreat was finished, Father Ciszek was invited to speak to the novices. Maruca went on to say, "He spoke for close to two hours! They just sat there absorbing everything they possibly could." Two of those novices would later recall how well he looked—more like a man in his thirties or forties than his actual fifty-nine years. They said, "He had a shock of white hair and was stocky, or full built." They also remembered how pleasantly he smiled and how he spoke with a peaceful gentleness, very slowly, quietly, reflectively; he did not lecture or boast but just told his story. They said, "We were inspired by the way he offered Mass, and we looked upon him as being profoundly spiritual, the ideal for a missionary who embodies the fiery spirit to do anything for the love of God." Their shared conclusion, that this was a very holy man, a saint, was reaffirmed later, in 1965, when *With God in Russia* was read from the pulpit at mealtimes. One of the young men present at the time was moved to say, "I was very inspired by his book. I read it three times on retreat."[10]

Dom Maruca continued to stay in touch with Wally (as they used to call him) Ciszek during the year they were together in Wernersville, serving as chauffeur for him and for Daniel Flaherty, S.J., who flew from New York to Reading every weekend to help Father write *With God in Russia*. Maruca, impressed by Ciszek's unassuming nature, remembers him as

> . . . a dedicated priest who loved people. He used spiritual terms and categories when he related his narrative to Father Flaherty. But ordinarily his manner was very simple, always people-oriented. He knew what to do because of what the needs of the people were. It was his cast of mind: he wasn't an intellectual dealing with abstract generalities; he dealt always, it seemed to me, in concrete realities. That endeared him to everyone. He had an unfailing good sense of humor.

An item of frequent and humorous discussion in the community was his dispensation from Tertianship, the somewhat unpopular final year of formation for a Jesuit, which came some years after priestly ordination and before taking final vows. Walter Ciszek was allowed to pronounce his vows without Tertianship on August 15, 1964. That prompted the comic remark, "Wally's twenty-three years in Siberia were considered equal to that one year of Tertianship!" Maruca concluded, "He enjoyed just being one of us." The possibility remains, however, that he, the Jesuit who had gone to Russia with the Pope's blessing, regretted not being allowed to take the special fourth vow of obedience regarding papal missions, presumably because he had not done his Tertianship and because he had failed his final theology exams in Rome in 1937. All of which must have contributed to the fact that he always felt a bit uneasy in the company of intellectuals.

In the autumn of 1964, Walter Ciszek was sent to the Russian Center at Fordham University, on the Rose Hill Campus. One of those who asked to meet him soon afterward was the Jesuit student Denis Como. He was interested in Russia and asked Father to give him a one-day retreat. "The way he prayed was right from his heart," said Como, then he continued,

> It gave you a feeling of peace and strength. I had the feeling he knows who I am and what I am going to become. It was like talking to a saint. I was

like a young puppy, eager and enthusiastic, but he was totally interested with plenty of time and no rush. I was aware that he was taking this time talking to me to encourage me. I feel God was really right there.[11]

What especially encouraged Denis Como to persevere in his desire to serve the Eastern Rites of the Catholic Church (as he later would, in the Chaldean Rite) was a story Father Ciszek told about Kayerkhan, Siberia, where he had been forced to dig manually for surface-level coal. Many of his colaborers died along with the children who were there with them. Eventually the Soviets stopped the project when no more children were born. They then transformed the barracks into a center for mother and child care. "What a change from the beginning!" Father concluded, smiling from ear to ear with a twinkle in his eye, as if to say God has his ways and made of it something good, so contrary to what it had once been.

Fr. Brian W. Van Hove, S.J., met Father Ciszek for the first time in June 1971.[12] He had entered the Society of Jesus in 1966 and had read *With God in Russia* as a novice during the thirty-day retreat. He remarked, "I completed the book, I believe, in one day." Van Hove was back at Fordham in 1973 for summer classes, where he regularly attended Father's celebration of the Divine Liturgy in Slavonic early in the morning. The community had recently moved to a new property just across the street, on Belmont Avenue, and had changed its name to John XXIII Ecumenical Center. Walter Ciszek was writing his second book, *He Leadeth Me*, so, naturally they would talk about the book. Van Hove relates the following anecdote:

> At one point, Father Ciszek came down from the chapel (which was on the second floor) fairly agitated. He said, "You know, I was writing and I just came to a block and didn't know what to say." He said, "I went to the chapel for fifteen minutes, and I prayed and I was just filled with what I should say, and I'm now going back and do some more writing." He said, "I've always been that way." His meaning was that he could always go to the chapel and be filled with inspiration.

Similarly, in the summer of 1973, Fr. George C. McCauley, S.J. (1930–2010) arrived. He was a theologian assigned to teach at Fordham University and would live in the John XXIII Center until the summer of 1979.[13] The community consisted of five or six persons, including Father Ciszek, although there were several non-Jesuits who regularly lived, worked, and ate with them because of their connection with the Center. In 1994,

McCauley, in an interview about his experiences with Walter Ciszek, related the following:

> In my first four years or so, Father Ciszek was in good health. It was easy to be friends with him, as he was a cheerful, kind, alert man. The living was modest, to say the least, but he and I would meet ten minutes before the evening meal for our Stolichnaya and bourbon respectively. I was with him at almost all meals and at the normal community occasions. His heart attack [in August 1976] slowed him down, but he was still fairly vigorous at the time I left the community. His work was mostly in spiritual direction, retreats, lecturing, and correspondence. He talked sometimes about his years in Russia, but anecdotally and humorously, not trying to draw any edifying messages from it for his listeners.

Since you already knew his background when you met him, what, if anything, surprised or impressed you about him?

What impressed me about him? He seemed to have moved to another level of humanity, which was characterized by an inner peace and by a spirit of befriending people. He was a magnet to all kinds of people, generous with his time and giving of himself. He spoke much of prayer, though to me he was always pleasantly inarticulate about what he meant by it. He had lists of people he prayed for regularly—and you would want to be on them!

The other thing that I often felt was his insecurity, tinged with a bit of envy or at least longing, in the face of people he thought of as intellectuals or academics. Sometimes this came out as an exasperated pity for them, but I always thought he would have liked to join their ranks. When he was in Rome studying at the Russicum, he was pals with John Courtney Murray[14] and Gustave Weigel,[15] who were at the Gregorian University, and he spoke of those days with enthusiasm.

Lastly, he often talked of his saloonkeeper father, a big man physically, whom Father Ciszek seemed to me to truly admire but was still chasing in a way, in order to deal with something unfinished. I asked him once why he spoke by comparison so rarely of his mother. He became very quiet, held off for a moment, and then said simply, "She was a holy woman."

Following his return from Russia, was his re-entry to American life and the Jesuit Society in America an easy or difficult adjustment?

I was told (not by him) on several occasions that when he first came back he was treated like an embarrassing country bumpkin by some. You have to remember that, among those in the Eastern Rite group, he was one of the few who had actually been east, spoke Russian, and administered the great rituals of that tradition in real life context. [. . .]

But, as I said before, he never traded on Russia as though that was his world. So he didn't need to draw parallels between what he was now and what he had been then. Once, some peregrinating superior came and told us that we should pray more together as a community. Dutifully, we organized a prayer session before dinner in our tiny chapel. One Jesuit thought we could jazz the session up with clouds of incense. This was after Father Ciszek's heart attack; the billowing smoke left him clutching at his throat in the pew. We finally gave it up. No nostalgia there for "the good old days" in Russia.

What do you suppose Father Ciszek believed he accomplished by going to Russia?

I would interpret his going to Russia as wanting to do the tough, difficult thing. Whether, at that time, this was for God or whether he was driven by inner demons, I couldn't say. My impression of him often was, "the Russians never had a chance." He often admitted to testing himself against the best in his work habits, physical endurances, and determination. He told me that in all his years in Russia he never got a cold and never lost a tooth. . . .

Did Father Ciszek strike you as a "saintly" man? In what sense?

Yes, I think he was a saintly man, even a saint. I would hope that I do not misrepresent him in saying this, but I thought of him as someone who had achieved a special insight about accepting and doing the will of God. The specialness and stark simplicity of that insight I would phrase this way: if something is *really happening* to you—some turn in your life, some burden of personality, some accident of health, some arbitrary political regime, some missed opportunity, or even some sin—then *that's the starting place* for any authentic spirituality. That's a kind of acceptance that I think few people achieve.

A summer guest at the Center from 1965 onward was Father Robert F. Taft, S.J., who taught at the Pontifical Oriental Institute in Rome.[16]He identified Fr. George A. Maloney (1924–2005) as one of the intellectuals who exasperated Father Ciszek most. In the full twenty years they lived together, George Maloney seems to have been a "dark shadow" to Wally Ciszek, just like in another way the memory of his father chased him. But in general he kept these matters to himself, sharing them with God in prayer. Father Taft recounted:

I have very fond memories of that community: we concelebrated the Russian Divine Liturgy every morning, sung in Old Slavonic, with full solemnity and incense, as is customary (though Ciszek couldn't stand the incense: he was allergic to it); we sang Vespers together on Saturday evening with equal solemnity; there were feasts and meals in the Russian tradition, etc. Probably the best community life I ever had in the Society. In later years, the community was housed in two adjacent apartment buildings [on Belmont Avenue]. Each of us had his own apartment, fixed up by "Brat Joe (Brother Joe)," as we affectionately called him. Brother Joseph Benkovsky, S.J., was a Slovak brother who earlier had spent many years working at the Russicum or Pontifical Russian College in Rome. The apartments were very small: a bedroom, a sitting room, and a bathroom and kitchen in one. The bathtub was in the kitchen, as in the old apartments of the working poor.

The community members were all talented men, strong characters. Ciszek had a streak of stubbornness. One of his former Superiors, Fr. James McCarthy, S.J. (†2012; he later left the Society and got married) found him a little bit hard to deal with. It was Father McCarthy's first job as Superior, and he was very meticulous, something of a nitpicker, probably too controlling. For Ciszek, with all his experience in Russia, McCarthy was just a boy. Regarding Father George Maloney, S.J., he was a man of prayer, a holy man and an ascetic, but much more distant from the community than Ciszek was. In many ways Maloney was the animator of the attempt to turn the Russian Center into a Center of Eastern Christian Studies. Ciszek looked upon Maloney, "the queen bee of the beehive," with some irony and amusement, but I never noticed any open conflict between them. Ciszek must have realized that the solution for the problems between the Catholic and Orthodox Churches is not intellectual but spiritual.

Wally probably wasn't interested in ecumenical practices that he didn't consider serious, if by that one means mere externals without substance. But he was, for example, instrumental in the foundation of one of the most important Eastern-Rite Catholic religious communities of the USA, the flourishing Ruthenian Carmelite monastery in Sugarloaf, Pennsylvania. He was their spiritual father throughout his life and was the heart and soul of that place. Walter Ciszek had no intellectual pretensions; indeed, no pretensions of any kind. But he was a man whose sufferings had given him a strength of resistance that probably at times led to a stubbornness. I think he was a wonderful man, and I think that anyone who knew him well thought so, maybe except Maloney and McCarthy.

Wally Ciszek was my confessor. He always impressed me as being a very normal man, a very simple man, like a *Gastarbeiter*. He was not an intellectual but a very spiritual man, a man of prayer. He had a great devotion to the Eucharist, to the Mother of God—standard qualities of Polish piety—and to the Catholic Church. He also had an iron will. I don't think he had any sense of inferiority because he wasn't an intellectual. He was very much the real American Jesuit, very masculine, one who hates anything that smacks of fastidiousness and pseudo-piety, who doesn't like pretense, who tends to be just a good manly fellow and companion. An example: when I went to confession to Wally in his room, in the hot and humid summers of New York, Wally would be sitting there in his underwear, without any irreverence; it just didn't make any difference to him. He was a very normal companion of Jesus. As a confessor he was the kindest man in the world, not probing, always encouraging, always smiling. I really and truly loved the man very much. It was impossible not to.

Another anecdote about Father Ciszek's unorthodox "summer apostolate" comes from Father Brian Van Hove. The story is set in 1975. Van Hove related it as follows:

If you've ever lived in New York City, [you know that] the summers are very hot and the kids in various neighborhoods open up the fire hydrants and watch the water gush down the street. Father Ciszek witnessed this and thought the children were just bored. Thus, he got permission from the superiors at Fordham University to use the playing grounds. He would put on his straw hat and a whistle around his neck, and in short sleeves and a clerical shirt went into the middle of Belmont Avenue and blew his whistle. All the kids in the neighborhood knew who he was; they lined up (girls and boys around ages eight to twelve, some thirty or forty of them, with their parents' permission) and, like a goose followed by the goslings, he would march them across Fordham Road. He would push the light, the light would stop the traffic, and he would take them over to the playing fields on campus—a grassy area with big trees—for about an hour or more. And when the time had come when they were tired, he would blow his whistle and escort them across the street again, and they would all go home, each to his own part of the neighborhood. He did all of that in the summers until his health would not permit. The last summer I saw him, in 1977, his lung emphysema (probably from working in the mines in Siberia) was so bad that even walking a short distance, he seemed out of breath.

Father Van Hove also remembers Walter Ciszek's regular apostolate of spiritual direction mostly to married women, how he would fix them a lunch Soviet-style—"bread and soup and not much else, maybe half a pear or half an apple"—and quietly have lunch together with them in the community dining room, which was generally empty around noon. In fact, he was very sensitive in matters of daily living. On his way to Fordham University for the feast of St. Ignatius, July 31, 1977, Van Hove met him on the sidewalk near the Center. "I refuse to go," Ciszek told him:

> I won't go over there. It's a sin. They eat all that rich food and they have all this opulence, it's lavish. It's a sin for religious to do that. When I was in Russia, we had a small piece of cheese, and all we could do was hide it under our pillow when we went to sleep at night and hope that the mice wouldn't eat it when we were asleep. And so, I refuse to go over there.

He felt guilty about it, because as a religious he was taught that community life is important, but he didn't want to be associated with opulence or a display of wealth that only rich people could afford.

In general, Father Ciszek would not bring up his opinions on Jesuit liberalism or on Church or world politics, nor did he talk about people, about bishops or cardinals, or even notorious Soviet politicians such as Stalin or Brezhnev. "But he would talk about things and give his opinion if it were brought up to him or if it came up, or he would not have an opinion," said Van Hove. He added,

> He made the point to me one time: "We were not able to keep up. We did not have books in Russia." And so he didn't read for many, many years. All he had in his head was what he had read in the remote past and what he could remember. He did not think it his place to comment.

With the same [kind of] modesty, Walter Ciszek made his final vows again, adding the fourth vow of obedience regarding papal missions, on August 15, 1977, in the presence of his Jesuit superior Father John Geary, Brian Van Hove, Brother Benkovsky, two of his sisters (Mother Evangeline, and Helen Gearhart with one or two of her adult children), and two friends, namely Sister Maureen O'Brien, O.C.D., and a layman, Michael J. Higgins, who had been visiting him earlier that year when Father was recovering from a heart attack. Two Jesuit scholastics did the singing. Van Hove described the occasion: "The day of the vows we were all having breakfast around 8:00 a.m. and by 8:45 the whole thing was over; it was early in the morning and almost no one was there. This was in the chapel of the John XXIII Center." Sister Maureen added,

Father shared later that the grace experienced was one of the greatest of his life. He said it gave him a new sense of being "sent" just where he was with new vigor. He spoke of being sent to the neighborhood and to the children in an increasingly hostile and dangerous area. Welcoming them, talking about God with them, and inviting them to know Jesus, teaching them catechism.

Some months later the Provincial said he wanted a "big" ceremony for his fourth vow even though Father said he'd already made it. In obedience, a bigger ceremony occurred, but Father said the graces came with the initial ceremony. In his words, "The more personal and quiet ceremony met the needs of my soul."[17]

In a thank-you card he sent to Sister Maureen's community, the Baltimore Carmel, Father Ciszek wrote,

> Your timely wishes for my profession gave me added joy. Since I wanted the celebration to be modest, your card gave it more importance. Your love and prayers enriched my soul. For your community was the only one to be united with me in spirit in spite of my efforts to make the occasion hidden. God has his ways that are always infinitely superior to what you expect. This I sensed as never before on Aug. 15th. What more could I wish in life than He gave me in my calling—the culmination of life and fulfillment of the soul's craving. Do I understand? It does not matter once my faith stands firm.

Apart from his own small community and the much larger Fordham community where he ordinarily ate ("He was always quiet and never talked about himself or what he went through in Russia," said one of the Fathers[18]), Walter Ciszek did not seem to have had a great deal of contact with his fellow Jesuits. At least twice, however, he spent more time with them. The first time occurred after the major heart attacks he suffered in August 1976. For his recovery he stayed eight months at Campion Center, the Jesuit house of retirement in Weston, Massachusetts, until April 1977. His fellow Jesuits there were quite impressed by what they saw as "his holiness, zeal, and energy for the apostolate that he had chosen so willingly" and about which they had read and heard so much. Some of their experiences with him seem to border on the classical legends of the saints; they included conversions of lay staff to the Catholic faith and reports of an "aura" seen surrounding him. Others were moved by his liveliness, acceptance, and kindness. One of them visited Father Ciszek and asked him to hear his confession. He commented, "His demeanor was 'all ears,' firm and gentle, straightforward and incisive."

Fr. George L. Drury, S.J., the then superior of the Center, said, "I found him to be a kind, gentle, and thankful person, definitely not self-centered, and so appreciative of his brother Jesuits and anything that was done for him." Father Drury stated that it was wonderful to meet him, and the Jesuits were all glad to have him there. Even though Father Drury's visits with him were limited, he recognized in Father Ciszek an exemplary Jesuit in his humility and love of God, "who by his faith and generosity showed how to live for the divine Kingdom."[19]

Walter Ciszek also spent time with young Jesuits on the few occasions between 1972 and 1981 when he was invited to Wernersville to give days of recollection to the novices.[20] Fr. James T. Maier, S.J., who was director of novices from 1977 until 1985, recalled how Father Ciszek awed the young men:

> He was so gentle in his approach, yet with an inner strength ("tough as nails") and a simple faith and trust in God that showed through. We received him with deep respect, and he really won the high praise of my fellow Jesuits. Walter was a master of obedience, very humble (grounded). He was, we understood, like a "fish out of water" coming home from one world to another, but still he followed orders and the directions of his superiors.

But not blindly, according to a lay collaborator of the Spirituality Center at Wernersville who reported,

> I was present at a light, but serious, discussion about obedience in the Jesuit tradition. Much to everyone's delight, Wally upheld the practice of moving ahead in a pinch and seeking permission or forgiveness later. He also approved of arguing with the superior as long as he had prayed about the situation.

When the director of the Center, the late Fr. George Schemel, S.J., called him in New York and teasingly told him, "Wally, the Holy Spirit told me this morning that you should come to live with us at Wernersville," Wally Ciszek responded immediately, "Well, George, if the Holy Spirit mentions it to me, I'll be right there."

The memories of those who met him in the summer of 1981 at Wernersville, when he served as the director of an eight-day vow retreat for the three novices, provide an apparently paradoxical image: " . . . short, stout, funny, very cool and calm, seemingly healthy and physically fit, walking in the brisk, chilly air outside on the ambulatory of the Jesuit House and eating hearty breakfasts." One of the novices noted his gentleness, modesty, and solidity, and then went on to say,

> But more than his person which seemed so "ordinary" and "normal" it was his story that really inspired everyone. Although quite conversational he was not given to talking about himself, and when he did speak of his ordeal in Russia he did so in a spiritual context. The homilies he gave at Mass were very long.

According to a Jesuit Father, "He was slightly stiff and formal when he said Mass," and so were his talks to the novices. Those were the days in which retreats were no longer preached to groups but given individually, with short introductions. As the aforementioned lay collaborator said, "We often joked among the staff that Wally's version of the directed retreat was a preached retreat given to one person."

"I believe at the end the feeling was that the newer format would have been preferred," said the associate director of novices. But one of the novices, twenty-four-year-old Joseph Lingan, who would become novice master himself, related the following experience:[21]

> I vividly remember knocking on his door every evening, and then hearing his gentle voice say, "Come in!" He sat at his desk, and I sat in the wooden chair right next to the desk. The first evening we met, I acknowledged and apologized that I had not read either one of his books. He looked at me with his typical twinkle and said, "Good, now we can get started." Over the next eight days, he shared his story, his novitiate experience, the "call" he felt to "go to Russia," his impatience with having to wait, and his joy at receiving the summons.
>
> Father Ciszek had a "fire-plug physique," a smile that suggested delight and mischief, and eyes that were bright and filled with joy. As a man of faith, he was tenacious. Clearly, he was eager to share his faith and his experience of and insights into the Spiritual Exercises of St. Ignatius Loyola. He spoke with confidence and gratitude, and as one who was clearly in love with God and with Christ.
>
> Concerning Father Ciszek's contribution to the Church, his inspiring faith and profound fidelity are a great example for all Christians, but especially for religious men and women. He was a humble man of prayer who loved God deeply. He desired nothing more than to serve God . . . and nothing less. As he shared his story, bit by bit, during the days of my retreat, he gave the clear impression that his life was not about him but rather a reflection of the

movement and action of God in his life. He liked sharing his story, because it allowed him to share about God. He was faithful because he knew to the core of his being that God was faithful, and he clearly enjoyed helping others to the same understanding. He was a living example of both the simplicity and profundity of what it means to be a person of faith.

5

Prepared for Total
Abandonment to God

On August 4, 1964, at the shrine of the North American Martyrs in Auriesville, New York, Father Ciszek began his annual eight-day retreat, in preparation for his final vows, which he would take on August 15. The retreat followed the common structure of the Spiritual Exercises of St. Ignatius: contemplating why we are created and how we alienated ourselves from God by sin; our call to Christ's kingdom and the invitation to follow him; our participation in his life, death, and resurrection, and especially our choice under the cross to seek his company in humility and in abandonment; and finally the prayer to obtain God's love. After having brought to mind some of the main principles that guide the one who is doing the Exercises, especially the aspect of personal contact and constant union with God, Ciszek stated:

The *purpose* of the Spiritual Exercises for religious is to deepen their spiritual life, broaden it, [in order to] arrive at a deeper conviction and appreciation of both God and the spiritual life, i.e., to know the true value of our own selves before God in the struggle for perfection and the absolute necessity of God in acquiring it. Great gifts received from God—such as love of him, deep faith, or martyrdom—are given irrespectively of our merits, efforts, cooperation, sufferings, determination. They are free gifts (supernatural) bestowed upon those whom God chooses. The disposition will follow if God chooses. It is an after-effect. Here cooperation is necessary. The gift received can be taken back by God at any moment, no matter how much we would like to retain it or not. Our attitude should be to praise God when we receive it and likewise praise him when it is taken away from us, not feeling in the least depressed but humbly praising God with or without it. Everybody praises and loves God in his own way, in so far as it is given to him by the Creator, be he a religious or layman. Hence, all praise belongs to God and wherever it is had should be humbly and wholeheartedly directed to God with joy and sincerity.

The next meditation is on the so-called Principle and Foundation, i.e., that we are created to praise, reverence, and serve God, and hence save our soul, and that all other things are created for us to attain this end. The main enemy of this God-established order is pride.

Time, place, and circumstance do not change our obligations to God. But one should always prepare one's self in time of peace and prosperity for all possible changes for the worse. That is, living one's full life for God, taking into consideration first of all the actual and then the remote possible good and evil, and then properly preparing oneself with the help of God for any occasion. This is done by prayer, vigilance, and knowledge. Knowledge leads us to God, gives us God, and [enables us to] have life in him. If somebody says he is happy without God, he lies. No creature can satisfy the soul of man which was created for God.

In the Spiritual Exercises, meant to help one order one's life, St. Ignatius gives great attention to the disorder of sin; he invites the retreatant to meditate on the triple sin of the angels, of Adam and Eve, and of ourselves. Walter Ciszek dedicated five meditations to this theme. His first reflections were of a more general nature.

Considering sin we must be objective: i.e., not influenced by our feelings, desires, and wishes, but in all humility considering it as it is, asking God's help for a better understanding. Our repugnance, shunning excuses, dissatisfaction, personal attitudes, or any such hindrance on our part are barriers to a good meditation on sin. Open-mindedness, sincerity, humility, and simplicity are required before we begin. Thus disposed, God will help us and reveal the malice of sin in its fullness.

The sixth meditation of his retreat, probably at the beginning of the second day, August 5, was as long as it was personal. Not "man" or "we" were its subject, but Walter Ciszek himself. It began, again, with the sin of the angels.

God condemned the angels for all eternity for one sin, while he has spared me in spite of all my sins. I'm still living, not condemned nor eternally punished. God had mercy on me. What striking contrast there is between the angels and myself, their sins and mine, God's treatment of them and of me. He condemned them for all eternity after their one sin and spared me despite my having sinned so often. The wrath of God afflicted them but spared me. Why? Am I better than they? No, they sinned once and my sins are many. The reason for such action on God's part is to be sought in his mercy, goodness, and love. The condemned angels are an example of God's wrath: they are deprived of his vision for all eternity, separated from him, tortured in hell without end. The fallen angels are an object of God's justice, receiving what they deserved, while I with my many sins am an object of his mercy, goodness, and love—pardoned, blessed, and tolerated again and again, after my repeated sins.

It seems there is no end to God's mercy towards me, though the possibility of being the victim of his justice is real, actual, and possible. Can I be certain that the next time I commit a sin God will not mete out a just punishment, in the same manner as he has punished the angels? The possibility of falling under God's justice is a fearful thought. One that should keep you on guard against sin, constantly imploring God for his forgiveness and mercy for yourself and others. That holy and salutary fear should not leave us for a moment. That fear will keep us from sin, or at least make us reflect before committing it. With this renewed spirit, thank God for all his goodness and in the humility of thy heart seek thy salvation.

The reflection that followed shows his insight into the dynamics of temptation to sin.

Reflection: Do not intensify or create temptations for yourself by simply suppressing or negatively reacting to objects which in themselves are not sinful but indifferent: a glance at some person, object, picture, etc. It's better in the simplicity of your heart to glance at that person or look at that picture, destroying by that very act the cause of a temptation, whereas restraining oneself by force evokes stronger reactions of curiosity and desires to satisfy the appetites, which in turn bring about moral responsibility and disturbances of conscience with a feeling of guilt. We ourselves often bring about temptations for ourselves by creating difficulties rather than acting simply and ordinarily as most people react without subconscious feelings of fear and perturbation. Psychologically, be yourself and as natural as possible. Do not create a doubtful situation for yourself, or be indecisive in acting, or permit fear or cowardice to influence you. A resolute, decisive, open, courageous character with deep faith in God is what you want to develop. Repeating the Exercises gives you a deeper insight into their meaning.

At the end of this sixth meditation, Walter Ciszek returned in his memory to his days in Russia.

Personal sins: The Lord did not punish me enough in the camps. Instead, when all was lost and no hope existed, he almost miraculously saved me from perdition. Why? I don't know, because there is nothing worthwhile I did for him, but rather the opposite. He regarded the good prayers offered for me, and the power of these prayers did the miraculous for me.

What am I worth in comparison with all men? Many excel me in natural and spiritual gifts. With angels and with the saints in heaven there is no need of making comparisons. And if compared with God, I am nothing—the most insignificant of creatures who dared to sin against his Creator. Vile, selfish, corrupt, yet sullen enough to live with people and presumptuous enough to pray to God whom I offended. Sin made me obnoxious, degraded in the eyes of God, a monster that only sin could make. Yet in spite of all this, the Lord regarded my nothingness, preserved me, cared for me, and delivered me from hell itself without my deserving this in the least. Where is God's justice? Where are his sanctity and other attributes, to condescend so low because of me and lavish his blessings on one so unworthy of them?

Why this for me? Why spare me, when you did not spare others far worthier than I? Confused, abased, humiliated to the depths, Lord, I express my deep gratitude to thee. You have done so much for me, let me do something for thee. Whatever you ask from me, I shall do, however humiliating, difficult, dangerous—or even most ordinary, but requiring hidden sacrifice, immolation, in daily insignificant and unrecognized actions. Or, with all sincerity yet modest and simple humility, if you call for a total sacrifice of life itself, your unworthy servant is ready. There is nothing I will refuse you, if you will it. You have conquered sin, evil, and death itself; that is why you are life and resurrection itself.

His response to the call of Christ the King came naturally. "He wants men of greatest generosity and self-sacrificing," he wrote, "who renounce their own will and embrace his will instead." So, "Lord, if that is thy will in regard to me, unworthy one, I embrace it fully and promise with thy grace to remain faithful to the end to thy most holy will. This is my life, my joy, my strength and courage."

Then for five meditations, on August 6 and 7, he contemplated the hidden life of Jesus, from his birth till the beginning of his public ministry. "The shocking reality of sin and grace, the dilemma that exists between the faithful and the sinner" was never far from his mind, nor his memories of his darkest moment in the Lubianka prison. But, "Christ has conquered sin. Faith in Our Lord will also conquer sin."

It all began with Our Lady's consent and the Nativity.

Christ's birth in the cave taught the world a perfect detachment from earthly things. And the poorest things, as Christ showed, are sufficient and desirable for one filled with the Spirit of God. His lesson given was not a verbal sermon or eloquent treatise but actual things that he chose to experience from the moment of his birth in poverty. It's the spirit of perfect detachment that is to be had by all who follow Christ, and the readiness to embrace actual poverty when called to do so. This spirit is kept burning in our hearts by a modest religious life [in which we are] always thinking of him and living for him. It's using but not owning. It's a desire put into practice, guided by prudence: to be poor as Christ was in the cave.

Reflection: While in Lubianka prison, I felt a surety about myself, that God was with me. This prevented me from the fear usually felt in prison about the danger of being executed. The constant efforts of the interrogators to influence me morally and weaken my faith in God, in the Church, and in the priesthood seemed to have no effect on me. My only anxiety was about how I could influence them to change their attitude towards religion and God. The unsuccessful attempts on my part in this regard used to make me feel sad and depressed, and when they would increase their efforts to break me down morally, my only concern was to be on guard and not give in. The naiveté and simplicity of my attempts to convert and influence these adept men, out-and-out atheists, was proof enough how inexperienced I was with the reality of things in Russia. Furthermore, my unreal plans, asking God to enlighten me specially, so that I might with brilliance of intellect show them how wrong they were in going against God and how true the Catholic religion was, gave me much difficulty for a long time. I prayed earnestly for the grace to convert them, even if it required a miracle, but my prayer was not answered as I wanted. Yet God constantly increased my faith—though I did not ask for this—and strengthened it so much that never did it waver during all my stay in prison and in Russia for all those years. This simplicity—the result of inexperience—puzzled them always. They thought I was pretending and, under the cover of simplicity, hiding some important political issue from them. But I was sincere and too simple and open-minded to be understood by their contaminated minds.

Reflection: Another example of my naiveté was the resolution I privately made to convert Stalin. I prayed ardently for him daily, and I truly believed I would convert him if only I got a chance to talk to him personally. I cherished this naive thought for many years, until his death proved to me the unreality of my simple and inexperienced mind. On the other hand, this boyish attitude in things spiritual saved me from many dangers and preserved me throughout many years of prison and camp life from excesses that could have hurt my health, caused a psychological imbalance of character, or brought about fear or depression in the harder trials I had to bear. Yet all this I was spared, because of this childlike spiritual attitude of mine. Thus I preserved my health and sound mind to the end, always however remaining a puzzle to those with whom I lived.

The eleventh meditation, on the presentation of the Child Jesus in the temple, became a meditation on Christian ministry, and specifically priestly work.

Even the coming of the God-man Christ here on earth would not save all mankind. What an important lesson this fact conveys to us followers of Christ who are engaged in apostolic work. Is the preaching of the Gospel going to save everybody? No. Christ came to spread the good news and that is also our main duty: preaching and teaching Christ. Salvation is not a thing that we can give men. We are not expected to. Nor have we the power. That is strictly God's work. Ours is to sow and cultivate in the best possible way. And this apostolic work for the salvation of souls is done while encountering many difficulties and contradictions. If we sincerely try, there is going to be some influence had. It matters not whether we see the good being done or not; that does not pertain to us. That is God's affair. The persevering in doing good is what ultimately counts before God and men. At times the "doing of good" will be little more than good intentions and secret prayer, yet these, objectively looked upon, have great value.

Simeon, desiring as a just man to see the Lord, waited long in silent prayer until the time came when he was rewarded for his faithfulness. Working for God means sacrificing self and all else, when necessary; enduring all sorts of sufferings, hardships, contradictions; not changing one's mind and efforts, though seemingly nothing is being done for his cause. This self-abandonment, patient struggle, and the suffering of all sorts of failures, humiliations, and persecutions is what constitutes the real work in priestly ministry. Simeon has foretold the truth about Christ and also about those following him. What happened to him can and will happen to all his followers. They, too, will experience the trials so closely connected with the work of saving souls, each in his own particular way.

Anna the widow was also rewarded to see Christ after so many years of faithful service in the Temple, years full of prayer and fasting. The Lord wants sacrifice from everybody, more so from his priests. The apostolic work in a parish, in the missions, is full of such occasions for spiritual work. The indifference of people, their tepidity, their antagonism, their simple negligences, and hundreds of other factors are objects we could handle, work on, and improve if we felt more zealous about our work for Christ. Our own person, our relations with others, our duties, material needs, all offer so many opportunities for improving ourselves and others. All this done prudently presents itself as a special field for creating something new for God, a work most attractive and beneficial.

Closely connected to the theme of doing God's will was the theme of obedience, exemplified by Jesus' obedience. After an exhortation to "renew our spirit of obedience, living the will of God every moment of our life, no matter what happens, convinced in doing so by a vivid and deep faith," Walter Ciszek most naturally joined the ranks of Christ in the so-called meditation on the Two Standards. When he tried to depict Lucifer's camp, the image of the communist society came to his mind: "How subtle men are in their propaganda, urged on by the evil spirit. Under the pretext of doing good, they build, educate without God."

Even though he did not mention its name, it seems obvious that he had the Society of Jesus in mind when on August 8 he meditated on the vocation of the apostles.

The Church divine is indestructible. Those called to rule the Church and serve God in a special way in religion are the true life of Christ's Church. They represent the spirit of the Church as a living and teaching body. In the hierarchy and in the religious orders, Christ prolongs his Church here on earth. As a human institution it is susceptible to changes, to weakness in its members, but not to deteriorate. The priesthood and the religious are the stronghold of that institution created by Christ, and he is with them until the end of time. Persecution has always assaulted the Church, scandals and human intrigues weakened its ranks and impeded its flourishing fully, yet, in spite of the evil and the human weaknesses of Christ's Church, he will never permit it to perish.

This faith, even against hope, should be the lot of everybody who received a calling from Christ. This is a personal obligation of every follower of Christ:

to grow strong in his faith. Years of training made the first apostles superhumanly strong because of their vocation. We too, the elect of Christ, have the same opportunity to be as strong in our faith as the first apostles. The strength of the Church is in her members. If we the leaders have not the strong faith, the faithful who are entrusted to our care will not have it either. In the long historical chain of the existence of the Church, let us see to it that the link we compose in this prolonged series be strong and firm.

Meditating on the Sermon on the Mount and the preaching of the apostles, Father Ciszek felt called to be one of those "great men of God who are not afraid to risk everything for his sake," for according to him it was a lack of such men that kept humankind "mediocre and very self-centered." Yet with the supernatural "unusual powers" of Christ's followers came the warning to be always on guard against the evil that surrounds them: "Have no desires or intentions not in conformity with the purity of an innocent man."

The heavy underlining in his notes on Christ's entrance into Jerusalem may signify that Walter Ciszek was truly moved by Christ's display of power and by the strong, contrasting feelings he evoked: rejoicing from the ordinary people, hatred from the learned Jews. The meditation finishes as follows:

The great advantage we have from this public triumph of Christ is always to seek the will of God in every detail of our life. Our human intellect is too weak to be able to decide what to do in various difficult situations. God, knowing all, will communicate to us his will in every case, if only we permit him to do so—and provided also we firmly believe in him. Living for God in religion is doing what he wants us to do. And that is his work: *to show us his will.* Blessed really are those who live in *close union and familiarity with God. There is nothing* so sublime, so satisfying, and *so inspiring.* When writing so, I mean the will of God whatever it may be: entailed with great difficulties, trials, dangers, joys, consolations, etc. This is living a full life, a true life.

St. Ignatius suggests that the retreatant, before entering with Jesus in the Passion, must embrace a certain degree of humility and choose a way of life accordingly. Walter Ciszek, on the sixth and seventh day of his retreat, expressed himself in two long prayers.

XX. The Three Modes of Humility

Lord, it is not for me to decide or choose what is better for me. I came to the conclusion that abandoning myself to your divine providence and seeking in it thy divine will is the only life for me. Hence the choosing of what is better for me, I leave entirely to you. I myself would choose to be like you in everything in so far as I understand and see; because you to me are life eternal. But having lived this long and having tried so often is proof enough for me that I need to select another method of life than I have been using thus far. All this time, my personal effort seemed to me to be the criterion of action and achievement. I had successes, but also many failures and—sorry to say—self was so involved in what I did, although at the moment my intention was sincere, as you know. That impulse, that desire, that conviction that I could do everything, did not always have you for the ultimate cause. Frequently (and one can say always) the "I" element was deeply and intricately involved in my spiritual life. However, all I did was primarily for you, not for anybody else or for self.

Yet this method of action did not give me the proper results, good achievement and full ulterior peace and contentment. It lacked the perfect surrender of self. You were there but not as you would like it or prefer it. Instead of fighting self to the full extent and the evil I encountered, a lot of the time was wasted in fighting you, in opposing your full plan. For this reason, the faults, imperfections, and other disorders in me seemed never to vanish. They continuously gave me trouble and, in spite of the resolutions I made honestly and sincerely, only gave me occasion for repeated acts of humility. I see now that there is a more perfect method to serve thee than before. A method which leaves everything to your direction. You decide, chastise, change, take away, give the hard and easy, the sweet and bitter, consolation and desolation, the Cross—in a word, your will as designed in your divine providence is manifested to me in its various forms, and I accept it as sacred to me.

This way of life I heartily want to accept now, because you want it from me. No more is self-reliance going to prompt me to action again. The very important decision I am about to take in regard to the modes of humility does not disturb me as previously. In the peace of my heart, I come to thee with that ease of a child, with a child's confidence and familiarity, totally unconcerned, and join you in company, content and satisfied being with you without the least disturbance in my soul, and enjoy immensely your presence. I have no desires, no cravings, no complaints; possessing you I want nothing. That is my life, that is my all, that is my happiness. Living entirely your life, not the life I thus far have lived with the "self" element prominent, I act in thee, move in thee, and do everything in thee. I'm living your life, not mine. What happens in me now is yours. It is the result of your operation in me. This is the new gift you gave me, a gift that you will receive back when solemnly I shall make the holocaust, the full immolation to you in the presence of my Blessed Mother and the whole heavenly court, pronouncing my solemn vows. This day shall be a public confirmation of your love in me and my love in thee, a union to which you have led me for so many years.

So then, the question of the third degree of humility: how does it stand? There can be no more questions in regard to you, Lord, any longer. You have solved every problem, every item in my life, by your infinite love towards me, by absorbing me in your divine life without any restrictions—and I, O my God, surrender totally to this wonderful act of your love. Nothing exists for me now but you and your love. Where is your love going to lead me? My answer I find in you and only in you. Act, Lord. I am ready to begin the new life to which you invite me. To you all praise and glory for ever and ever.

XXI. Making a Choice of a Way of Life
Lord what can I give you that I did not receive from you? You moved me to embrace a new life of self-abandonment to thy divine providence. I responded to your call as best I could, according to the understanding and grace you gave me, without making any reservations whatsoever. It was the purest act I could make, prompted by your love, [an act] of total surrender to your love with all its consequences that will take place on the day of my last vows. A perfect renunciation of self and the world, simply because of you, and of you wanting this. To me this will be a day of experiencing the apex of your love towards me, a love that has guided me for so many years through great dangers and perils. Your love for me was so strong that sin itself was impotent in the face of it. The love that you poured into my soul, unworthy as I was—though sincere and honest as a child—reflected itself not in the sublime acts of the soul proper to a soul filled with thy divine love, but in a strong and deep faith in thee. Though sin has pierced the soul with its pungent sting and destructive force, and permeated it deeply with its venomous influence ready to poison the whole soul and carry it off to the gates of perdition, your wonderful gift of this strong faith in thee has saved me.

At the very moment when sin was ready to rejoice in a full victory over the soul and claim its full rights and possession of it, it met the shield of faith on its way to conquer and was retarded at this very moment of contact by the superhuman power of faith—and then was pushed out with inexorable force and driven out, completely crushed and crumbled. Faith again revived the soul, instilling in it a deep compunction and humble depression. Yet in this humiliated state it felt justified and kept you in possession, in spite of the repeated attacks of the evil onslaughts of sin to never let you alone again in spite of its degradation and utter unworthiness. The power of faith is untold. Even thee, O infinite God, could not free yourself from its critical and decisive grip.[22]

Nothing then is fearful for men of faith, because nothing in this sinful world of ours is capable of destroying this vital faith with its deadly grip. Even the most horrible sin is as nothing in opposition to this vivid faith.

You have worked so wonderfully to my spiritual and better good. Even when everything was absolutely against me, no human spark of hope remained, and total moral ruin was imminent to devour me as a victim already destined to perish, you, O Lord, in all serenity have directed this inevitable tragedy and disaster to a goal of salvation. You have brought freedom where there existed not the least pretext for having it; you have shown your power where no human power in existence was available to bring about this wonderful change in the freedom restored me. All this was hidden from me for a long time, and now you deign to reveal your secret workings for me out of the infinite bounty of thy love for me. Today, having received this great grace from you, O Lord, I abandon myself entirely to you and a life in union and possession of thee. In this spirit do I proceed to make my last vows. In this spirit I humbly desire to remain to the end of my life.

———

In that same spirit Walter Ciszek entered the series of nine meditations on the passion of Christ. They became meditations on true love, self-abandonment to God's will, and patient suffering. On August 10 he wrote,

In suffering it is a great grace to know how to conduct one's self rightly. Of course, those who live in union with him will rarely make mistakes in this regard. Jesus showed by his conduct in Herod's house that silence, too, is an effective way of showing your own truthfulness. What is your own, means it is forceful. It carries the message directly without any fear.

However high your desires may be, however morally solid, to influence others you must receive special help. No matter how humble and degraded you are, if the Lord chooses you, then you are going to be effective, but only in so far as you firmly believe that the work done is Christ's and solely take care that he gets maximum glory from it. Our Lord in the passion is such a striking example of total immolation for his Father's cause.

———

While meditating on Jesus' being taken from Herod's house to that of Pilate and being scourged on Pilate's orders, Father Ciszek wrote some reflections on God's ways with him in the retreat. The context was that of Jesus' passion: "Christ feared no more, but suffered acutely: his desecrated body, sad heart, and tired mind."

The facility to pray comes solely from God, but the peace that comes from faith is always in the soul, whether we find it easy or difficult to pray.

A good retreat is not considered such because of many ideas and thoughts, but because one had self-abandonment and experienced, with humility and faithfulness, what God gave him.

The peace had during the retreat is like a barometer. If one commits the least fault deliberately, the peace of the retreat, like something physical, is disturbed and is ready to vanish, with commotion arising, if one does not reject immediately the small evil out of his heart. Other actions may come or go—not deliberate incongruous actions—and the peace of heart is not in the least disturbed. But suffer the slightest deliberate fault to enter the heart, and peace recoils quickly.

————————

He then returns to the matter of Jesus' passion and concludes,

Although he abhorred all this unjustifiable brutality, Christ was consistent in his sufferings: the intensity, duration mattered not. He never weakened in spite of all, but remained faithful to his Father unto death. A wonderful lesson for us sinners is hidden in Christ's passion. From Christ suffering, from Christ humiliated, we should learn. To serve God well is to remember that everything received from him is a gift, whether it be consolation or desolation, hardships, or whatever. Even for one committing sin, the gravest sin should not separate us from God. The moment we are conscious of it, that very moment our faith should hold on to God and let him not depart. Strong faith is powerful enough to keep God from parting from us after sin, because faith, being a gift from God, is God himself. Holding our Lord back at the same time and seeking reconciliation with him, we are again in full possession of him.

————————

The following meditations, one on August 10 and three on August 11, were dedicated to the passion of Christ and his resurrection.

Love is the infinite power of God, which produced and preserves all creation. To this love all belong. Jesus gave us an example of this heroic love for us, for me personally, sinner though I am. He wants us to imitate him in this heroic way in so far as he gives us the grace. Christ on the Cross showed to the whole world the power of the spirit, the divine qualities of the divine soul. The unlimited power of prayer coming from the soul. In the most utter of sufferings, the soul is capable of pardon. His Father was always in his mind; the love he had for him burnt until the end. And for this love of his Father, the mystery of the Cross was perfected.

———

What touched Walter Ciszek most were, on the one hand, the themes of patient and humble acceptance of suffering, and on the other hand, the fight against evil that will last till the end of time. "The Church after the resurrection rose from the persecution she suffered. Now, with the spirit of the resurrection, the Church is going ahead, opposing the attacks of her enemies with the courage and strength of Christ, the founder. The time for battle is still on and will last to the end of time. In union with the Church is our victory and final resurrection in Christ."

He concluded his vow retreat on the evening of August 11 with the so-called contemplation to obtain divine love. It became a long, personal prayer:

Lord, the numerous blessings bestowed upon me through the redemption and creation are a sign of the love you have for me. The particular graces I have received from you from my childhood until now are your special favors towards me: the blessings in the Society are most conspicuous; the strong vocation you gave me to go to Russia. The special care you had over me there, the strong faith you filled my heart with, kept me from being possessed by sin and, when all hope disappeared from the horizon, a spark of faith still lighted my soul.

This wonder worker—the faith, I mean—preserved me for thee. And you, out of sheer love, delivered me from the evil and hopeless situation I found myself in. It was all the interior gift of faith that you prized in me, that faith which had power over you, to which you yourself had to succumb as life's experience has shown so many times. The faith that works wonders: the spiritual uplifts which even had power over your infinite omnipotence because that spiritual power of faith deeply seeded in the soul was nothing else than your infinite power operating in me freely, because you willed it so and gave me that greatest of all gifts: to will as you will. Sin, death, and earthly power were impotent in the face of this power. Weak as I was, the faith you gave me operated. When I was in no way responsible for it, it was strongest in me. When sin overwhelmed me, faith crushed sin again and again. All that was mine was weakness and sin; yours was the power of faith in me. Death continuously threatening to destroy me instilled no fear in me because your faith within me operated.

The questions put to me often by those doing their best to destroy me—such as "How are you still alive?"—were a source of wonder. And even here in the U.S., the most frequently asked question "How did you survive?" can be answered only by the response "Faith preserved me." It worked wonders. Earthly power decided not to allow me to return to the U.S. Up to the very last moment they held out. I personally hadn't done the least thing for my release; nobody I knew in Russia gave it a thought. No one imagined I'd ever return to the States. Yet, seeing the dangers, I only had faith in thee. Finally faith triumphed. So simple did it work to a successful end.

Lord, how can I ever repay you enough for what you did for me? Will this be enough: to express my sincere gratitude and to praise thee to the end of my life in prayer, sacrifice, and labors? If I give my body, my mind, and my soul all back to you, will this be enough for you, or for what you have done for me? If I make the best promises and resolutions that can be made, Lord, this is still not enough for you. I know that your love is still manifesting itself so strongly towards me. Unworthy as I am, you are permitting me to take my last vows. In these I want to make the perfect sacrifice. Not that I myself thought of it but because you have inspired me with your grace and suggested the best possible way of serving you. All promises, all efforts, all good works aside, Lord, all that I can do and achieve even with thy grace are not the best offerings I can make for you. There is still something better. All these good works, though perfect, have something of self in them.

You prompt me to go further, and, though I do not realize fully the meaning of what I'm going to offer you at present, in the spirit of faith I do this because it comes from you. No matter the cost or the risk. This offering made now is exactly what I wish to make on the day of my final vows. In advance, Lord, with all sincerity and honesty of heart, in the deepest humility, with vivid faith "I abandon myself simply and totally to thy divine providence." This is what you want from me; this is what I give generously and irrevocably. Nothing do I ask, nothing do I fear, nothing else do I want. You yourself have prepared and led me to this, and I now respond freely to your invitation, having only the faith that prompted me to this. Amen.

6

Working for God

For as far as we know, Walter Ciszek never kept a spiritual diary, but occasionally, either during a retreat or on other occasions, he would write down some personal reflections, especially in the years immediately following his return to the USA. An important theme for him was his apostolate as a priest and a religious and how best to serve God. Time and again the key concepts are God's grace freely given and our constant need of humility. His thoughts on these matters are both analysis and private exhortation, based on his lived experience.

Personal Reflections Written April 29, 1964
The tension you feel before talking publicly is something that you cannot control entirely. Yet this nervous tension should not so influence you as to interfere with your thinking. The consciousness that you are doing the right thing and doing it solely for God should be the force penetrating every word you say.

Of course, you have limitations, and in the course of the talk you will make blunders, saying something not exactly as you should have, or even praising yourself publicly, which is humiliating. Yet all these insufficiencies, shortcomings, and defects are so human that, in some way or another, they will always manifest themselves in your speech. But to feel discouraged by this, or to be too touchy about committing them is a sign of pride and a sin against God. The faults you have, and which you may commit, not deliberately and maliciously but because of your frailty and limited intellectual capacity, should be a source of true humility and a cause for betterment.

Your principal inspiration should be a sincere desire to promote God's work as best as you can, by prayer, long preparation, union with him, and absolute faith in his cooperation. Every good work you try to do will be colored by the spirit you possess, with all its defects and limitations. This does not impede God from attaining his end through your good efforts. The success of any enterprise depends on personal effort, persistence, prudence, and basically on deep faith in God. Acting in this way will make our actions wholly good not only from the natural perspective but from the supernatural as well; all our actions in life should be considered and understood totally from these two perspectives.

Doing so, however, will not exclude failures, mistakes, and even errors. These are not necessary for true success; their absence only adds to the intensity and fullness of success. The ultimate criterion of all success in our life should be God—a greater union with him, a stronger faith, a purer prayer. The success we should strive after is to reflect more perfectly God's will in our actions. Our apostolate should not limit itself only to direct contact with people or to public activity. Our whole life, every minute of it, should be an apostolate in itself. First of all, by our prayer, by our very presence, we should help others come closer to God.

The more effort we make, and the more preparation and interest we show in the spiritual life, the more we will like it, see its astounding beauty, and, above all, live it. The spiritual is attained [in the same way] as the natural. How much physical, intellectual, and psychological work is necessary to achieve something [in the natural order]? Yet every natural achievement, as a good work, can be improved and perfected. That is why man is always making progress in his works, entering new fields of enterprise where [the possibility of] perfection is unlimited. The same can be said of the spiritual. Yet every good act is a unity and the result of a process within the soul; it is a good worthy of praise and admiration whether it manifests the highest possible perfection or not.

For every good action we should thank God, rejoice that he gave us the grace to do it, and strive to do better. The secret is not to be discouraged but ever to do God's will and not pay too much attention to your own self.

Personal Reflections Written April 30, 1964
The feelings of man easily change. If you permit yourself to be carried away by them, your attitude towards people, things, God, and the spiritual life changes and becomes an inferiority complex. This changed attitude should not be simply suppressed but rather led into another channel that leads you to union with God. By doing this you evoke new feelings or, rather, the changed attitude effected by this new relationship with God takes on a new form, meaning, and intensity, eliminating the old feeling of perturbation. As a result, peace and satisfaction ensue, together with deep faith that this is the right conviction one should have. Its strength becomes so great that the verbal expression of this state of mind and soul carries with it and conveys to others the inner force one has. The result is a strong influence on others. The ideas conveyed and impression made on others tend to evoke the same reaction in them, prompting them to imitate and develop similar characteristic traits in their souls.

The guiding principle in such movements of the soul should always be the intellect helped by the will. All this, however, implies that the principal cause and motivating power is God—union with him, his divine providence and most holy will. This entire psychological process, with the effort made and the facility of doing it, is considered an act of the highest prayer. This form of prayer belongs to the unitive way, a friendship with and a possession of God, which becomes a second nature. It depends on a constant renewal of spirit and mind, which so preserves the union with God that not even the surrounding distractions that are continuously present can lessen or change that interior strong disposition of soul.

The true humility that arises from this does not consist in feeling oneself discouraged—shunning difficulties, having doubt, uncertainty, or an exaggerated estimation of one's limitations—but rather in a positive, certain feeling of possessing God and the good God is doing through you while not attributing this to oneself, but entirely to God alone.

Personal Reflections Written in Philadelphia, May 14, 1964

What life has in store for you is impossible to know. The wise are prepared for every occasion that might arise by being united with God and keeping their souls in order. The fact, however, that the precautions taken are not always a guarantee to prevent mishap is evident from experience. The great asset, however, is not to get perturbed easily or, if possible, ever. If you do not lose sight of God's Providence, you can succeed in remaining in control much more easily, than if you do not think of God.

The outcome of an incident depends upon maintaining your presence of mind. This moral power is felt by others as much as by yourself. However, this does not mean that you should expose yourself to dangers without reason, or for insufficient reason. Such a way of acting borders on presumption, and it can happen that God will withhold his help in such cases. Depending totally upon yourself, there is little chance of success.

Working for God will often put you in difficult situations because this is the will of God. If you want to be faithful to God and his will, you must take the risk of not being afraid of the consequences, knowing that God is with you and that the hardships and sacrifice needed to promote God's cause are a part of God's plan. They must be received with the same disposition as success. In the final run, we are just instruments in God's hands to be used as he wills, not as we will. The strong and sincerely devoted will prove themselves faithful in his service. The selfish will shun difficulties, put their own reasons before those of God, and will impede, by this, the work intended by God.

Change of place, circumstances, people, and environment can influence you and distract you greatly, if you submit yourself to their influence. It depends on how you prepare yourself for these occasions; how you react under them, and how much personal effort you use will decide the degree of failure or success. Be prepared always, so that nothing finds you off guard, and you can be sure of controlling yourself and the situation in which you may find yourself. These are the kinds of apostles needed now to spread God's teaching. The fearful have no place with Christ. He ended up on the cross; perhaps you will have to pay the same price for his cause. Be willing. Be prepared through prayer, recollection, and union with him.

Personal Reflections Written December 31, 1964: "Thanksgiving for the Year"

The world with God, and without him, are two different worlds entirely. Where there is God, men have a spirit that is developed according to the principles of Christ. Christian virtue is what distinguishes them from people who do not believe in God.

Looking back on my life, after living a little over a year in the United States, [since returning from Russia] I can really thank God for what he has done for me. It is his divine providence that protected me throughout the twenty-three years in Russia. He prepared me for that mission, led me into that country when it was most dangerous, protected me all that time, and when it became critical (morally, physically, and socially) he returned me to the U.S.

Lord, I am thankful to thee for all you did for me in Russia. You know I was sincere with you, and though I accomplished practically nothing at all for you, I still remained faithful. Though I was weak and showed this many times, you were most dear to me. You were first in my thoughts and desires. Nothing attracted me so strongly that I would not change it for you. Never have I forgotten my priesthood, nor did I interfere in the plans that your providence had ordained; and you blessed me, though I was unworthy. You did not forget me in times of danger and in times of peace. The spiritual friends I gained, who helped me continuously with their prayers, were and are numerous. You continue to bless me now, showing me that my mission is not yet finished. And, in all this, there is so little that I have done. All I can say sincerely is that, realizing your goodness, I am constrained to remain humble and let you work in me to the end. I rejoice in you alone, for in an unostentatious way you worked great things against the powerful of this world. Though I do not see your plans for the future, I am ready to be with you to the end, to do what you want me to do, even if it be your will for me to die for you; because what you ordain is true and necessary.

I am really thankful and grateful to you, Lord, for letting me realize what great blessings I enjoy now in this new life: the blessings of the religious life with its peace, its deep spiritual gifts, its consolations, simplicity, freedom, sincerity, goodness, its abundance of graces, the dignity of the order, respect of the priesthood, and all the spiritual benefits of religion [. . . .] The material benefits, likewise, are great: the home to live in, privacy, the good food, order, the religious atmosphere surrounding me always, with chapel, Mass; all physical necessities of life taken care of (doctor bills, expenses); no family or children and all the worries that come from them, no money worries, no physical labor to gain a piece of bread; the company of my brethren, who also seek to serve God, the sympathy of people always ready to help the Society of Jesus and show interest in me.

Are we worthy of all this, Lord? Are we not [already] living, enjoying the hundredfold you promised to all who leave mother and father for your sake? Yes, Lord, this is all yours, and I deeply thank you for all of it, appreciate your goodness, and am perpetually grateful to you. But this can all be taken away from me. [. . . .] Lord, grant that I be faithful as before, if the time comes to suffer for you. I am the richest man, in all respects, as a religious. I realize this, but I enjoy all this because you have given it to me and favored me so much.

Lord, I am particularly grateful and thankful to you for having filled me with your spirit of charity and [the desire for] Christian perfection. How different is this spirit from the one possessed by the people in Russia. Instead of Christian virtues, the passions of those people have developed enormously, for they do not have your full help as we do. They hate each other so strongly; they are so quickly envious, jealous, and, above all, lack the charity of one who follows thee. How much they are losing, how severely they are punished, yet they do not realize this. Lord, with all their sins, faults, and defects, I still like them all for your sake alone. The evil that overcomes them, I reject, but their souls I bring to you as an offering, for you have chosen me to know their spiritual needs and misery, and, as a consequence, they are mine. For them do I beseech thee, asking you to bless them and have mercy on them. You know how to bless. You know how to deliver from evil. This is my prayer to you for the abandoned and afflicted Russian people. I firmly believe in you because I have already experienced your special providence.

Personal Reflections Written in July—August 1965

Friday, July 2, 1965—The American people eat too much and have too much of a variety of food stuffs. This is all good, if we remember God and thank him for his gifts and be always ready for the worst. We are baptized with the Holy Spirit, the teacher of all truth.

Saturday, July 3, 1965—Every intellectual being by living develops and has his constant experiences which increase his knowledge. This progress may be negative or positive—with or without God—bringing him joy, happiness, or misery and dejection. All this must be taken into account when dealing with people in order to be able to understand and help them. Therefore in every case which brings you in contact with people, you will find something new that you do not have and you also can give something new to others from your own experiences. The attitude is respect; it can develop later into love and a spirit of sharing with others.

Saturday, July 24, 1965: In giving retreats you must be recollected, prepared, avoiding all willful distractions, and even then God's inspirations come when he wills. This is a condition that is more proper but not a guarantee that God's grace will follow. Hence the constant need for humility, knowing that we are at his mercy and that whatever he does is good for us. That is the unrestricted faith and love we should have in God. Such faith and love come after many trials. This will prove one's sincerity. To realize that God is free, and to serve him as such without expecting a reward or recompense from him after every sacrifice is the true understanding one must have to serve him best. A spirit of total unselfishness—my unworthiness. If you have done everything possible for God, consider that you have only done what you ought. Many times you plan to do something for God, and then you see that you did not do it—conscious of what you ought to do and what you are actually doing, a proof of our impotency and the might of God's power over us. That holds not only for particular actions of ours but especially for actions of others, nations, and events in this whole universe, in all actions good or bad. Hence, the great meaning of prayer in the life of man—my life, the lives of others and all belong to God—the obligation is to act that way. Those affected by a retreat or sermon show that God, not man, has worked.

Monday, July 26, 1965: One may be very close to God, but this is simply a pure blessing and gift of God's grace. If it is taken away, you shall feel as miserable and helpless as any sinner. Our actions in regard to God are not ours but God's; hence, the constant need for humility in the spiritual life. It is essential always to be conscious of and to confess our inability and sinfulness. Yet the unshaken faith in God's Providence over us should never leave us. During a temptation, you're full of [what is tempting you] and feel guilty. It's not in your power to free yourself from it immediately and entirely until God steps in with his grace. No matter what you experience, or how intelligent you are, God is all, God the absolute. All else is meaningless without God. Sin is our misery, yet God conquered it. God is our only good.

Friday, July 30, 1965: God is good and loves everybody, not only those specially consecrated to him. This is something that brings joy to the heart and disposes one more to appreciate the spiritual life of the lay people.

Sunday, August 1, 1965: Do not make resolutions as if you are going to keep and do them, but make them as one united with God, believing he is going to perfect them in you in whatever he wishes, while you humbly accept and do his will, knowing that whatever happens, it's God's will. Always possess him and rejoice in him with all your shortcomings, weaknesses, and sins, forgetting self absolutely, as you are, and perfecting your knowledge and love for him, and in him alone. No matter where you are, what you do, what happens to you good or bad, you are his and he is yours, your all. You should have no other desire but for him alone, in spite of your fallen human nature.

Friday, August 6, 1965: What people or nations are, they are such because God wants it. He is the giver, the ruler, and the chastiser. You are genuine if you are mighty in word and *deed*.

7

The Idea of Priesthood

Among Father's notes there is an undated sheet with the title "Faith of Priest," possibly an outline of a speech he gave. It contains precious personal information on how he maintained his priestly identity in Russia, how he kept faith in the mysteries of religion, prayer, sacraments, and celibacy. Prayer is always needed, he says, and strength of spirit and heart is more important than theological clarity and accuracy when we are explaining what we believe. In Russia, when he argued with atheists, it was not intellectual reasoning that affected them but the faith he manifested regardless of the difficulties.[23]

In another undated set of notes, probably from the 1960s, Father Ciszek came back to this topic, again in the context of his experiences with the ideology of atheistic communism. Talk in the Soviet Union regarding the world is always insufficient, he says, but faith in Christ shows us the direction in which truth is to be found; it teaches us that we are more than mere humans and permits us to look at guilt and sin with the eyes of God, who out of love created us and the present world as we know it. For Walter Ciszek, as a Jesuit priest, his "noble mission" is to bring people to God, that they may serve him too.

"Faith of a priest"

As a priest I believed what I had been taught: that I was an *Alter Christus* and that Mass was the greatest act in the world (purity of angel). I persisted in my belief in the priesthood and the infinite value of Mass, in spite of my incapacity to explain it all or of the lack of others' interest. I said Mass in spite of not seeing any immediate value, profit, or satisfaction. I held on to the priesthood in spite of disadvantages: being deprived of an apartment, being looked upon as physically impotent. I did not respond to the love of women and was thus considered a man without a heart, cold—I was offended by this, suffered, for I knew my physical capacities, my violent character. I rejected a marriage proposal in the garage where I worked [...], all simply to keep my original idea of priesthood intact, pure, sacred. This cost me and I could not explain it. I firmly believed that if I forsook saying Mass, I would succumb and be unfaithful. I felt I did not belong to that society, I felt out of place with my spiritual conviction—they did not understand it, yet they respected me. I said Mass, though unworthy, so as not to lose faith. I prayed to the Blessed Mother and complained, for I have made mistakes. I never, however, depreciated the priesthood, Mass, the spiritual life, religion. I suffered, yet I felt something superior in me that elevated me above it all—atheism, hatred for religion; the system could not satisfy me, not enough. [...] I feared being unfaithful and saw no hope for the future, yet I believed in God's Providence. Still, my idea of priesthood has not changed, neither of the Mass, nor of celibacy, nor of spirituality.

"Call of the Infinite"[24]

As a religious priest following the call of God in faith, I dedicated myself to his service, which requires a lifelong effort. It's the religious priestly life with all its demands that should concern me most. The idea of God, who in his providence is leading me to my final destiny, should permeate my whole life from morning to night, day after day, week, month, year, till the very end, in rising and going to bed, in praying and working, in assisting at saying Mass or other spiritual duties, in eating, resting, recreating, sleeping, being with others or alone. In all these and other minute details of my exterior or interior life I should be always inspired by faith in this unfailing Providence. The spirit of such an apostolate will draw and attract others to God, and that is our aim in serving God and his people. The things at our disposal, given us abundantly or in a limited measure, will be used for that purpose.

Growing in the Spirit of such dedication will develop a strong disposition of will, totally grounded and united with the creator's will. It will confirm us in the habit of ever rising in spirit, directed to eternity, accepting everything that occurs in our life, good or evil, sins, failure, as his Will: success, catastrophe, hardship, suffering, trial, enemy persecution, misunderstanding. Even death will not divert us from the initial grace given us in our vocation, because faithfully living from moment to moment in grace is the power in us leading us to our destiny, which is God himself. We came to existence because of God's infinite love, and we are sustained as what we are, and what all else around us is, thanks to that love. Our very nature then tends to reproduce in us this inborn tendency of love for our Creator, God the Father, and for his Son, who exemplified to us ungrateful ones that unchanging love for us on the cross, also for our fellow man, created like ourselves, children of God. All else that this wonderful world has in it is a direct gift of his goodness for all men without distinction. What prevents us from serving God in love? Only sin.

Not that I'm narrow minded, but to me a mystery is a mystery for all time; you either accept it or not, with all its consequences, believe or not. I believe in God because I know who man is, what the world is. Yet I love the world, in God only. I'm not afraid of changes and know they will and must come. In regard to liturgy, and everything in the Church, nothing will phase me, but the fundamental ideas will not change; in those I believe, and I serve God acting on first inspiration, knowing that in the natural order, all changes produce friction and tension, so, also, do they in spiritual order. Grace is continuously changing, elevating us higher and higher. The results—pain, depression, uncertainty—may be unintelligible to the intellect, yet they are fully acceptable to faith.

This simple attitude is based on faith in God and finds a solution for all in the interior and exterior problems confronting me and other people. Communicating this spirit is my apostolate—sharing my experiences with others, my love for them. God is pure, simple act. This simplicity he reproduces in us through faith in him, which brings hope and flourishes in love. All these three virtues go together; they do not exist separately. It's not confusion that results from faith, but simple trust in God, factually and actually, amidst the turmoil of the world. To keep this simple faith in God alive and crystal clear, as grace gives it, is the lifelong task of each and every one of us. Prayer again is the means of keeping us in this state of purity, always uniting and fortifying us in God. God gives and does for us, and we accept and follow where he leads us; that is our role in his divine plan of salvation for us.

Purity is not the intactness of the virtue itself but rather the interior estimation, attitude, appreciation of the ideal found in God and the Blessed Virgin compared to my weakness and possible unfaithfulness expressed in concrete action, or better, sins committed in this regard. A humble admittance of one's sinfulness before the merciful ever-loving God is the strength received from such action. God's infinite power is reflected in such humility, compensating for my utter nothingness. This is my joy and consolation. The constant need to keep this humble relationship towards God, by never forgetting my sinfulness and his holiness, revealed to me in the eyes of faith, is the purity of the ideal imparted me by grace. If I fail, God again humbles me by letting me fall, to restore the proper relationship of creature to Creator.

That is why, although I see the good of communism, present and future, it never satisfied or convinced me, for it lacked entirely the power that faith had, resulting in peace and joy. Faith gives you a foretaste of eternity, the divine life. Hence, no cold, suffering, hunger, slave labor, loss of freedom, sickness, degradation, lack of comfort, want, need, hardship, difficulty, discouragement, feeling forsaken, failures, abandonment, or any other human mishap can deprive one from a well-grounded faith; neither sin nor death, the world, the powers of evil or good. For simple faith in God is above all these. Bringing God to people is the noble mission of the priest. Where you have failed, bring him again; if guilty, repair your guilt. This is done through a spirit of prayer and sacrifice.

8

A Voice from Eternity

On September 23, 1976, Walter Ciszek suffered, for the second time in a month, a major heart attack and cardiac arrest, which he miraculously survived. A registered nurse who was present remarked later how amazed she was that he had no residual effects at all; she added, "[It was] incredible, because he was not in good health to begin with." During the five hours he was unconscious, Walter Ciszek had a near-death experience that would determine the remaining years of his life; he had "come back" for a reason, and he firmly believed God's providence made it happen. Nevertheless, he spoke or wrote about it with great discretion.[25] The following text was composed by Walter Ciszek around 1978.[26]

I just passed out, and during that time I know I wanted to go to God. That was my whole disposition, because I came to the brink of this world where eternity began, and I had to pass over that. Yet, I felt that, though my spirit was outside the body, there was a certain kind of drawing of the body and the soul to each other. It was [...] the body that was not functioning. I went off and said, "Here I come, Lord, here I come." I was trying to get over [to him] and I saw the Blessed Trinity—the Father, the Son and the Holy Spirit.[27] The Blessed Mother was [also there, but] turned sideways, so I didn't see her face. I really wanted to get over to the other side, but nothing happened, [even though] I tried and tried. I was going into a deep depression when I saw I couldn't get over, and my willful efforts were getting weaker and weaker.

Then, when I became kind of frustrated, from nowhere it just happened that *I felt infinite peace* and, right after that, *perfect reconciliation*. The infinite peace I understood, but the perfect reconciliation I didn't understand. Then, out of that [sensation], again I heard a voice speaking as if from eternity. It was a *loud* voice that filled the whole world with the splendorous light of eternity as it said, "*I am going to cure you, and, at the same time, I am going to teach you how to live.*" Then, when that voice disappeared, I heard within it a voice resounding like a thunder. I then saw Our Lord, appearing just as we visualize him in the New Testament. He was pointing at me and said, "I am going to teach you how to live"; then he began to tell me precisely what he meant. He said, "I am going to teach you how to be pure, how to be simple, how to be modest, how to be poor, obedient, prayerful, and believing. I am going to purify you, and, after that purification, I am going to enlighten and elevate you through compunction, sorrow, and repentance, by uniting you with me in my passion, in my suffering, sacrifice, reparation, and hope in the resurrection; all these together will be your act of love for me." And that was so convincing.

When I finally got out of this unconsciousness I was in for all those hours—I don't know how long it actually lasted—those who were with me thought I'd never pull through. When I opened up my eyes, they all came over and asked me [how I was]. "I'm not going to die," I told them. When they asked, "How do you feel?" I said, "I feel OK because I'm not going to die." They didn't know what I was talking about. Then I told the woman, who was with me all the time [...], "The moment I get out of here I'm going to write about this." That's what kept me from relapsing into another heart attack after that, because I had the conviction that, no matter what happened to me, I'd get out of it. It took me almost a month [...], but I did get out of it.

When they let me out of the hospital, I kept growing in the things [I had experienced]. What I did was to repeat all this in my Masses, actually, before I said the Mass. Also, I always mention this experience in my examen of conscience. I have been doing this for two years, and there's an added growth to all this, [...] in the inner center of it all; it is the consciousness of God's love for me and the infused love for him, which he has given me. And that is what I'm working on.

Yet, it does not eliminate the weakness of your human nature; but it does give you a conviction of what God really is, and this is what I tell the people: that God loved you first, and he's loving you now, and he will love you for all eternity.[28] Yet, to become conscious of that is not *your work*. Your work is, I would say, [to follow] the pattern he gave me—it's a pattern for everybody: be pure, simple, and humble. You have to be that: pure, simple, and humble—that is, each of us in his particular state in life. I'm a religious priest, I can't get married; it's out of the question for the religious. But for those who are married, it means to be pure in the married life—that is, *live* the married life but in the right way, in the way God wants [you to live] it; that's the purity, that's what we're talking about. But you have to be poor in spirit, you have to be obedient to the will of God, you have to have a life of prayer, a life of deep faith.

To have that, you must always be undergoing purification. You're always going to be enlightened [by the knowledge of] God's ways and elevated [to live] in his ways, and being in it always passes through the purification that we call sorrow, compunction, repentance, and union with Christ in his passion. That's why I always talk about his passion so much, because without it you don't have anything. And [sharing in his] passion means nothing else than that you're going to have to suffer to make reparation, you have to make sacrifices, and you have to have hope in the resurrection; all these put together make one great act of love for God.

So it's not just one little thing but everything working together, and what he promises [as a help in this work] is faith and prayer. No matter how bad I feel—so close to a heart attack, just about dying—I say, "Lord, I still believe, even though there's not a bit of chance that you're going to cure me." Not that that may be true—in the sense that I know that now I'm cured, I have no trouble. But that's my faith in him, and that is my act of love [for him]. I accept that I have to go through all this and see that this is the way he loves me, and I have to love him back with that, with this suffering that I now have. This is real love. It is this that I see as an invitation: "If I love you so much, why don't you show me your love? My Son showed me his love by all that he did for me. Why can't you do the same?" So that's the motivation for me. I ask for help. I ask for a cure, while leaving it all up to him. Healing and curing mean nothing else than knowing how to live with your illness and knowing how to handle it. Further, faith tells me that he permits me to have this problem. And if he permits me to have sickness, he has a purpose [for doing that], and that purpose is always [the achievement of] a deeper and greater purification. That's my belief, and it comes from him—I have to accept that.

Yet, I know my prayer is always heard. Every time I pray, I have no doubt that he hears my prayer, but he doesn't give an instant cure, so I'm not asking for that. I'm just asking for healing, and that healing is nothing else than my consciousness that whatever I ask for is accepted by God, and God responds to it in the way God wants. I see that in the way things are happening to me. God has slowly made it clear that it pleases him for me to suffer, just as it pleased him when his Son suffered, because he was doing his will. Yet it remains my strong and unspoken belief that he can change my sickness into health in a moment. But keeping this to one side, I know there is another side to it: my understanding of the whole economy of God's salvation. And it is here that I see an invitation, which is a grace given in this kind of healing, [the awareness] of how to live with this illness and how to handle it properly. It's an invitation to love God in my illness as he loves me and to be grateful for his gift of my love for him. And this is the whole thing.

Every day that I repeat this, I have a deepening in that perfect reconciliation; I see what it is now. It's the constant renewing of yourself in faith and hope. And now I'm [at that stage] that it's not only faith and hope but it's also love. So I'm working on all these, on the basis of grace. I had had all these before, but not with the same depth, which I now have in these things. It's not the same conviction [I once had]. It's to be one with yourself, never losing the sight of his presence, and sensing his presence, you see. This is different. And yet it's a deep humility, a deep poverty of spirit. I cannot produce anything unless he gives it [to me; I am,] therefore, like a patient waiting for him to get [what I need], not for me to take it in advance, as I did before: I always took things in advance.[29] Now I don't, and I find the greatest peace in this.

It's not only the belief. It's not only the hope. It is love that puts something in faith and hope that gives the full operative power that's supposed to be in faith and hope [. . .]. There is a difference; yet having this [inner power], you're very humble, you're very obedient, you're very prayerful. You have deep faith; you're poor, because you gave up everything you have, and you're waiting for him to give to you. That's an interior thing. As for exterior things, such as, I'm here tonight, but, if I were out in a jungle, if I had to eat leaves, I would eat leaves; [if I had to] eat grass, [I would] eat grass, or sleep on the ground—it's up to him. If he sends me [to do something,] he'll have to send me from my bed, because I'm not capable of doing what I did before I had that experience—that is, those twenty-four years [in which] I did everything in extreme conditions. And it was he who sustained me. So I know that now, and [once you know that,] you're very humble; you want to bring others to him, to let them start their whole life for him and believe in him, and he'll direct it the way it's supposed to be. So that's my life now. And yet you're given an absolute certainty that you have the certainty, of what? of faith, of hope, and now you even have love.

Now you don't want, you *cannot* have heaven on earth. This is the best you can get in this world: *live* faith, *live* hope, and *true* love. I want him, and yet I'm just as human as anyone else, and I always look at myself as I am, and what I am; I see everybody else as better than me. That's the way I feel, and I pray for that—to see the greater grace in the other, not me. That's humility. Do I want it? No. I'm inspired that way; that's why I pray. And what he asks for me is not going to be initiated by me; I never question his way of leading me. Because He's the Lord! He's God! and I'm content. I couldn't do anything. If you make a mistake, they're just passing things, like gusts of wind coming. You don't know where they come from, but they hit you and knock you over. And when you fall, it was just a gust of wind, that's all. It didn't change my disposition [with regard] to the Lord, or my act of faith. But the suddenness of it all just knocks you over, that's all.

So, in this way, you live and communicate with others and lead a life, a very simple life, but a true life of prayer. Nothing extraordinary, nothing sensational, because sensational is not in keeping with Christ's spirit. It's a simple and true-to-life effort, seeing things as they are, seeing through eyes of faith, hope, and love, and seeing God as a Good Samaritan, and rejoicing and having peace, and, then, having him do the rest.

9

Living God's Gift

Another, much shorter account, focusing on the spiritual fruits of the experience, is found in a letter written in 1982 to one of his spiritual daughters, who had heard that he had a vision of God when he was in the hospital and wanted to know more about it.

Two years later, a few months before his death, the same person wrote to him again. She had always thought him "beautiful and very holy and very Christlike," but recently, when she visited him for a day of recollection in July 1984, she had noticed something different about him. "Father," she asked, "if it's possible, could you tell me what is the difference I sense in you now?"[30]

Letter Written May 8, 1982

Concerning the vision, or experience of the Trinity, [I had] when in the hospital suffering from a cardiac arrest, I remember well only my own reactions to the grace I received, and I still remember the message communicated to me from within, but nothing beyond that. It was so personal, so direct, and so emphatic that I remind myself of its contents every day, in my thanksgiving prayer said after Mass.

Such a grace is given for greater dedication and faithfulness in following Christ, for humble and total obedience to the will of God, and as an invitation to be more and more like Christ in following him in one's own calling.

Whatever I said, while still in a coma, was mentioned to me by others later, when I was recuperating. But the personal message I received from Our Lord was so overpowering that I did not remember what people told me, nor did it ever interest me to ask about all that happened during the critical days of my illness.

So what interests me most is the strong desire to be totally given over to God and to bring others to such a life of abandonment in serving God.

Letter Written August 26, 1984

The difference in me now is simply what is happening because of God integrating me into the mystical, which means sharing his goodness and holiness personally. It's all his gift, grace, and blessing—a gesture of his love for me, permitting me to be centered on him and see everything else in all creation as it is in him; i.e., to see God in all things and his love saving all men through, with, and in Christ. It's being filled with the love of Christ in infused prayer while contemplating him as he is, the eternal loving Christ, and filled with his love returning to earth and sharing that heavenly love received with others whom he sends. It's a confirmation in his love, changing one's being into something new within.

Part Three

THE SPIRITUAL
TEACHER

10

Walter Ciszek among Religious

For Father Ciszek, contact with other religious began at home, in the John XXIII Center, where in the late 1960s, staff and community were made up of Jesuits and diocesan priests and religious (Franciscans) of the Eastern Rite.

Among them was young Philaret Littlefield, a Byzantine Franciscan brother-monk who would stay in the Center from 1969 until 1973.[31] He recalled that such a distinction was made between the priests and the brothers that there were many priests who would not empty an ashtray or do anything that was not strictly their duty, but Father Wally (as they always called him) was not like that. Brother Philaret explained:

> He was as comfortable doing janitorial work as he was preaching. He worked with us brothers a lot and helped us with the physical things of the Center. Jesuit Brother Joseph Benkovsky, another member of the community, and I were constantly cooking and cleaning and preparing stuff, and if Father Ciszek was around and had nothing else to do, he would be with us, doing what we were doing; so we became friends. The thing I remember most is that nobody knew who he was. When people would come to the house, they would think he was a janitor or possibly a lay brother or something like that. He was very ordinary in his behavior, but once he got on spiritual topics, you could see in his eyes and his whole demeanor that he was the real thing—the real deal!

Brother Littlefield also recalled noticing how in the old Center (before 1971) Father Ciszek would sometimes pace back and forth in the dark of night in the chapel on the top floor. He asked one of the fathers about this and was told how Father Walter had done the same thing when he was in Lubianka prison, continually reciting the Divine Liturgy so that, if he ever had the opportunity to celebrate it again, he would remember the words. He said, "He wouldn't be kneeling on the steps of the church or something like that; he wouldn't call attention to himself. He was also very accepting." Littlefield remembers that there were times in the house when there was tension between the Jesuits and everyone else. But Father Ciszek did not take part in any of that; he was always supportive of everyone. He went on to say, "My recollection of him is that he was a man of the community—very pious, a great sense of humor, and not particularly delicate with his daily language, the vernacular. He was just very affable, very much at ease with all kinds of people."

Father's compassion was also well illustrated by the way in which he dealt with a particular parishioner of St. Michael's, the Russian Catholic church in New York City, where he used to assist. This man, who had been married and had a son, became a pariah because he had decided to undergo a sex-change operation. One of the priests from the John XXIII Center actually refused to visit him in the hospital. Father Ciszek, without being judgmental of the other priest, found out where the man was hospitalized and went to offer the sacraments and the encouragement he needed. "For him," Littlefield concluded, "this was a spiritual matter. Put your prejudices and your condemnations aside; there is a soul that needs to be taken care of."

Remarkable from another point of view is the story of the Jesuit brother Francis Butler, who had entered the Society of Jesus in 1956.[32] He explained, "As brothers we were tailors, cooks, etc., but we did all for the glory of God and his Kingdom." In 1963, when Father Ciszek came back from Russia, he was working at Fordham. Brother Butler went on to say,

> I was so impressed by his saintly manner. On occasion, when he began to speak here and there and offer days of recollection, I would go there and help him set up the microphone, pass out literature, *et cetera*, and this allowed me to be present in the back of the hall and listen to his holy reflections.

In the second half of the 1970s, when Brother Butler was teaching at Xavier High School in Manhattan, he felt less and less at ease with certain developments in the Society of Jesus—liberal moral teaching, experimental liturgy—while his defense of the position of the Church on certain issues isolated him more and more. About the same time, he spoke with his spiritual director about a priestly vocation. Whereas the latter encouraged him, his superiors did not favor the idea. He explained, "If I wanted to continue with this desire, I was more or less being told to pack my bags and go elsewhere." He then asked to make a retreat of discernment, and, having received permission, thought of asking Father Ciszek to guide him. He explained, "This was the last day of exams in May of 1980, and I was in the middle of my work in the bookstore. I wanted to leave everything in proper order. So I called Fr. Ciszek and asked if he could suggest someone for the retreat; he responded, 'I'll do it.'" Butler continued,

> In our phone conversation I told Fr. Ciszek of my need for discernment, as to whether I should stay in the Society or whether I was being called to the priesthood. He agreed that some Jesuits had fallen from the ideal of "the glory of God." He said that the Jesuits had to be careful because some had lost their way.

On July 6, 1980, Brother Butler began a ten-day retreat with Father Ciszek and lived with him at the John XXIII Center. Describing the experience, he said,

> All the spiritual books that I had brought were of no avail. Father said, "Get rid of those; I will tell you what to read." The retreat consisted of meditation, reflection, and prayer. We would start at 7:00 each morning in the private chapel where Father would say Mass; I was the altar server and did the readings. I would spend four or five hours before the Blessed Sacrament each day reflecting on notes from my reading, and I kept a diary of every thought. We would try to discern the pros and cons. It was a special time when we celebrated Mass. One day, at the washing of hands, he held on to the finger towel and said, "Do you realize that someday I will have to answer to God for how I guided and directed you in this?" I replied, "Father, the same God that is guiding you is guiding me. I'm praying for you every day." In the evenings between eight and nine o'clock we would go through the points, and during this time Father never indicated which way he was leaning.

On the final night, Father Ciszek said to him, "Brother, before God, I believe that you are being called to the priesthood." Recalling the event, Brother Butler later said, "He said this with a warm twinkle in his eye, and I was filled with a sense of peace and joy. I thought, 'If this holy man believes I am being called, then I am going to be a priest.'" Butler then asked Father for the purificator used at Mass and said, "I'll use it for my first Mass." Father replied, "Just as God led me through my time in Russia, so the Lord will lead you. Stay firm, hold on, and he will take care of you." Brother Butler, not without sadness, left the Jesuits and became a Josephite Father, inspired by their ministry to the poor. He was ordained a priest on May 25, 1984.

Going forward from the time Walter Ciszek arrived at the John XXIII Center in June 1964, he would often be away a month or two at a time, giving retreats and conferences, mostly to women religious. Maureen O'Brien, who was accepted into the cloistered community of the Baltimore Carmel on October 12, 1963, the same day Father Ciszek had come back from Russia, remembers how she stood there, holding in her hands both the letter of acceptance from the Carmelites and the *Washington Star* with the news of Father Ciszek's return, and thought, "If that Jesuit can do that, I can at least enter and give it six months!" Several weeks after her entering the monastery, Father Ciszek wrote to the community saying he had learned that their Carmel had been praying for him at the Provincial's request after the Jesuits learned he was still alive in Russia. In gratitude he offered to give them his first retreat after being released. This first retreat, preached in 1965, was so much appreciated that the prioress wrote to all the other Carmelite monasteries around the country; he received twenty invitations after that. According to Maureen O'Brien,

> Walter Ciszek felt so close to the Carmel because there he found the focus on prayer as apostolic service and contemplative surrender to the allness (sic) of God, values he had learned in Moscow's Lubianka prison. He personified the Jesuit "contemplative in action," saying that real spirituality had to be lived.[33]

The Holy Annunciation Monastery at Sugarloaf, Pennsylvania, would become the religious community most graced with his attention. The Discalced Carmelite Nuns of the Byzantine Catholic Church living there still regard him as their spiritual father. He used to call the sisters "my little ones" or "the kids." A few months before his death, he wrote to them:

> Your calling is such a blessing, permitting you in an atmosphere of natural environment to give yourself fully to a life of prayer and communion with God and concern for priests and all humanity. Your growth in holiness, as life daily affects you amidst the passing events of life, lets you learn quickly the ways to perfection. Your total dedication to God in sacrifice and suffering will help tremendously those who are most in need of divine mercy. It's the lofty ideal of love of abandonment to God that sanctifies and perfects in himself and others.

Mother Marija of the Holy Spirit, one of the three founding Sisters of the monastery, founded in February 1977, relating the story of their twenty-year friendship, said,[34]

On October 15, 1963, a visitor to our Morristown, New Jersey, Carmel (where I entered in 1946) told of the return of a Jesuit from Russia, exchanged for some Soviet spies. Some months later, Fr. Paul Mailleux, S.J., through whom I was regularly borrowing books from Soloviev Library at Fordham University, sent me a book "hot off the press." It was entitled *With God in Russia*. That was a great one! One nun stayed up all night reading it, and then it was read in the refectory.

Father Mailleux, then superior of the Russian Center where Father Walter was to be stationed, and our dear friend, Fr. Joseph Ledit, S.J., who had taught at the Russicum in Rome when Father Walter was a student there in 1932–1933, wanted me to meet Father Ciszek. The meeting they proposed in December 1965 never took place, but I finally met him at a retreat in October 1966, after I had been transferred to a California Carmel. In the summer and autumn of that year, Father was giving retreats on the West Coast. He had been back from Russia about three years. His English left something to be desired—the words were there but some re-arrangement was needed!

Father Walter was a realist, and once back in the United States, he turned his heart, mind, and energy to the American scene. Still, he always retained his love and conviction for the suffering Church in the Soviet countries, which he believed would produce a harvest of holiness because of the "blood of martyrs." He had no hatred for the Communists, nothing harsh to say; to those who harbored animosity and expected to find this in him he would say, "You can't love God and hate what he loves." One time someone asked, "Would you go back to Russia?" He replied, "If God wanted me to go back to Russia, I'd go back in a bathing suit." He kept matters light.

Father Walter navigated so beautifully in the troubled waters of the 1960s and 1970s! Here was a priest just returned to the U.S. church scene of the Vatican II era after twenty-three years of prison and exile that should have damaged his mind, heart, and body. Yet he had such openness to every situation. His vigilance and humility enabled him to be completely himself because that self was completely subjected to God's will. And so he paddled relatively untroubled through the rapids that overturned many a boat in those days. And so, too, this monastery of the Holy Annunciation took shape under his guidance and was ever sustained by his encouragement.

When the time arrived for putting foundations under "ideas" that had been discussed for many years, and we requested the approbation of episcopal authority, Father Walter recommended us to Bishop Michael J. Dudick, D.D., head of the Byzantine Catholic Diocese of Passaic, New Jersey. In all likelihood it was on this recommendation that we were accepted by Bishop Michael. I wrote to Father Walter constantly; I saw him often. One time I felt he did not understand me; perhaps, after some years my attachment to him had become too "naturally" affective. I penned an angry letter to him! His reply was so humble; he said he kept my letter on his desk for three days, adding that he was happy to be of service to help me and my community. This was not an end but the beginning of a new relationship.

Father Walter was never self-indulgent. Faith and charity were uppermost in his mind. He cared little about frills. He never looked for comfort. After our retreat in July 1976, our foundation was launched, but the next month and October of that same year, he suffered two major heart attacks. It was about twelve months before he was again in sufficient health for apostolic work. What a transformation in love he underwent in the sufferings and blessings of those months! What a new guide I found for a young community when he was able once again to take on the burden of spiritual father to the young women God sent us here and whom Father Walter called his "kids."

Some people were in awe of him, but he wasn't looking for anything, nor was he needy. He would deflect attention from himself in a spontaneous way. This was his way of keeping his real self hidden. But he welcomed love and friendship and used his power to inspire and bring others closer to God (and his "kids" were among these very fortunate ones). In *He Leadeth Me* he explained his mission: to let people know how important is their faith in God, how to hang on to God. He did not have time for intellectual intricacies. I mentioned the famous German theologian Karl Rahner, S.J., and he just said, "Not my *forte*." Prison and arctic camps were not conducive to intellectual pursuits, but his simple faith in God and Christ was brought to great perfection. Nothing else was necessary.

Of course Father Walter's spiritual journey continued here in the United States. Father was very humble, but not naturally humble or self-effacing; he was a gregarious, outgoing, and headstrong personality. Yet, in Russia, his whole person was purified. I think of two aspects as "moments." When I first met Father Walter, he spoke of love, as a son of St. Ignatius would, as the summation of all the virtues. Love, for him, meant doing the will of God in any and every given situation: now obedient, now patient, now silent, etc. Years later, this "moment" was followed by his personal realization of the final day of the Spiritual Exercises, the contemplation to obtain divine love.

He seemed to emerge from his several heart attacks, subsequent hospitalization, and his experience of the Blessed Trinity as a "lover." And he knew it! From then on until his death, he seemed to have an abiding experience of the goal—purpose—of life and, while he remembered how the first steps were to be taken, he more and more communicated the glow of the "living Flame of Love," in the words of our Carmelite Father St. John of the Cross.

The young sisters who were introduced by Mother Marija to Father Ciszek did not know what to expect.[35] They were in awe when they heard they would be meeting him, expecting "a living saint," a rather grim, austere person, or someone large and imposing, given that he had survived all those years in a labor camp. But he was not as they had expected; he was small and not physically imposing at all. "He had a smile that lit up his eyes," said one of them, "and an expression that said, 'I'm so glad you've come!'" "His good humor won me over right away," said Sister Mary of Jesus, who entered the monastery in 1980 and met Father Walter for the first time in January 1981. She went on to say, "He impressed me then and on all subsequent interviews as the happiest person I'd ever met. To look into his merry, twinkling blue eyes, one would never suspect the ordeals he had endured in his lifetime."

Sister Andreja Vladia, who first met Father Walter in the fall of 1983, found herself realizing, during a retreat she made with him, that he was the type of person with whom you could be totally honest, you could freely reveal yourself. She said, "Father made me feel so comfortable: no rejection, no judgment, no refusal of love—he was so Christlike." The secret of his strength and his compassion, according to one Sister, was his faith. She observed,

Father Ciszek truly believed in the inherent goodness of people; he looked beyond their exterior, to where he knew God dwelt within their souls. This faith is what I saw shining in his eyes and on his face that first time and each subsequent time that I met him, and it is that faith which will always stand out in my mind when I think of Father Walter.

One of the Sisters wrote, "He was the most delightful person I ever met," to which Sister Mary of Jesus added, " . . . fully human and totally in love with God, dedicated to His service." Another Sister wrote, "The more time you spent with him, the softer and warmer became your heart."

Between 1981 and 1984, Father Ciszek visited the monastery five times, and just as the Sisters did not have any difficulty talking to him, so also could he speak to them on religious subjects at great length without causing tedium or boredom. He would often interject humorous anecdotes into his talks to illustrate the point he wished to make. And, although his homely examples were easy to understand and remember, they were always filled with a wisdom that allowed one to "see deeper" as the years went by and as growth in the spiritual life took place. One of the Sisters wrote, "I had the privilege of sitting at his feet and listening to his words of wisdom." Quoting him, she went on to write,

> The Spirit of God given you in baptism, together with faith, are your most precious gifts from the heavenly Father. When we listen to the Word of God, our minds are filled with light. It is the lowly heart that understands. Inspired by faith and love for Our Lady, you will be able to rise above illness, above future uncertainty, and above temptations so strongly opposing every serious attempt to dedicate one's life to virtue and holiness.

Asked specifically about the retreats Father Ciszek gave, Sister Mary of Jesus answered, "Father reminded us at the beginning, and throughout the following days, that just to be on retreat was a great grace, that it was planned and designed by God's Spirit and not human will. He stressed our limitations and God's faithful love and mercy."

These seem to be the two points best remembered from his conferences and retreats: our weakness and God's strong love. Sister Andreja recalled Father Walter explaining that if you are in a situation or difficulty, you can make a U-turn; instead of putting the blame on something outside or on someone else, look within yourself to see how you have contributed to the problem, and then find a way to restore peace to the situation. When she was having serious doubts about her vocation, shortly before her taking the veil, Father Walter saw that she was troubled and asked whether this was really what she wanted. She replied that she was worried because she wasn't sure that it was what God wanted. He answered, "You couldn't want something so good on your own, so of course God wants it. He wanted it first *for you*." "That taught me a lesson," she concluded, and went on to say, "We must remember that when we want something noble and good, it is God's grace making us desire it. On our own, we are incapable of wanting anything noble and good."

Surprisingly, Father Ciszek hardly ever spoke about the ordeals he had endured in his lifetime. When he did, it was not to draw attention to himself but rather to teach a spiritual lesson and to glorify God for sustaining him in those circumstances. To illustrate a teaching on Old Testament retribution, he would tell the Sisters how, when he got into some mischief as a boy (stealing apples, for example), his conscience would bother him at night. He would not dare to go upstairs alone or to the outhouse, fearing God might strike him dead, but his pride would not permit him to tell anyone that he was afraid! He would also share with them how in Russia he was subjected to all sorts of temptations, but that he always prayed never to lose the gift of faith while surrounded by atheism. He would say that, when in temptation, "it is important to turn your back on it and look at God's will. It's subtle, but you can always smell the sulphur."

It was Sister Mary of Jesus who recorded the above sayings, to which she added the following:

> Father said, "Do God's will whole-heartedly," and, "Faith is inseparable from love; out of these two twins *hope* is born." He spoke often of God's providence and the "sacrament of the present moment" and of how faith and love must underlie all our works. He would say, "Love equals the Passion"; i.e., one must love even when it hurts. He also said that it is very wrong to sin out of malice, but to sin out of human weakness; "Just ask God's pardon, and He will provide a similar (and slightly tougher) situation to repair the fall." Father Walter stressed that we are each made in the image and likeness of God and that God cannot unlove (sic) himself, and then he went on to say, "God preserves his own. He let me struggle, and only years later could I see his presence."

The following series of eight conferences were given at an unknown date to an unknown group of apostolic religious sisters. The text has come to us not as a manuscript but in a typed version; in fact, it may well be a transcription of a tape, for Father Ciszek was not in the habit of fully writing out his talks or of underlining words or capitalizing them for emphasis, as is the case in this text.

11

Generosity

Conference given by Fr. Ciszek to a group of apostolic religious sisters

Lord, make me an instrument of your peace.
Where there is hatred, let me sow love;
Where there is injury, pardon;
Where there is doubt, faith;
Where there is despair, hope;
Where there is darkness, light;
Where there is sadness, joy.
Oh, Divine Master, grant that I may not seek to be consoled, as to
    console;
to be understood, as to understand;
to be loved, as to love.
For it is in giving that we receive.
It is in pardoning that we are pardoned,
And it is in dying that we are born to Eternal life.

Would you not say, my dear sisters, that this beautiful prayer of St. Francis sums up the most sacred day of your life, the day of your religious profession: the day when you told Christ that you were his in body and soul and heart and mind, the day you solemnly vowed to your God that you would serve him in obedience, and poverty, and chastity, all the days of your life, *for him, and for his love, and for his glory, and for his people* as long as you should live?

"Lord," you said, "make me an instrument of your peace. I give you my body in chastity, my will in obedience, my comfort in poverty, my pride and self-love in humility and charity." "Take me," you said, "Lord, I'll do anything you want, go anywhere you wish. I'm yours, Lord, for the asking and for the taking. *Do with me, as you wish.*"

Yes, *generosity*—the will to give and give and give, never asking the price, never expecting a reward—this sums up your profession day. On that day, you really did not know what this giving of yourself to him would demand, this giving to his People. How could you? You had only just given yourself; you could not look into the future and see what this totally generous gift of yours would mean to day-after-day living. You knew just one thing, that he, your Master, your Lord, *wanted you, needed you,* your life. He *needed* your strong young hands, your heart on fire with love of him and the people he had died to save, and *he needed* the kindness, the charity, and the holiness of your life; and we gave ourselves to him completely.

On that day, did you think how much this gift of yourself would cost you? A foolish question, for who thinks of cost when it comes to love? On that day, did you even dream of the possibility that you might be sorry you ever gave this gift; another foolish question? Does true love ever grow cold and repent of its love?

No, you could not see into the future. You did not know, really know, *what* your Christ would ask of you, *how* he would take you up on your gift, *when* he would demand every ounce of your strength to live up to your promises. But this did not make any difference in the giving. There would always be the same Christ, no matter what came up. You could give him, in the unknown future, no more than you were giving him on that sacred day; your soul and body, everything you had, everything you were, that his People might live in peace and love, and because of you.

And now, the years have passed by, and I wonder how much all of us have forgotten about that unforgettable day. I wonder how much generosity, the very keynote of that day, has been pushed farther and farther into the background of our minds and of our lives, so that the uncomfortable comparison between that day and this may not gnaw at us so badly.

But surely, you may say, "We're not expected to have the same generosity today as we had then. After all, we had just finished novitiate. Our fervor and love were running over. Our cup was filled with the happiness of Christ, and we would have gladly died for him, yes, even as we wanted to live totally for him. Time brings changes: fervor grows dim, love cools."

No, you are not expected to have the same generosity you had on that day. Christ expects to see in the lives of you women a deeper and greater, and a much, much wiser generosity. Then we did not know what Christ would ask; now we do. Our life—mine included—is a failure if we cannot say today that we are just as anxious to give Christ our lives—in our work, in our sufferings, in our prayers—as we were on the day of our profession.

This, my dear sisters, is the keystone of the religious life. Our whole vocation is summed up in this one word: *generosity.* And to the extent that we have lost this generosity in our daily lives, to that extent has our vocation grown dim and our love cold. I suppose many of us think as we meditate: "Well, I did have such generosity at one time. I was willing and anxious to do anything Christ asked, anything my superiors asked me to do. But I guess, somewhere, somehow, in the shuffle of the years I've lost this gift that makes the religious life the happy, peaceful thing that I know it should be."

I do not agree that most of us religious have lost this gift. Oh, there are a few religious who have entirely lost their generous hearts, who have become the worst possible scourge a religious community could have: a cynic. Who, if they were listening to this talk, would say to themselves, "This priest is just feeding us a line. He says these things because he knows that he is supposed to. But he does not really believe them." "Let's face it," they say: "the innocence and the fervor and the high-blown idealism of the novitiate, and of the day of our profession, are things of the past. We are leading hard, practical lives now with hard, practical work to do, and such past ideas have no place in our lives." There are such women in religious life—both you and I have met them—unhappy, miserable people who have denied the generosity of their own hearts, *who have stopped loving Christ* and souls in him, and who have no one else really to love. May God have mercy on their souls, and may God deliver any community from having such a one in its midst. The poison of such a person gradually seeps into the very heart of a community, and young, impressionable religious are destroyed, and the joy and laughter and peace of Christ, slowly but surely, steal away from the hearth of such a home.

And there are, then, the ones who just cannot seem to care anymore, who cannot get themselves excited about Christ and his *cause* at all, who have let the seeds of lukewarmness grow in their hearts until the will to give, the spirit of generosity, is all but a dead thing, and life has been for them a boring, empty thing.

But, my dear sisters, you and I know that such religious are the exception. We are not all cynics, thank God! We are not all tepid or lukewarm, though we are weak and not holy. What I think has happened is this: this generosity of our profession day is still in us; we have just forgotten to call upon it as frequently as we used to. You don't lose such a gift as this; you deliberately erase it by cynicisms, or chip it away by tepidity, or just forget it is within you. And I think this is what many religious have done: we have forgotten there ever was such a gift. For, let's face it, sisters, the gift of generosity is not a comfortable gift to have around. It demands too much of us. Then it means that you and I have (right up) to this time the *stuff* of which holiness, total dedication, is made. We still have this dedication to Christ and to souls. Christ doesn't choose ungenerous and selfish souls to serve him. I know there are very few saints among us, but this I say again: we have the *stuff* out of which sanctity is made. We have the generosity, hidden now perhaps deep within our hearts and minds, but for most of us it is still there; if we would call upon it, we would slowly but ever so surely begin to find in us the holiness we saw as in a vision on the day of our profession.

But herein lies the problem. Do we still want to be generous; do we sincerely want *now*, *today*, to go *all out* for Christ as we did on the day of our profession? Is it not true that most of us are afraid of the gift that is within us, that we almost deliberately forget it because we fear it so much, because we fear what it might do to our lives, that it might take away our little comforts, our little pleasures, the little round ball of pseudo-happiness that we have managed to form for ourselves?

Are we not afraid really to *give* Christ *everything today*? Are we not afraid to love him too much, to serve him too much, to live up to our promises made on the day of our profession too completely? Afraid, because as the poet [Francis Thompson, "The Hound of Heaven"] has so beautifully put it:

> For, though I knew His love who followed,
> Yet was I sore adread
> *Lest having Him, I must have naught beside.*

And the years have done this to many of us, I am afraid. They have somehow convinced us that life with Christ, but with nothing else, would be an empty dreary sort of thing—too hard, too uncomfortable, too terribly, terribly austere for which to live our lives.

What I think has happened is that we also become afraid to give up not only the things, but also the people who seem to us to make up much of our happiness. The little comforts have gradually gathered around us; what are they? Not very much really: perhaps a special place in the community room, perhaps a special pen or typewriter, a favorite holy picture, a special crucifix, a rosary, a watch—things we can secretly call *mine*. We fear to say, "Christ, I really don't want these things." We fear to give them away, lest in giving them away we be empty, we have nothing.

Strange, isn't it, that after we have given up everything for Christ, we hold on with great possessiveness to the little things we have gathered in our religious life, the friends to whom we cling with the very same possessiveness. Why? Well, we know that these things give us a little bit of comfort; we know that we like having them around. And we are so terribly, terribly afraid that if ever we just let go of these things and people, our hands and our lives and our hearts will be too empty. We are afraid to give Christ the *chance to fill them*.

You see what these things do to us. Christ invites us every day of our lives to make the one total, all-out gift of ourselves to him, to take the one plunge into the depths of his heart, to find the love that is there and the peace that is there, but, like little children holding on desperately to their teddy bears or their security blankets, we won't let go. "What if," we say to ourselves, "What if I let all these little things go and then there is nothing?" Sounds silly, doesn't it? And, yet, you are not willing to give up your most treasured possession, your most treasured comfort—even, perhaps, a friend—if these are harmful to your life with God.

Strangely enough, we are even afraid to pray too much. Let's say I have ten or fifteen minutes free today. I can do what I want with it. Is it not true that we are afraid to give these minutes to Christ today, for fear that he will make a habit of asking for these precious few minutes of ours, and are we not afraid—yes, afraid—to make a habit of giving our extra minutes to him? *Why?* Is it not that, deep within us, we fear that the minutes given to Christ will not bring us as much happiness and joy as minutes given to a favorite book, or radio program, or TV program, or minutes given in conversation to a friend? And yet, " ... though I knew whose love I followed, yet was I sore adread, lest having Him, I must have naught beside."

And we are convinced of our own opinions and are afraid to give in too often to others, lest the good feeling of pride in one's own knowledge be slowly erased from our minds, and once this feeling is gone, again there is the fear of emptiness. We know what we have, but we are afraid to reach to the unknown Christ.

Many of us, strange as it may sound, are even afraid of being too charitable, lest others take advantage of us, lest others not respect us, or fear us. We know that if our tongue is sharp enough, no one will dare cross us or speak uncharitably to us, *so we keep the sharp tongue.* We know that if we are not especially charitable in our words and actions, that we will not be asked to do special jobs by the superior or by other sisters, so we shy away from too much charity.

We know that if we practice self-denial and mortification too often at table, for example, that if we constantly take the lesser piece of meat or the staler piece of bread, or pass up a piece of pie occasionally, or eat the things we don't particularly like, we know that this, too, could get to be a habit in our lives, and the habit scares us off. Doing a thing once or twice is not too bad, but doing it all the time, always practicing some self-denial, some mortification: "After all," we reason, "our lives as religious are mortification enough."

Do you see the pattern, my dear sisters? Most of us run from generosity, because we are afraid of it. We are afraid to pray too much, too fervently, lest Christ ask this all the time, afraid that if we give too much, we'll be empty or half-filled; "[Yet was I sore adread] lest having Him, I must have naught beside."

And yet, my dear sisters in Christ, what is there really besides Christ? Can personal comfort or the little pleasures, or personal pride, or the pleasure of another's company, or the half-asleep feeling at prayer, or the desire for respect and even reverence—can any of these fill our lives with peace or joy or happiness? *Christ promised to fill our lives.*

When we run from our own generous natures, we are running from our own happiness. When we are afraid to give because of what the cost might be, we are letting peace and joy slip from our lives.

Remember how Francis Thompson expressed it. God finally catches up with the poet who has fled from Him so constantly, fearing "... lest having Him, he must have naught beside," and God says:

Ah, fondest, blindest, weakest,
I am He Whom thou seekest!
Thou dravest love from thee, who dravest Me.[36]

And each one of us drives love from our lives, drives the longing, the desire for happiness and peace from our lives, each time we run from generosity. There is no love, there is no peace, there is no joy without him. He and he alone is our reward exceedingly great; no physical comfort, no thing, no person can ever truly fill our lives. The emptiness we often feel in our lives, the just hunger and longing, can be filled only by him. He made us especially for himself, and our hearts and minds must be restless until they rest in him.

Your vocation is to give:

Your life in your work,
Your heart in your love,
Your soul in your prayer,
Your hopes,
Your fears,
Your joys,
Your little loves,
Your little pleasures,
To give everything to Him.

Take the one great leap in the dark. Give everything all over again, and you will find yourself once more the generous, loving, eager, happy woman who once threw her life with complete abandon into the deep, deep sea of Christ's love.

12

Patience with Ourselves

Conference given by Fr. Ciszek to a group of apostolic religious sisters

In the past few years, much has been written about love: how it is the central teaching of Our Lord, how it sums up the whole of Christianity. We know that to meet Christ—really meet him—to have a daily encounter with him, we must first love him as he is, and then him in our neighbor and friends and in all men and women, because they are the image of God. However, I wonder, when was the last time we were told that we are also obliged to love ourselves?

Self-love as it is described in the spiritual books is, of course, a vice, but real love of ourselves, of the soul and body, of the mind and heart, is a sacred and wonderful virtue. Without it, we really can't give God our full service and our full love. There are many different ways we can show this real love [for] ourselves, but I don't think there is a more practical way than by the simple, seemingly unimportant virtue of patience. I don't mean patience basically with others but patience with ourselves, with our lives, our faults, our weaknesses; patience with our own sufferings and temptations; patience with our lack of perseverance, our inconsistencies, and our sins—patience with our very humanity.

Isn't it true that one of the things that bothers us most is the fact that we are so weak spiritually and physically, that we are so *human*??? How many times, I wonder, have we hated that body that is ours—yes, truly hated this very humanity that God blessed us with? Somehow or other, in the years of our spiritual training we got self-denial and mortification mixed up with self-hatred and detestation of this body that is ours. Somehow we've read in the lives of the saints—written by men and women like ourselves, who secretly are ashamed of the bodies and heart and emotions God made for us—and have found *proof* in these books how much we should hate and despise and, most of all, fear our human natures. For no other reason than this, I think most of the old lives of the saints should be quietly disposed of, and men such as St. Thomas More and women such as Teresa of Avila, who loved the nature God gave them, should start a whole rewrite job.

The impatience that most good religious show others is nothing compared to the impatience they show themselves. When they find themselves distracted in prayer, lazy in their work, imperfect in their love of God and man, immediately they blame themselves and their weak bodies. I think that if most religious had their way, they would rip their bodies off and wander about in their souls—with, I am sure, a feeling of great relief that they are free at last to really love God, free of the weak, insignificant, totally useless thing called body and human nature. They forget, of course, that without the body they could not whisper one word of love to this God or shed even one tear of sorrow for their sins or feel the slightest tug at their heartstrings of pity for others or compassion for the suffering Christ and his sorrowing Mother. For all these are human emotions and human activities and belong to this body we often are so impatient with.

I suppose one of the main reasons for our inner impatience is our very vocation. We're called to serve the untouchable, love the unseeable, believe the improvable, and trust the unhearable, and do all this with a human nature that longs desperately from its very make-up to touch and see and know and hear. We are always reaching out beyond the limits of our own human nature to grasp our God and hold on to him. However, our *hands* can't reach that far, and our human nature, all too often, fails when we reach. We know as professionals—professional "pray-ers," professional God-lovers and man-servers—that we ought to be totally dedicated to our spiritual life. Yet, we cannot touch, or see, or hear the God who is the very heart of this spiritual life. A doctor can know what he is after and spend his life, every minute of it, seeking a cure for one tiny form of cancer. For he knows that if he *looks* long enough, he'll find the *seeable* thing that causes that cancer. A musician can get himself totally involved in writing a new symphony or looking for a new sound in music, for he knows, too, that, if he studies and works long enough he'll find this *hearable* thing that is his symphony or new sound. But we, we can never, though we search the whole of our lives, ever *see* God, really in this life, as human beings. We can never truly hear his voice as just human beings.

Yet, this is the only work that we can become *totally* involved in: our search to find God. We can never let ourselves get totally involved in things that we can touch, in people we can see and hear. We can't teach so completely that we forget about our God about whom we are teaching, nor care for the bodies of people to such an extent that we forget the Christ who lives in them, or get so involved in making things for people that we forget, even for a moment, the untouchable, unseeable, unhearable, unprovable Christ to whom we have dedicated our lives.

You see, we are, as religious, as professional God-lovers, living a paradox with very real, very con-spiritual, [sic] very invisible, very untouchable God. It's no wonder, I suppose, that we tend to get impatient with our human nature and the faults that flow from this natural, and, to us, known "self." No wonder we say, "Things shouldn't be like this! What's the matter with me, with this body of mine? Why won't it work the way I want it to?" It's no wonder that this human nature *seems* to stand in the way of our truly serving him, truly loving him.

But "seems" is the magic word in that last statement. For God made us to serve and love him, not as pure spirits, like angels, but as human beings, with flesh and blood, with heart and emotions and passions. He gave us everything we have. Every feeling, every tear, every sorrow, every joy, every inconsistency that is so much part of being human is in us, because *he wants it there*, because he wants us to love him, not like angels but like humans. And angels can't feel love; we can. Angels can't feel sorrow or pity or compassion; we can. Angels can't cry over sin; we can. God gave us our human natures, not as punishment, not as a millstone tied around the neck of our souls, but:

> As our way to love him,
> As our way to serve him,
> As our way to hold him in our minds and in our souls,
> And as our way to walk to Heaven with him.

You see, when God made us, he blended the spiritual with the material, and in this blending found a way to have a completely material universe serve and love him. For when we use things for his honor—our hands, our hearts, our flesh and blood—then we are making even material things part of the great love song of the spiritual universe. And when we use physical words to praise him or build great churches to honor him or write books to make him known, then we are reaching into every nook and cranny of this physical universe and making it, because of our human natures, capable of praising and honoring and serving God through us and in us as human beings—beings with soul and body.

Moreover, when man fell, the sound of praise and love could no longer ring from a praying, honoring universe. God so missed this honor and love that he sent his Son to take on this very flesh and blood that he might redeem a world, a universe, so that he, in our flesh, might bring a whole world back to God.

Hate this flesh! Despise this human nature! When it is God's instrument of love and honor and praise and benediction? He loved it so much that he made it, loved it so much that he redeemed it, loved it so much that he brought his Son and his Mother with this same flesh and blood, this same human nature into his very home of heaven.

I think that much of the impatience we show towards our human nature flows from the way we think we ought to be accepting things, like suffering, and the way we actually are accepting them. Too many religious think that in imitation of Job, and then of Christ, we ought to stoically and even joyfully accept all suffering, perhaps with peace, yes, but not with jumping-over [sic] joy and happiness. They think of how Job said in his suffering, "God gives, God takes. Blessed be the name of God." They forget he also said: "My soul is weary of life. . . . I will speak in the bitterness of my soul. I will say to God, 'Do not condemn me. Tell me why Thou judgest me so. Why didst Thou bring me forth out of the womb? Oh, that I had not been born.'" They think of how Christ said, "I have a baptism wherewith I am to be baptized, and how I am straitened till it be accomplished." They forget he also said, "Father, if it be thy will, let this chalice pass from me"; and, he was sweating blood in fear of the pain to come! On the cross, [he utters] a cry that breaks the heart of a world: "My God, my God, why hast Thou abandoned me?"

You see, we don't have to like suffering; we don't have to get impatient with ourselves for not wanting it. All we have to do is to *take* it, take it for the good it can do to our lives, and for the benefit of those desperate, lonely, totally unhappy men and women who walk so far away from God.

In addition, when temptations come, we don't have to be—because we cannot be—as *strong* as Christ was in the desert. All we have to do is fight them. Sometimes it will seem as though we are fighting a losing battle. Sometimes we will come so close to the edge of sin that we will feel the hot breath of hell and almost taste the sin in our lives. But as long as we fight, we will be all right. To be impatient with our weakness, to curse ourselves and our human nature because the thought of the temptation delighted us; to feel shame and sorrow because we were on the verge of sin is all wrong. For all Christ asks is that we fight. This and this only is enough to win his love, no matter what our feelings.

For if we were not human, we could not *be* tempted. And if we never really have the opportunity of a temptation, then we could never have the opportunity of fighting. Yes, opportunity for every temptation is our opportunity, offered to us to grow in virtue: in kindness or thoughtfulness, or prayer, or zeal, or purity, or obedience, or trust. Each time we conquer a temptation, no matter how unclean we feel, no matter how close we have come to sin because of the strength of the temptation, we have grown in virtue, grown closer to Christ, and Christ simply will not take such an opportunity from our life. He wants us to stay human because it is as human beings, growing in all virtues daily, that we will grow in our love for him. Remember what St. Paul said about the sting of the flesh that he himself had: "Three times [a symbolic number, meaning 'many times'] did I beseech the Lord to take this thing from me, and three times did he say, 'My grace is sufficient for thee.'" And St. James tells us, "My brethren, count it for joy when you shall fall into difficult temptation, knowing that the trying of your faith works patience and patience has a perfect work."

I suppose one of the greatest areas of impatience is personal illness. So many of us just cannot stand being sick. It seems as though we should simply be able to make an act of the will for the sickness to go away. But it does not work this way. And we have to pamper this human body of ours, give it medicine and better food and especially *rest*. For as soon as we start working again—*bam*! there goes the body clamoring for attention, clamoring for rest. Again, you see, it's as though we see our bodies as some enemy agent to our love of God and our service to him. But *he gave* us our bodies. He knows they wear down. He knows they get weak. He knows they sometimes don't work too well. If he made us, our whole being, body and soul, then why should we be impatient with these same bodies? Do we not really indict God and blame him for a bad job? Are we not in effect saying, "God, if you had done a better job of putting me together, you'd get a lot more out of me." But, you see, he doesn't want a "lot more out of me." He wants us simply, in all we are doing, to love him with our body and soul, with our whole human nature to the *best* of our strength, whatever that may be at any particular moment. And with this love he is satisfied, though sometimes all it may consist of will be a very weak, "I love you," for, "strength is made perfect in weakness, and when I am weak, then I am strong."

Well, maybe you can agree with me so far. But certainly, when it comes to sin—I mean real *sin*—then you say we have a right to be impatient with ourselves. After all, God is not going to put up with sin, no matter what our human nature! So here we can join him and be patient with ourselves and our weaknesses. But can we? Oh, I agree we ought to be mighty impatient with malicious sins, such as gossip, unkindness, and meanness, for these flow from a real lack of Christlikeness. And I am sure that God does not have much patience with such people. Remember how he dealt with the Scribes and Pharisees, whom he called hypocrites and blind guides?

Then, on the other hand, notice how gently he dealt with weakness, "Woman, who is there to condemn you?" "No one, Lord," she said. "Neither will I then, [he said,] go now and sin no more." For you see, he understands weakness, for *he made us*. And the faults and sins from our own weakness, our prayer distractions and lack of perseverance in good, our laziness, our intemperance, and even sins against purity that sometimes even the holiest people fall into, find, I am sure, a merciful forgiveness. Remember the beautiful Psalm 77: "But he is merciful and will forgive their sins and will not destroy them; many a time did he turn away his anger and did not kindle all his wrath. He remembered that they are flesh: a wind that goeth and returneth not." So to get terribly angry with ourselves, to get disgusted with this human nature that God gave us, to live in impatience with our own lives, is not called for even in sins of weakness. All he wants us to do is to say, "I am sorry, God." That's all he wants, all that he demands: "Go now and sin no more."

Patience with ourselves flows really from the virtue of temperance, the habit of being moderate or reacting moderately when trying circumstances rise up against us. Though it flows from temperance, it is, I think, intimately connected with faith, hope, and love. For when we are patient with ourselves and the human nature God designed and made, then we prove in action that we believe we are a voice of praise to God for this material universe; then we know he will help us not to sin and [will] forgive us when we do. Most of all, it will prove that we love him enough to offer him the many, many imperfect acts of our day and know that Our Father made us because he loves us. He will accept these acts as sacred and sublime gifts with a blindness that only love can achieve.

13

The Mystery of Suffering

Conference given by Fr. Ciszek to a group of apostolic religious sisters

One of the greatest mysteries in this whole world is the mystery of suffering, the mystery of evil. People have been looking for the answer to this mystery from the beginning of time. Before Christ, suffering was considered the greatest punishment that God could send a man or a woman. Read the psalms, such as Psalm 119; suffering was not accepted, it was rebelled against, it was seen as a mark of displeasure on God's part. Remember Job; the best that that good man Job could say was, "God gives, God takes away, blessed be the name of God." The whole book of Job simply says: "Who are we to question God? We can't question God. Suffering exists, and that is all there is to it." The pagans, like the Stoics, saw suffering as a reality and considered it a virtue, too. So much has suffering been part of human life that many, many tribes, even tribes who have no concept of Christianity, make their young men go through many whippings and beatings as proof of their manhood. A man is one, they think, who must be able to accept this thing called pain.

Then Christ came, and he changed the very nature of suffering. He did not take away the pain of suffering. That's still very much around. That will never change as long as we are human. Headaches and stomachaches still hurt. A slap in the face still hurts, and always will. Rejection still hurts and always will because we are human beings. But he gave the whole world, if it would only listen to him, a reason for suffering, and he did even much more than this: he showed us by his example *how* to suffer. I think that the great thinkers of the world, and the real saints of the world, would have been satisfied had he simply *told* us why we are to suffer. But not us ordinary people—hearing why we are to suffer would not have made any difference to us at all. Jesus had to show us in his own life, in his own flesh and blood, in his own hurting humanity, *how* to suffer.

Had Christ been like the Stoics, I don't know what we would have done; but he wasn't. He did not accept suffering manfully[37] as the Stoics did, without a word, without a gesture. He cried, yes, cried at the tomb of Lazarus. He felt hurt many times because of ingratitude: "Where are the other nine?" Many times, he was hurt by people, hurt when people walked away from him, when he told them about the Blessed Sacrament [the "Bread of Life"]. "Will you," he said to the apostles, "also walk away?"

He was hurt by the refusal of so many to accept him. "If you do not believe my words," he once cried out, "believe the works that I do." He was hurt because men had made his Father's Temple a den of thieves. Imagine the hurt it must have taken to force him to make a whip and drive people out of his Father's home. And how desperately he was hurt by Judas's betrayal, by Peter's denial, and by the apostles abandoning him! "Judas," he said, "dost thou betray the Son of Man with a kiss?" [Similarly, the Gospel tells us,] "When Peter had finished speaking, Jesus, turning, looked at him." What that look must have said; the hurt in those eyes must have been a terrible thing, for, Peter, seeing that look, went out and wept bitterly.

At the Garden of Olives, when Jesus knew the apostles would run from him, when he knew what would happen, he begged, begged God to take it all away. "Three times," the Scriptures say, but three times is the mystical [symbolic] number; Jesus could have prayed a hundred-times-three times: "Father, if it be possible, let this chalice pass from me, but not as I will but as Thou willest." And he said no other prayer; he couldn't, you see, because he was hurting too much.

And the pain was so great on the cross; he hurt so much there on the cross that he even complained to God: "God, my God, why hast Thou abandoned me?" This is the only prayer that the Evangelists tell us he said on this occasion. He was hurting too much, you see, to say anything else.

Yes, thank God, Christ did not accept His sufferings stoically! I don't know what we would ever have done if he had. But he showed his complete humanity: he cried, he showed hurt by his words and by his actions, he begged to be relieved, he complained to God, and he didn't make up even one beautiful prayer in all his sufferings; he scarcely "prayed" with words at all.

Yet, he finally accepted [his suffering]; and this is the important thing, isn't it? He accepted, not because he wanted to prove he could take it—this would have made Him a pagan athlete. He accepted suffering not because there was just no way out—this would have made him a Stoic. Rather, he accepted it because he knew that his sufferings would purify the world and save it; this made him our Redeemer.

Although, as God, he needed no glorification, as man, he did bring about the glorification of his human body through his final suffering. He rose because He died; he was glorified because he suffered. He could have had the glory and the peace and the unending joy in his body at any time, because he was God and he had a right to it. But the fact remains that he had none of these things until after he suffered.

We have many, many examples from the life of Christ, but there is none greater than his suffering. He taught you and me how to live with it. If he cried, cannot we? If he showed hurt in his life, cannot we? If he begged to be relieved, cannot we? If he even complained to God, will God punish us if, in the midst of our hurt or pain, we complain to him, Our Father?

If we find it impossible to pray when we are hurting—I mean, really hurt-ing—do you think God will mind very much? For how much closer can we get to him, how much more can we raise our minds, our aching minds, to him, and our hearts—perhaps even, for a while, bitter hearts—to him, than when we are suffering? We may not be saying prayers of love and devotion, but we're close to him; we're with him even as Christ was with him.

I think too many of us have the notion that resignation in suffering means stoic acceptance; it doesn't. We don't jump up and down with glee when things, or people, or situations hurt us. I'm sure many of us can remember being so sick, hurting so much with physical pain that we asked God to call it all off, that we asked God to take us because life was just filled with pain. I'm sure many of us have been so sick with hurt, so bitter, that we haven't asked God anything. I don't think God was displeased with us; after all, His Son had done the same in his pain.

When you come right down to it, it is not *how* we physically accept pain—bodily or mental pain—but what we do with it when we have it. How we *use* it is the big question. So, we are not masochists; we don't accept pain because we like it. Nor do we accept it just to be better and stronger people. Me, I like being weak; I'm a coward, I guess. Nor do we accept it as the Stoics did because there is nothing else to do about it. Christ accepted pain and suf-fering in order to *use* it for our redemption; to be our Redeemer. This is the only reason, finally, why we should accept pain: to be co-redeemers with Christ.

St. Paul said a bold thing: "I fill up those sufferings that are lacking in the sufferings of Christ." If Paul had not said this, under the inspiration of the Holy Spirit, it would never have been believed: Something lacking in the sufferings of Christ? Something that we can *fill up*? Yes, this is our part: to be part of Christ—to really belong to the Body of Christ, to work with Christ for the sal-vation of human souls—we have to suffer with Christ. There is no other way.

For here is the heart of the mystery of suffering in the new revelation of Christ: it is the necessity for redemption—our own and that of others. If we would work with Christ—be part of him, redeem souls with him—then we must suffer with Christ. Why? Only God really knows. Suffering? Why not some other way? Herein lies the mystery of suffering.

However, even though there is still a mystery to suffering, at least Christ has given us a reason for it; at least we are not living in the darkness of the Old Testament times when suffering was the greatest curse that could happen to a person. At least we know this, that we fill up those sufferings that are lacking in the sufferings of Christ and that we redeem with him when we suffer with him—redemption gained, redemption applied.

Many say that there is no comparison between Christ's sufferings and our little sufferings. Yet, in a way, there is. He was by far a so much greater person than we: it took the vision of a crucifixion, the vision of millions and millions of souls rejecting him to make him cry out for surcease; it took the agonizing thirst and pain on the Cross to make him complain to God. Sometimes, all it takes for us to beg God for surcease is the rejection from one friend. All it takes to complain to God is a blasting, unending headache. But we're little, little children compared to Jesus; we can't take nearly as much. And God, I think, understands this and listens as carefully and with as much hurt in his great heart for us his children, as he listened with great hurt in his heart to his own beloved Son.

And He will finally comfort us; he will finally send *us* his angels to minister to us. When the pain and the heartache have run their course, when the souls that needed saving have been saved through our humiliation, or rejection, or hurt, through our temptations, or worrying, or pain, then will the comfort of God overwhelm us. When we have cried out in our own abandonment, in our own inability to raise our hearts or our minds or even our eyes to God in prayer, then, somehow, peace will come; somehow, we will be able to say: "Father, into thy hands I commend my spirit."

Then, through this suffering—a suffering we neither asked for nor desired, a suffering we would have totally rejected had we been able—through this suffering God will redeem many souls. And, when it is all over, at the end, he will raise us up once more, even as he raised his own Son, and he will give us—yes, even us—that peace that was in Christ Himself that first Easter Sunday morning.

We have heard, over and over again: There can be no Easter Sunday without our own Good Friday. We believe this. But not until our own Good Friday comes will we know how much pain and heartache can really hurt. Not until then will we ever be able to imagine Christ's pain and Christ's abandonment. Yet, not until then, and indeed, only then—only on our own Good Friday—will we be able to imagine and even experience, in some way, Christ's joy, Christ's peace on his day of resurrection.

14

Humility

Conference given by Fr. Ciszek to a group of apostolic religious sisters

The spirit of Christianity and the real spirit of our own religious life can be summed up best in the words of St. John the Baptist: "He must increase, and I must decrease." This is really our whole goal in life; it is the message of every day of our life.

But how do we let him increase in our lives, how do we *decrease* day after day, so that he can live more and more fully within us? "Christ," says St. Paul, "emptied himself, taking the form of a slave"; but how do we slaves empty ourselves so that we can take on the form of Christ?

We can, of course, meditate on and practice different ways for as long as we live, and, each day that we do live, we will see, more and more, how far, far away we are from having him truly living in our lives. But the one basic and essential starting point must be the sacred and wonderful—yet often despised—virtue of humility. Oh, for him to truly increase and grow in our lives, we need deep, deep faith, great confidence, and a divine love. But before any of these virtues can grow in our lives, before we can really believe, or hope, or love, we must have basic humility.

It is, indeed, basic to such an extent that there is no real joy here on earth without it, nor is there heaven without it. One day when we walk the streets of heaven, we will see many, many men and women whom we may well be surprised at seeing. We'll see repentant sinners of all kinds. I am sure that there will be more Magdalenes and Augustines than Little Flowers and Gonzagas. But we will not see even one proud man or one proud woman in heaven. For one has to stoop low to enter heaven. A man or woman has to say, "I was wrong and I am sorry," and you see, the really proud man or woman cannot say this. Thousands and thousands of years ago, God had to create a special place for the proud, a place of horror and loneliness, the everlasting fire of hell. Heaven could not tolerate, even for a moment, the presence of Lucifer and his followers once they rebelled against God—not so much because they rebelled but because they were too proud to say they were wrong. No, you may look as you walk the streets of heaven for all eternity and meet repentant sinners of all kinds, but you will never meet the proud man or the proud woman.

Yet, as basic and as necessary as humility is, I don't think that there is any [virtue] more difficult to work for, nor any virtue less appealing to us of the twentieth century. There seems to be some sort of stigma attached to this beautiful virtue, as though humility is the substitute for decisive action or the full expression of one's own personality. I think when most think of humility—even we religious—we tend to think of some meeky-mousy character who never "puts herself forward," never dares to try something new, never puts herself in the limelight for any reason at all. But this isn't humility; this is laziness. Christ told us not to hide our light under a bushel basket. He said, "You don't put a city on top of a mountain so that it can't be seen." He said, "Let your light shine before all men."

It takes, I think, a lot more humility than pride to try a lot of things: to be willing to make a fool of yourself for Christ, to give yourself totally and completely to some job that has never been tried before. It takes humility, I think, to put yourself in a position where others will take advantage of you and think you some sort of "easy mark," to do this so that others may love Christ more. Actually, many times the truly humble person will look very proud, for she isn't thinking of her own image or what others are thinking of her. She'll be out to give her total self to the job she has to do and to her whole life and not care what others think, or don't think, of her, or care whether others talk or don't talk. This looks like pride, but I think it takes a lot of real humility to act like this.

Some of the older spiritual writers, especially those tinged with the heresy of Jansenism, have done a great disservice to us in many of their writings. But their words on humility really take the cake! Were we to believe some of these writings—and we do, I think, tend to believe them—we would have to believe that only the sticks of the community, only those who never *do* anything, are the really humble ones; that, as soon as someone begins to do something in and for her community, she can never really be humble. I think that the influence of these writers, plus of course the whole attitude of the modern world on humility, have made the sacred virtue of humility an unappealing thing in our lives today. . . .

But humility, true humility, is simply, as you know, the recognition of what we are in God's eyes. It's the virtue that gives us the power to say, and know, "Everything I have, every good I do, comes from God." I can't even say, "Jesus," as a prayer, without him. I can't lift one finger unless he gives me the power. I can't do anything without him except sin. This is the only power I have by myself, to rebel against him.

The great St. Teresa of Avila says that humility is truth. But it's the most difficult form of truth for which we will ever have to work and attain. For it is a truth that will demand total self-knowledge, total realization of what we are, and this is something that we never fully realize. But the working for it, the striving to attain it, is not a humiliating thing or a thing for "little" people—who are not going to "do anything" in life—to worry about. It is a completely ennobling thing and, really, the most wonderful thing that can happen to any person's life. For the greatest gift that God could ever give to any one of us is to know ourselves, and this [is what] humility tries to do. Christ knew absolutely and perfectly who and what he was. So he had perfect humility and was, therefore, the perfect man. Mary knew, as well as any creature can ever know in this life, who she was. So, hers was the most perfect humility ever known in a mere creature. All we can do is imitate from afar this perfect gift of self-knowledge in Christ and Mary; but the imitating is well worth the effort.

Even after that, humility is something very well worthwhile in our lives: something that can make any job we are doing an even better job; something that will make us "put ourselves forward" for the sake of God's cause many, many times. Even after we realize all this, humility is the hardest virtue in the whole spiritual life to work for; for it is, I think, the virtue of paradoxes. When I think I'm humble, I'm probably proud. When I accuse myself of great pride, then I am reaching toward humility. But when I realize that I have reached a certain degree of humility, then in this very realization there is danger of pride. Sometimes we laughingly say, "I'm humble and I'm proud of it." But there is, I'm afraid, a lot more truth to this witty saying than a lot of us would dare to admit. Humility is the most elusive of all virtues. It's like trying to grab a handful of water or trying to pick up a blob of mercury. On the one hand, I have to be humble while not realizing that I am humble. On the other hand, I can't deny that I have gifts, because this would be denying my own self-knowledge, and self-knowledge is the very aim of humility! I have to have pride in my work, yet I have to work with a humble spirit! Pretty confusing, is it not?

Actually, the best way to work for practical humility—beyond praying for it, of course, and dutifully meditating on who we are and who God is—is to go to humility through the back door, not thinking so much about working to gain humility but rather by fighting against those sins that stem from pride [...] whether they be sins of unkindness, or thoughtlessness, or disobedience, or gossip, or laziness. We will grow in humility if we recognize our own sins; see that they come from pride (attempting to let ourselves increase [...] instead of Christ); and then try, with God's grace, to cut them from our life, so that Christ can truly increase in our daily living. But of all the virtues, this one especially is one we will be working for, wondering whether we have advanced even slightly in it, right up to our deathbeds.

Yet—and here is another paradox—though we are never certain we have any degree of humility, without it, we can't teach or pray, or really learn about God and ourselves. All of us, each in his or her own way, hopes to be able to teach the world a little more about Christ. That is why we religious wear these habits. It is for that we have given our lives. But unless we are at least aware that we must be humble people, unless we see that we are still very far from the humility of Christ or Mary or the great saints, we can never be teachers about Christ. You see, only the humble man or woman can teach Christ, can give him and his love to others, because the proud man or woman just can't really *have* Christ. The proud person is so filled with himself that there is no room for Christ. And I can't in any way give what I do not have. I can't give Christ if I don't have him myself. The wonder of humility is that it teaches us that we are nothing: that we have nothing of ourselves to give to others; that no matter how brilliant or holy we are, all this is from God. If we try to think that we are giving ourselves, we are sounding brass and tinkling cymbals. But when we know that we are nothing, then Christ comes into our lives and fills us with himself, and we have the indescribably wonderful grace of giving Christ to other men and women, no matter what we are saying to them or what we are teaching.

Only the humble person can truly pray. Oh, anyone can say a lot of words, whisper a lot of set phrases and forms, but only the humble person, the man or woman who knows that he or she *must* be humble, can really pray. For the humble person sees herself in prayer, sees that she has hurt God by her sins and says, "God, I am sorry. I'm really not going to sin anymore. I'm really going to give up this sin that has hurt you no matter what it costs." Then the bridge to God is up again and the humble man or woman can walk in his [or her] prayer right up to the heart of God and know him in a way that is intimate and at which even the angels wonder. But the proud person refuses to see sins or faults, or, seeing them, refuses to say that they are really wrong and so tries to push those sins to the back of his conscience. But he can't. They force themselves right up front. They say, "Get rid of us, before you go to God." If pride stops a person, if it says, "I can't give up my unkindness, or my disobedience, or my faults against poverty," then the bridge to God can never be really built and God can never be really reached.

And humility gives us the sacred gift of being able to learn from everyone. It gives us the ability to take advice from any person who gives it, not just the brilliant or the holy or the great, but from the simple and the ignorant and from those who may be far below our own position or station in life. It gives us the power to imitate Christ himself, who *learned* from Peter how to catch fish, and from Joseph how to make tables, and from Mary how to eat. It gives us the power to learn, even from those who do not appeal to us at all, whom we may not like very much. The humble person knows he doesn't know all things, knows that good advice, no matter what the source, is a rare gift, a gift that helps develop the wonder of self-knowledge. Very often, it is from people we may not like very much, or from people who are a little nasty and mean, that we learn how deep our pride is in reality and how far we still have to go before we have reached any real degree of humility. For such people will tell us what they think of us, will give us advice without bothering to be nice about it, will show us quite brilliantly and quite cuttingly, too, by the way, how proud we really are. Real humility will give us the power to accept such words, and though they may hurt because we are still human, we will be able to take them and because of them grow even closer to Christ.

I haven't spoken much about pride today because there was so much to take into consideration about the positive side. But if humility is the foundation of our spiritual side of life, then pride is truly, as we have learned so many years ago, the root of all the evil in our own lives. It's frightening to realize that every fault we commit, every sin we fall into, ultimately goes back to our pride, to our lack of humility.

Yet, it is wonderfully encouraging to realize that if we pray for humility, meditate on this sacred virtue, do everything we can to develop the depth of this virtue in our life, then we are preparing for the greatest joy—for ourselves, our puny insignificant little selves. And we are preparing to fill the emptiness with the wonder and the sublimity of Christ himself, so that each succeeding day of our lives will be a new Christmas, when Christ will be born ever more and more in our lives.

May he increase. May we decrease!

15

Faith

Conference given by Fr. Ciszek to a group of apostolic religious sisters

We take a lot for granted in our religious and Christian life. I suppose half of our lives have to be spent reminding ourselves *not* to take things and people for granted. For the danger in taking things for granted is that, slowly but ever so surely, the wonder that should surround such things as God's grace, or the gift of life, or the love of a friend, begin to lose their splendor and become not just ordinary and commonplace but even tiresome and boring.

I suppose if we were to try to list the things that we religious, especially, take for granted, we would be here all day busily writing away. But you know, so insidious is this [vice of taking things for granted] that we are very liable to overlook something that is more common to *us*, more part of *us*, indeed, than the very air we breathe. Yet, it is the most sacred and the most basic of God's gifts to us: the gift of divine faith. We'd overlook it because we live with it all day, every day, because we just can't imagine living without this gift, because it is as much a part of us as our minds that think and our hearts that love.

It is not just by accident that the theology books and the catechisms list the virtue of faith first; it *is first*. It is the foundation stone of everything else in our Christian and religious life. I can't hope, I can't love, I can't see Christ in others or know that he lives in me, without faith. I can't be wise, in the Christian sense, or prudent, or chaste, or patient, or strong, or kind, without faith. I can't live even one moment for God and in him and with him, without faith. If I have no faith, then life, every second of it, is a rat race, a treadmill, a boring, useless, hopeless existence, going nowhere, accomplishing nothing—a taste, indeed, of hell itself. Yet, of all God's sacred gifts to us, this gift of faith is the one we are most positively apt to take for granted.

I am sure that each of you can define faith; you have known this definition since you were little children: faith is the virtue by which we accept all the truths that God has revealed *because* he has revealed them. And you can take each idea apart and explain it fully because you have read so much, and taught so much, about it. But the problem with this definition, and the problem that comes simply from taking those words apart for a further understanding, is this: We tend to think of the wonderful virtue (which means "power," by the way) of faith as a "knowledge machine" about God. "Faith," we say, "gives us the power to accept all the wonderful truths about God, about Christ, about our religion." Put faith into the mind and heart of a man or a woman and, Zammie! Bang! Wham! . . . in goes a lot of knowledge about God.

But, oh, the power of faith is so much, much more than this. Faith doesn't just give us knowledge about God; it introduces us to him. It is our constant meeting ground, our trusting place, with Almighty God, the Creator and Redeemer of the universe, where we stand on God's level and know him and love him as a sacred, wonderful Person, know him and love him as our closest friend. Faith isn't just knowledge; it's encounter. It's not just knowing; it's meeting and facing and accepting, not some cold bundle of truths but meeting, and facing, and accepting, and so possessing God, Christ, the very source of these truths.

This is the sacred gift we take for granted. This is the power (the power of knowing God) that is so much part of our Christian lives that we rarely even think of it. Yet, my dear Sisters in Christ, of all the powers God has given us, the one that can weaken the fastest when taken for granted is precisely faith. Because we know God through faith (blindly and with our human eyes, and human minds alone) there is great, great danger that our *real* encounters, our *real* meetings with this hidden, *unseen* God, can become rarer and rarer in our lives. [As a result,] that which goes by the name of faith in our religious lives can become simply sterile, impersonal knowledge.

Think, sometime, of the days in which you did not pray, in which you let your prayers become formal, soulless things, in which you did not see the real reason for prayer, perhaps because God did not grant you a special favor that you were asking. Think of those days, and I am sure that you will remember how far, far away God was from your life and your thoughts—far away, because you had stopped praying. The lifeline between you and God was down. You see, you stopped believing in him on such days, because you stopped meeting with him. The encounter with God just did not exist on days of *no prayer*. So, faith had to be a weak and almost dead thing. Do you see what our Lord meant when he said, "You ought always to pray, and never to [grow] faint"? We must constantly be in the attitude of prayer, no matter what we are doing or how involved we are in our work. If we are not, if we have, in effect, turned from prayer and are doing a job for the glory it brings us, or the pleasure it brings us, or doing a job just because it has to be done, or totally out of routine, then we have ceased to pray always. We have ceased to make our work prayer, and there is real danger that our faith will grow weak.

Faith, you see, is very much like our life itself. We either nourish it constantly with the food of prayer, or we starve it. It either grows strong, and so we *meet* God more and more intimately every day, or it grows weak, and God becomes some impersonal being we read about in theology books or hear about in sermons and conferences.

If you study the Gospels, you will never find Christ talking about faith as just some cold body of truths. With him, it is always a trusting faith, an acceptance not just of truth or word but an acceptance of *him* as a Person who can and will change our lives, if we let him in. The faith he demanded, over and over again, was this living, trusting faith, this faith that said *not*, "I believe in God," but, "I know you, God, but in addition I love you. I know you're with me, over and over again. I know that you will help me, because you love me." "If you believe," said Christ, "*action* this belief and I will save you." Remember, he said to the man who had a sick child, "If you believe, your child will be cured." What did he mean but that if the man accepted *him as God* and so knew that this God would and could do all things, then, and only then, could Christ work a miracle for his child.

Remember when Peter was walking on the water to Christ, Christ said, "Come," and Peter began, but then, realizing where he was, he doubted, not some work, some code, some canon—no, he doubted Christ, and fell. Or remember when Christ was sleeping in the boat during the terrible storm on the lake? They had to wake him. "Save us, Lord; we are perishing!" You see, they doubted *him* again; they weren't quite sure that he loved them enough to care for them even while he apparently slept. [That was why he asked,] "Why did you doubt, O you of little faith?"

And throughout the Old Testament, the story is the same; it is a living faith, a personal encounter with God that the psalmists, for example, proclaim over and over again: "The Lord is my shepherd, I want for nothing; He is my fortress, my deliverer, my exceedingly strong defense; God is our Lord, and there is none like to Him; Behold, God is my helper; The Lord is the upholder of my soul; Though a thousand fall beside thee, no evil shall come near thee for he has given his angels charge over thee." The faith that Christ talks about and demanded, the faith that God inspired his prophets and psalmists to write about, was always this trusting, living faith in the God who lives in us and with us, through real faith, this personal meeting and accepting of God himself, not just occasionally but always, every minute of the day; for only this kind of faith acts and lives. Knowing God's revelation means nothing, but knowing *him* in every action of every day, this is living, acting, trusting faith.[38]

We know that God has graced us with the sacred gift of faith. It is, as I have said, so much part of our lives that we take it almost totally for granted. And in taking it for granted, perhaps for too long, for too many years, I wonder, is it the living, trusting, acting faith Christ demands of us, is it a constant encounter with God, the very source of life, and love, and grace, and pardon; or does it sleep too often in our lives?

In your private prayers, for example, do you believe, I mean really believe, that you are talking to God: that he, the Almighty Creator of the universe is really interested in every word you whisper, every thought you have, that you are meeting with him on common ground, with every prayer you offer? Oh, if we believed this, really believed, imagine the brilliance and the splendor of every prayer on our lips, in our hearts.

Every day, you have the privilege of offering the prayer of the Divine Office. Do you know that you pray in conjunction with all the voices of the full praying Church each time you pick up this holy book, that you meet with God, not just as a single human being but as the official "pray-er" for the whole human race, that God hears your voice joined to a million others and is pleased with the whole human race because of your words of praise?

And each day, at the Mass, you with your priest offer Christ in sacrifice for the needs, for the redemption of a world; yes, you offer this sacred sacrifice. You meet God and hand him this most perfect gift. You say each day, "Father, here is a gift, a sacrifice that is equal even to you. Bless the world. Save us. Have mercy on us." *And, do you know*, God *must* hear you because of the dignity of your gift! Do you believe in this way each time you offer Mass with your priest? Do you believe that here at Mass is your greatest encounter, your most intimate meeting with God that can ever take place on this earth? If we believed [with] this living, trusting faith, every Mass would contain this wonder, this splendor no matter how you felt or how tired you were.

If we have a living, trusting, acting faith, then we know that God is around every corner of our life, that he does indeed walk with us and talk with us and love us, so deeply, so immensely that our *life* for him, our dearest friend, is like a tiny flame of a match compared with the burning world. Do we act on this all day long? Don't we so often act as though God is somewhere out there in the vast, impersonal sky, too concerned with the really big things of the world to be thinking of us? Aren't we so very often like the apostles in the boat, thinking we have to wake God up so that he will pay attention to us? For we just can't believe that we are so important to him because he loves us, and that his love is part of every second of our life. As this second goes by, God loves me and cares for me; no second of the day is different!

If we have faith in God, then we know that we meet him not only in our own lives but that we encounter him also in every person we meet. So, when we treat others with a living, trusting faith, we are treating them with the kindness and the gentleness with which we [would] treat Christ himself, because they are Christ and God lives in them; this is what our faith teaches us. But how many, many times (because our faith has become but a bundle of dry truths), how many times do we treat one another so shabbily, so unkindly, so unlike God treats us? Do you see, if we believed, if our faith was a living encounter with God, then every second of every day, we could never be unkind, never hurt [others]?

A trusting, living faith gives us the power to move mountains. When we realize that, our faith puts us in direct contact with the very God of the universe, our Creator, who makes us *be* every moment. Such faith gives us the power to cry out with St. Paul, "I can do all things in him who strengthens me!" This is the kind of faith Mary had. This is the kind of faith that makes us touch God every minute of any day. This is the kind of faith that makes living—every minute of it—a sacred mystical, sublime experience. And this is the kind of faith, my dear Sisters in Christ, that I pray you will have from this minute on.

16

The Love of God

Conference given by Fr. Ciszek to a group of apostolic religious sisters

"And a Scribe wishing to test him said, 'Master, what is the greatest commandment?' And Jesus answering said, 'Thou shalt love the Lord thy God with thy whole heart, and with thy whole soul, and with thy whole mind, and with all thy strength. This is the first and the greatest commandment.'"

Often, we talk so much about our lives and the lives of our neighbors—what we should do to fill our lives with God's grace and peace and happiness, what we must do to make our neighbor's life happy—that we forget the basic reason why you and I and all men live. We live and breathe and have our being for one reason only: *to love God*. God created us for this one reason, to love him. He gave us power over all things of the earth for one reason only, that we may love him. He gave us our lips to be voices for the stars and the sun and the birds and the animals and the trees and rocks and mountains, and the exotic orchids and the simple dandelions, so that they can sing their hymn of praise to their God through you and me: "God, we love you!" The world would echo with this cry: "God, we love you!" It should be the song of every man, the whisper of every child: "God, we love you!" There is no reason for living, no sense to life, no reason why our heart should beat, or our lungs should breathe, or our minds should act, without this love. We have been made "God-lovers," and our lives are restless, empty, barren things unless they be filled in every part with the song of songs, "God, we love you."

[Jesus told us,] "Thou shalt love the Lord thy God, with thy whole heart, and with thy whole soul, and with thy whole mind, and with all thy strength; this is the first and the greatest commandment." Christ came to earth as a little child, was born of a Virgin in a cave at Bethlehem for but one reason: to teach men to love their God. He made the deaf hear, the dumb speak, the blind see, the lame walk, the dead live again, he was betrayed by a friend, spat upon, scourged, crucified on a Cross, for only one reason: to bring men back to the love of their God.

He brought grace and pardon into our lives so that we could do what we have been created to do by God, so that the world could sing the song God made it to sing: God, we love you!

He founded his Church, taught us to pray, gave us the Sacred Sacraments, gave us his flesh to eat and his blood to drink, gave us the power to offer him in Sacrifice every day of our lives for this one same reason: that we might love God more completely in our lives; that the echoes of this Son of love may be heard in every land, among every people, in every language; that all the power of our lives may be spent in singing this one great song of praise: God, we love you!

And Mary his Mother has come back at Lourdes, at La Sallette, at Fatima in Portugal, and to many, many other spots throughout the world to set the hearts of men singing again, singing the only song that God can hear: "Oh, God, we love you!"[39]

Why is this command to love God the first and the greatest commandment? St. John the Apostle answers this question in just a few short words: "Let us therefore love God, because he loved us first." He created us, redeemed us, and lives now intimately in our hearts and souls. Because he loved us *first*, you and I are living and breathing at this moment. If he were to stop loving us for even a moment, you and I would cease to be. Where there is life, there would be utter nothingness, if God were to halt his love. This, then, is the important reason for the first and the greatest commandment: we are to love God, not because we fear him, not even because of what he has done or will do for us, not just because his commandment insists that we love him, not just because he is Almighty God, the Creator of the universe, but, because he, God Almighty, thought enough about us—about you and me—to love us *first*. And love demands love in return, for he loved us *first*.

This love of God that I am talking about is not a mere sentiment or an emotional feeling (somewhat like the feeling we might have after reading a particularly warm book or seeing a sentimental movie or television show), nor is it the sentimental love of two young lovers. No, true love of God is a deeper and stronger thing than just feelings. Feelings and emotions pass away, but true love lives on. For real love of God is anchored deep in the mind and heart of a person, set so deeply that no thing, no person here on earth can ever destroy it. [It is] set in wisdom and knowledge, the wisdom that life's whole reason is to love God, and the knowledge that he deserves to be loved *because he first loved us*. Love like this, though it sometimes experiences good feelings and deep emotions, lives beyond these feelings, beyond these emotions in the very bedrock of our being.

Such love gives us the power to say and to mean, "God, I love you" when sorrow has torn all joy from our hearts, when pain is like a living thing in our lives, and when the hatred and unkindness and treachery of so-called friends and even irreligious [people] has sickened the very core of our souls.

Such a love gives us the power to say, "God, I love you" when it seems that he, yes, even he has abandoned us, and when the devil has made our lives his plaything and has tortured us with every imaginable temptation. This is real love of God, a love that is not measured by fervor and piety in prayers but by a faithful daily devotion to prayers that may seem cold and lifeless things. [It is a] love that is measured by doing things for God when discouragement and even despair and disgust and all types of shame have made it almost impossible to do anything for anyone.

This is real love of God, a love that is constantly and completely a *devoted love*: with a willingness to give God everything, even life itself, just for him, just for his glory; with a willingness to forget oneself, one's own needs, one's own desires out of love for him; with a willingness to *do* anything he wants, just because he wants it and to see him loved and glorified and praised above everything else in life; a willingness to love him deep, deep in your inmost soul, to want him in your life, sincerely and truly, more than you want comfort, or respect, or success, or health, or human love or anything else this world can give to you. [This is real love of God,] to love him without measure, without stinting, without ever considering how much it will cost you to love him. For true love never considers cost, never says, "It is enough." We are [only] beginning somewhat to love God when we can say and truly mean, "My love of God is never enough."

Obviously, of course, the first requirement for the love of God in our hearts is that we be friends of love, that we be in the state of sanctifying grace, that we be free of all sin that is serious. For a person cannot say, "God, I love you!" with her lips, and mean this, when her heart and mind and soul are turned to sin relative to some person or thing. Sisters, herein lies the real evil of mortal sin; it destroys the very reason for our existence and makes a heart that was made to sing a song of love for God mute and silent and useless.

Does it surprise you, good women, that I should even bring the idea of mortal sin into a talk presented to you? Perhaps it does, and yet, my dear Sisters, the more you and I meditate on the horror of mortal sin, the more we will try to avoid even a first tiny step towards this terrible evil. And, surely, you—you who have taken upon yourselves in a special way the vocation to love—surely, you can see that of all the terrible effects of mortal sin, this one I have just described is the worst. Mortal sin in a bride of Christ makes her—who by her very habit professes to love her God every moment of her day—makes her a sham and a faker, and makes her totally unworthy of her vows and of her habit and the very house in which she lives. For all these say, "This woman is a God lover," while, deep within her heart, she has given the lie to these things by

[even] one mortal sin. Oh, my dear Sisters, to die a thousand deaths, to suffer tortures unimaginable: all these would be as nothing compared to committing even one mortal sin. For in dying and in suffering, our dedicated souls can still sing their songs of love; but in sinning mortally, we make our hearts as silent as the corridors of hell.

The next greatest enemies to God's love in our life are the so-called "little sins," the little venial sins of gossip, unkindness, lying, impatience, envy, anger, disobedience, criticism, and the so many little faults we scarcely even notice in our daily life. We can also add to this list our constant lack of thoughtfulness. Yet, these "little sins" chip and bite away at our love of God. They gradually but, oh so surely, push him and his love into a small corner of our life. A little lie told to avoid difficulty in the community, or with a superior, a word of anger or of impatience with the young people you teach, a word of unkindness to a fellow sister, and carelessness in your daily prayer: all these "little sins" are the greatest evil in the world, next to the evil of mortal sin.

But avoiding mortal sin and avoiding, at least, all deliberate venial sin is only the beginning of our love. Our love of God becomes real when we *do* everything out of love for him. When you teach a child that two and two are four or teach a college philosophy major that the ontological proofs for the existence of God are more existential than they are essential; when you wash the face of a hospital patient or administer the whole complex organization of a hospital; when you put a new light bulb in an older sister's room or lecture brilliantly on atomic fission; when you do all—great things and little things, big things and little things—when you do all *just and only out of love for God*, then your love of God is real.

Every simple act of every day, and every great act of every day, done out of love, can grow because we love God, can be changed into so *great an act of love* that the angels themselves will be dazzled by the light of this one little act. The more that you do everything for your God, the more do you love him. The more you offer every act of kindness, every pain, every sorrow, every smile, every tear, every joy, every worry, every good thing to him, the more you love him. Each time you say throughout the day, "God, I love you!" the song of your love of God fills the halls of Heaven itself.

It is not easy to love God with such a devoted and selfless love. For we are born with selfish hearts, and there is constant pressure to put our pleasures, our comforts, our needs, and our desires above everything and everyone else, even God himself. One of the most terrible effects of venial sin is this: it turned the heart of man, which was made to be God-centered, into a self-centered heart. God made us to love him. Sin turned us from him. This means that every time we want to love God and not ourselves, every time we want to do something for God, such as avoid mortal sin or venial sin, say some special prayers, be kind or patient or understanding, each time we will have to do violence to our own human nature. We will have to take our lives and our hearts in hand and turn them forcibly away from what *we* want, to what *God* wants. This is what Christ meant when he said, "The Kingdom of Heaven suffers violence and the violent bear it away." The violent ones are those who constantly say *no* to themselves and to their wants in life, who pull themselves filially and violently from what they want in life to what God wants in life.

You see, this is the reason there is, and must be, penance in our lives. For the only way we can do constantly what God wants us to do, the only way we can do things for God and for his children and not for ourselves, is by constantly practicing penance in small things, by constantly saying *no* to our own desires. And *this* is penance, as you all know so well. This is why Christ told us, "If any man will come after me, let him take up his cross *daily* and follow me." [This is] why St. Paul said, "They who are Christ's have crucified their flesh" and, "If any man love the world, the love of God is not in him."

Love of God is not an easy thing in our life. It demands suffering and penance, much, much prayer, a constant repeating of the good inten-tion—telling God that you want to do everything for him. For the more you repeat your good intention, the easier it is to *do* things for him. Love of God demands giving up the many comfortable "little sins" of our life. But all that you do to make your song of love echo through the streets of Heaven will be well worth it. For, my dear Sisters, you will begin to find an unimaginable peace coming into your lives. You will still want success in your work, and health, and human love because you are human, but you will begin to want them, really, only if God wants them. You will be able to say, and really mean it, "God, any-thing you want is all right by me. I'll do my best," and the rest is up to our lover, God. Humiliations, failures, and the unkind actions or words of fellow sisters will still hurt, because you are still human, but they will never hurt enough to make your soul sick and disgusted with life or with your vocation in life, because in all these things you will truly possess your God.

For when you love him, then you truly possess him, and possessing him, you will be able to say with St. Paul, "Who shall separate us from the love of Christ? Shall tribulation, or distress, or persecution, or hunger, or nakedness, or the sword? But in all these things, we overcome because of him who has loved us. For I am sure that neither death, nor life, nor the powers of hell, nor the things present, nor things to come, nor height nor depth, nor any other creature will be able to separate us from love of God which is in Christ Jesus our Lord."

17

Mystical Body

Conference given by Fr. Ciszek to a group of apostolic religious sisters

"Know you not that you are the Temples of God, and that the Spirit of God dwells in you? You are Christ's, and Christ is God, and God is all in all."

One of the most beautiful of all the doctrines of our faith is the teaching on the Mystical Body of Christ. I know that you must have heard many conferences on this subject and read many books. What I am going to tell you this day will not be new to you. But the beauty, the sublimity of this doctrine bears as much meditation as you and I could possibly give it.

Of all the doctrines the Bible teaches us, the doctrine of Christ living intimately in our lives is one of the most clearly expressed. There are the words I have already quoted. Then, St. Paul also says, "All you who have been baptized into Christ have put on Christ, that you have Christ dwelling through faith in your hearts, that there is no longer Gentile, or Jew, or slave or freeman, but that Christ is all in all; that we, the many, make up the one Body of Christ." He tells us [in another place], "My little Children, I am in labor until Christ be formed in you." And, finally, [there is] his great cry of triumph, "It is no longer I that live, but Christ lives in me."

Our Lord Himself tells us: "I am the vine, you are the branches. Abide with me, and I will abide in you. If any man love me, my Father will love him and we will come to him, and take up our abode with him." What can these words mean, what must they mean, except that you, you have Christ living, in every part—in your hearts, and in your lives? Wherever you walk—whether you walk to do good or walk to do evil—you carry [with you] Christ, the Second Person of the Most Holy Trinity, the all-Holy Son of God. [This means] that, as long as you have his sacred gift of sanctifying grace coursing through your soul, he who formed the universe and flung the stars in the sky with a mere flick of his fingers and fashioned a world for men to live in, and died upon a Cross, he lives intimately within you.

Even as I am talking to you, he lives within you. He is closer to you than a beloved mother or father, or the closest of friends. You and he are united in a union so close, so intimate that there is nothing, nothing here on earth, that can compare to this union. The first kiss of lovers, the union of lifelong friends, the married love of a lifetime—all these are as nothing compared to the union between you and your Christ. *At this very moment,* though you cannot feel him, or see him, or touch him, his life throbs vibrantly in your life, in your soul, in your heart. The things you touch, he touches. The things you look upon, he looks upon; the words you speak, he speaks; he is with you in everything you do, except sin. You so-called ordinary weak human beings, you are Christ bearers to a world. The scientists say that we are but a speck, an infinitesimally tiny speck in this tremendous universe of ours. But tiny, insignificant though we may be compared to the universe, in the eyes of Almighty God we are the greatest, most marvellous, most sacred work of his hands, for we—you and I—carry his Son in our lives. We are Christ bearers.

And because we are Christ bearers, we have received a destiny beyond all imagining. We are God's *chosen ones,* his instruments [chosen] to bring love and peace back to the world, by bringing Christ back to that rugged world, a world that had become rotten with sin and gutted with hatred and war. The pitiable thing [is] that Christ was scourged at a pillar, crowned with thorns, spat upon, betrayed by a friend, blasphemed, and killed upon a Cross to bring holiness and love into the hearts of men, and peace to the countries of the world. It is a terrible thing to see the precious Blood of our Christ wasted on the lives of so many of his children.[40]

We have given our lives to him to help him fight the real and terrible evils that do exist *now*. Satan stalks the earth as someone who is very real. Only if we understand this, *only if we recognize the immensity of sin into which our world has sunk, only then will we see how desperately our good lives are needed.* For God, only through your lives as Christ bearers, only by your lives as his instruments of love and peace, will destroy such evil in the world; God will cast Satan back into the Hell created for him and will wash men's souls with the precious, healing Blood of Christ.

He wants you, and needs you, to carry Christ to this our world of the twentieth century. For, my dear Sisters, Christ must live intimately in our world *today*: in its shops and offices, in its homes and schools, in its clinics and hospitals, in its senate buildings and law courts, in its room of presidents and premiers and kings. For only if he lives among us, only if men can touch him—as the poor, sick woman touched him so many years ago—can they be cured of their sin and suspicions and hatred. Christ living in heaven, today lives here on earth, only through you and me. If men of our day must touch him and feel him to be cured, they can touch him and feel him only through you and me. And, [in order] to live fully in us, so that his presence is never hidden by the sin of our lives, Christ asks us to be saints—yes, saints, great heroes for Christ, heroes whose faith is burning, whose hope is immense, whose love is divine. [Christ asks us to be] heroes, women who have learned so deeply the secret of prayer that they live and breathe in the constant presence of their God, women seeking for penance in their daily lives to save the souls of those who have walked far, far away from the heart of their Christ.

You see, it isn't true to say, as so many spiritual writers seem to say, that Christ does not need us to save the world. He does need us. He needs you and me—our bodies, our lives, our hearts, our souls, and our love—to live among men today, to save those men by his healing, holy presence. He needs to touch the world with your hands and walk the world with your feet and look upon the world with your eyes, and talk to the world with your lips, and love the world with your hearts, and save the world again today in you and with you, and *because of you.*

This, then, is our task. This is our destiny: to give Christ new hands, new feet, new lips, and new eyes, new hearts, and new bodies, to live intimately in the world to which we have given our lives to save and make holy. Oh, how little time there is to preach a negative Catholicism, a negative asceticism, to you, the chosen ones of God: don't be careless in your prayers; don't ignore your rule; don't violate poverty; don't gripe and complain about superiors or appointments; don't be lazy and halfhearted in your work; don't be petty and uncharitable. For there is no time for such a negative or "don't" asceticism. Our world *is* falling apart at the seams. Hatred and sin and greed are now rapidly destroying it. And it is you, the intimate friends of Christ, who must hold this world together and bring men back to the heart of Christ by bringing the heart of Christ back to a world.

There is but one measure of our success in life and of each day of our life, and it is this: How fully did I let my Christ shine from my life today?... How fully, how completely did I love him? Did the children I teach see Christ even as I taught? Did the person I spoke to about a school bill, or a hospital bill, see Christ even as I spoke? Did a little child whose coat I straightened out feel the hands of Christ as I dressed her? Did a hospital patient see the smiling Christ as I ministered to his needs? Did a businessman hear Christ's voice talking as I discussed a point of business over the phone with him? Did my Sisters hear Christ laughing and joking as I sat at recreation with them? Did I do anything—anything at all—that hid *the presence of Christ within me?*

So many of us get involved in the work we have to do that we see *this work* as the reason for our existence. We measure our success, even in the religious life, on how successful we were in the work we did on any particular day: how well we taught, how brilliantly we took care of a business matter, how wisely and prudently we handled another's problem. *Do not the pagans also do this?* The work that we do is just a secondary thing. Whether or not, after trying with our whole heart, we are successful, makes no difference at all to our real vocation. We are *not* just professional people, different only from the other professional people in the clothes we wear. We are not dedicated to teaching, or to hospital work, or to administration. We are dedicated—or at least we should be dedicated—to giving Christ new bodies and new hearts with which to live in our world today.

It's time we took a good look at our lives and stopped measuring them with the yardstick of the world, the yardstick of material, tangible success. We are the chosen ones of God, and we are a success only if the Son of God shines brilliantly in our daily lives, in our daily work. The children of the fourth grade or the young woman of the four-year college will little remember what you teach about arithmetic or about atomic fission, but they will remember all the days of their lives how much of Christ they saw in you. And your hospital patients will little remember the efficiency with which you ran your hospital, but they will never forget the face of the smiling Christ they saw as you walked into their suffering lives.

We can hire fine teachers, efficiency experts, guidance directors. We cannot hire—at any price, even for a moment—a body, a heart, or hands, or lips, or eyes for Christ to live in again. Only a deep, dedicated, constant love can give Christ a new life with which to touch and heal the men and women he once died to save. And unless each man, woman, and child we touch, even so slightly, touches Christ through us and because of us, then we have failed Christ; we have failed to live up to the only *profession* we have, the profession of being Christ bearers to a world sick with sin and aching for the healing hands of Christ.

It is a startling and frightening thing to realize that people will not touch Christ in us unless we are sincerely seeking holiness in our daily lives. Every deliberate venial sin, every act of pettiness or nasty meanness or lack of charity hides Christ's presence within us. Every angry look, every angry word, muffles the voice of Christ within us. Every deliberate violation of your rule, every sin against your vows, holds Christ back from the people with whom you work.

It is a task that will demand great sacrifices in your daily lives. But if you love the world you live in, if a great pity wells up in your hearts for the people of the world who are living a sinful, bitter, cynical, humdrum, boring existence because they do not know Christ, then you will take up this task joyfully and willingly, out of love for the souls he loved even to the death of the Cross.

My prayer for you, then, is that Mary Immaculate, the first Christ bearer to our world, will give you the great grace to be like her, a monstrance for her Son, that she will help you to so manifest Christ in all you do and in all you say that you may *make him visible* to the world in which you live. And oh, Mary, give these, God's chosen ones, the grace to sacrifice themselves all day long so that sin, greed, and selfishness, and unkindness, and impatience and gossip may never hide the presence of your Son within them. Oh, Mary, make the lives of these religious Christ bearers such that the presence of your Son may shine from them, wherever they walk, and heal our sick and ailing world of its sin and of its hate. Let this be their chief and only task.

18

The Presence of God

Conference given by Fr. Ciszek to a group of apostolic religious sisters

I bind myself today to
God's power to guide me,
God's might to uphold me,
God's wisdom to teach me,
God's eye to watch over me,
God's ear to hear me,
God's Word to give me speech,
God's hand to guide me,
God's way to lie before me,
God's Shield to shelter me . . .

Christ with me, Christ before me,
Christ behind me, Christ within me.
Christ beneath me, Christ above me,
Christ at my right, Christ at my left.
Christ in the fort,
Christ in the chariot seat,
Christ in the heart of everyone who thinks of me,
Christ in the mouth of everyone who speaks of me,
Christ in every eye that sees me,
Christ in every ear that hears me.

—St. Patrick's Breastplate

I know of no more beautiful words to sum up the doctrine of God's presence in our daily, minute after minute living than these of St. Patrick. How aware—even minutely—must he have been of God's presence in his life? How conscious he must have been of the sacred indwelling of God: Father, Son, and Holy Spirit. No wonder he was a saint; for the deepest definition of saint is *one who has united himself or herself so completely with God that this is his or her whole life*. God acts in a saint so totally because the saint has so completely emptied himself of self that God has complete possession of that person's life. "I live," cried St. Paul, "now, not I but Christ lives in me!" St. John of the Cross, surely describing his own life, said of this union: "The soul's understanding is the understanding of God; its will is the will of God; its memory is the memory of God; its joy is the joy of God."

I suppose the teaching that God is in our lives—and sees us, and is with us every second of every day—is one of the first things we learned as little children. "God is everywhere," we heard, "and there is not a minute of the day that he is not watching over us." Perhaps, too many of us heard, or at least understood, "watching us" as though God were a watchman with a stick in his hands; but, at least the fact that God was everywhere, was certainly part of our earliest childhood.

Since we have become religious, we have learned that our whole life should be taken up with increasing this presence of God in our lives and in living *constantly* in God's presence. We know that here, as I have said, lies real sanctity; when we can cry out with St. Paul, "I live, now not I, but Christ lives in me," *then we are on the road to holiness*, the road to sainthood.

Before we look for ways to increase God's presence in our lives, I think we should try to understand the *how* of God's presence—that is, what we mean when we say that God is present in us, that God is united to us.

We believe, of course, that God is everywhere. We read in the spiritual books that *his immensity fills the universe*. But the trouble is that as soon as we talk of God's immensity, we almost try to conceive God as so *big* that he fills the universe in the same way as water fills a bucket. But though God is immense, though he is everywhere, still he is a pure spirit, and once we talk of spirit, then, we can't be talking about size, about bigness or littleness. Our own soul is not divided up into different parts, as is our body; it is one thing, giving life to all the different parts of our body. In very much the same way, God is in every part of the universe, giving it the energy—the life, you might say—to keep on going. But God is not in parts, either. He is *one*, whole and entire, in every part of the universe, because he is pure *spirit*, and a spirit isn't limited by space as we humans or material things are.

If God is in the universe, supporting it, giving it the energy to go on—continually creating it, as a matter of fact—then he is in us, too, in the very same way. He is in us giving us energy, continually creating us so that if he took his presence away from us, even for a minute, we just would not *be* any longer. So because God is the Creator of the universe, because he is our Creator, he has to be wherever there is something or someone created. We call this presence of God in the universe (and in us) God's "ordinary" presence. But there is another kind of presence of God, a presence that is beyond the ordinary. [It is] a special, supernatural presence in which God is not just giving us life, not just upholding us, but is also giving us a new life of sanctifying grace; God is present now as a person who is to be known more and loved more. And it is this special, "supernatural" presence of God in us that can be increased and intensified more and more. There can be (and God wants this) a continued growth in this, his special presence. The more this special presence of God grows in us, the more we are united to God. And the more we are united to him, the holier we are.

How does this union grow? How does this special presence of God become more and more intense? There is a saying today: "I want to be where the action is." And this is just what we can say of God: "God is where the action is"—where his action, his activity is. Where he is acting more, he is present more. So, [just as] our soul is more present in our mind than in our big toe (because there is, or at least should be, more activity, more action in our mind than in our big toe), so also, God (in his special presence) is more present in a saint than in a newly baptized baby because there is more action, more of his action going on in a saint than in the baby. [This is so] because the saint is constantly turning his mind and heart to God, [while] God, for his part, is turning to the saint and filling that saint's soul with his own life of sanctifying grace. In the baby, there is simply the steady, special presence of God through sanctifying grace, which will neither grow nor decrease until the baby grows up. But God's presence is surging in the saint, because each time the saint prays (or even thinks of God), God fills that soul with ever more sanctifying grace. And each time God fills a soul with grace, he himself is in that soul more; for God is, and must be, where the action is—where his action is.

Every time, then, that we turn to God in prayer, he turns to us. Every time we think of God, he thinks *more* of us. Every time we look at a [holy] picture or think of one of his saints, or of his Holy Mother, he turns more to us, fills our own souls with more of his grace, and, consequently, is *more present* to us, is more part of our lives, is more and more the center of our thoughts. And as he becomes more and more the center of our thoughts, he becomes more and more present. A beautiful vicious circle, is it not?

If we ask, then, what is to prevent God, who is all-powerful, from becoming present in our lives, the answer is frighteningly simple: "No one but ourselves." "Open thine heart, and I will come in like a torrent," says God. So the only thing that stands in the way of God—Father, Son, and Holy Spirit—totally living in us, is *us*. He becomes more present the more we turn to him, the more we think of him. There is nothing but ourselves that keeps him from acting in our souls, so completely, so utterly that we can dare to say with St. John of the Cross, "The heavens are mine, the earth is mine, and the nations are mine; mine are the just and the sinners are mine; mine are the angels, and the Mother of God; all things are mine and God himself is mine for me, because Christ is mine and for me. What then dost thou ask for and seek, O Lord? All is thine; all is for thee."

"Wow!" might be the first reaction to these words, the words of a saint caught up in God's transforming union. But here is the road we can at least begin to travel, when we see him everywhere in our lives. I have said that God is everywhere. I have said that God is everywhere in his ordinary presence, but the more conscious we are of his ordinary presence, surprisingly enough, the more does he become present to us in his special, supernatural way, as friend and Lover. So when I think that God is upholding me as a human being—and also upholding the bed that I sleep on—then he becomes more present to me in a special way, for I have turned my mind to him, and he has turned to me, and then I must not fall asleep but with God.

And when the wandering thought comes to me that he is present in the very air around me, making every atom in the air exist, then have I turned my mind to him and he has turned to me, and I no longer just breathe but now I breathe in God's very presence.

He is present in the pen I hold to write this talk, or a sermon, or a letter of sympathy. When I know this—remind myself of this constantly—then God is present in my soul in a deeper, greater way, and suddenly the words are no longer just mine, but somehow, they are his, because he is acting more in my soul and mind.

He is present in the bench I kneel at, the fork I eat with, in the books I learn from, in the paper I write on, the desk I sit at. And as I see his upholding, sustaining, creating presence in all these things, then he is with me, I mean really with me, as I pray, or eat, or read, or write, or study.

We are often startled into realizing that God is present in the world around us when we see an extraordinary beautiful sunset or the wonder of a perfect flower. What we too often fail to realize is that God is present all the time, in everything we use, or touch, or see, or smell, in every word we hear or speak, every sigh we whisper. Joseph Mary Plunkett, an Irish poet, brings this truth out in a beautiful poem. He centers his thoughts on Christ, especially:

> I see His blood upon the rose
> And in the stars the glory of His eyes,
> His body gleams amid eternal snows,
> His tears fall from the skies.
> I see His face in every flower;
> The thunder and the singing of the birds
> Are but His voice—and carven by His power
> Rocks are His written words.
> All pathways by His feet are worn,
> His strong Heart stirs the ever-beating sea,
> His crown of thorn is twined with every thorn
> His cross is every tree.

What we must do, if God is to be the all-important person in our lives, is find ways constantly to remind ourselves of God's double presence. Why not write it on cards you have in missals or breviaries: "God is in the words I am speaking, in this book I am using, in this card I am reading. He is in the voice of the sister praying next to me. He is in the heart and soul and mind of each sister praying with me—now, at this very minute." Why not take five minutes from every meditation time to think just of this? Why not spend at least three particular examinations each week asking yourself how often you thought, during this day, of this all-pervading truth?

Actually, once you but become aware of this truth in your life, then every spiritual thing you do is turning you to God, is making him more present within you, is making him—or at least *can* make him—live more vibrantly in your life. But isn't it true, when we're praying, that we have to kind of pinch ourselves to remind ourselves we really are turning to God and that he is turning to *us* as we turn to him? You see, we must first be vibrantly aware of this truth of God's presence. We must believe it with every fiber of our being. Then, and really only then, will all our prayers and holy readings, and Masses, and sacrifices truly turn us to God—really make us aware that he is living and acting more totally in our lives. Only then will we be convinced that even by a simple sigh can we draw God—Father, Son, and Holy Spirit—closer to us.

There are, we all know, many powerful reasons we should pray for an increase of faith daily. But there is none more powerful than this: as faith increases, our realization of God's Holy Presence in us and in the world and people around us, grows ever deeper. As our faith increases, God takes over the very activity of our souls more and more, so that after a time:

> His understanding is our understanding,
> His will is our will,
> His memory is our memory,
> His joy is our joy.
> And it is no longer I that live, but Christ lives in me.

May God and Mary bless you always.

Part Four

THE COUNSELOR

19

Counseling through Letters

When Walter Ciszek was not on the road giving lectures or conducting retreats, he spent his time counseling the many people who wanted to share with him their joys and sorrows and ask him for advice. His spiritual guidance took several forms, but the common thread was his availability, his kindness, and the individual attention he gave to all people who came to him, no matter who they were.[41]

Brother Philaret Littlefield, a Byzantine Franciscan member of the John XXIII Community in the early 1970s, recounts that Father Ciszek was comfortable with bishops and ordinary people. "If a drunk came to the door, he would tell him to come in and sit and talk with him and give him a sandwich. There was just no fanfare at all." Littlefield also noted, "He had spiritual children from all over the world," and "He gave spiritual direction to many influential people in their respective fields or stations or class." Carl and Marie Siriani recounted that when they would bring Father Ciszek back to Fordham from visiting their home, there would be people sitting on the doorsteps waiting for him; they said, "These were people he knew and had been helping, but they needed to talk, so he let them come into his apartment because he could not turn them away. And so many times he was exhausted." Fr. John Catoir, another spiritual son of Father Ciszek, also echoed this: "He would accept anybody! He put God's will first and did this with anyone he encountered. He would not read bad motives into anybody."

The spiritual direction that Father Walter provided also took the form of a voluminous correspondence that he maintained until his death. As a novice, Fr. Joseph Lingan, S.J., made an eight-day retreat with Father Ciszek. He recalls entering Father's room and marveling at the boxes of letters:

During our meetings, I noticed he had several shoeboxes on his desk. He shared that each box was full of letters and cards he received in the mail, and that he was taking the time between meetings with us novices to write a personal response to each letter and each card. It was apparent that he was moved by the fact that people took the time to write to him, and he wanted to show them the same consideration. He shared that many included the request for prayers and/or advice, and he wanted to offer his encouragement, support, and advice. Imagine, taking the time to respond to each letter and card. I suspect if he were alive today, Father Ciszek would be using a personal computer, and likely would be using Facebook and/or Twitter.[42]

Sister Rosemary Stets, O.S.F., a dear friend and spiritual daughter, fondly recalls his letters to her:

There was a time, years ago, when I would anticipate, with many prayerful thoughts, a letter from Father Walter. When I got one, I almost didn't want to read it, so as not to end the joy of knowing it finally came. His letters were like telegrams from God—so precious to me, and so meaningful. I kept them all, and now, when I read them over, I am still finding help, inspiration, counsel, direction, and a great degree of comfort.

Letter writing, for Father Walter, was a ministry, especially in later life. He spent hours at his desk writing letters. He never went anywhere—on vacation, or on a retreat, or to help out at a mission or a parish—without taking along a few (quite a few) letters to answer; and the letter writing was not just a quick dash or a short note, it was not a superficial letter or a mere social contact. First of all, he saw very clearly why people were writing. The bulk of his correspondence grew after he published his first book, and especially after publishing the second one. People were writing because they were deeply affected by what he wrote, and they needed or wanted to hear more. They felt he had a grasp of the essential in life; he knew what was important, he understood the mystery, and he had grown very close to God. People trusted him, trusted his judgment and his counsel, sensing "he did not preach like the scribes and Pharisees—he taught them with authority."

Always, Father Walter mentioned specifically in his writing the letter he had received, e.g., the Mass stipends (and mentioned when the Mass had been said), or expressed thanks for prayers. He was very grateful for the concern of his many friends—always amazed at their gifts and donations. And in turn, he gave himself tirelessly to each one. He always read over the letter or letters a second or third time before answering. He continuously prayed for the many intentions recommended to him and mentioned by name whom he was praying for. This personal interest and the seriousness with which he embraced these petitions spoke to all of us so clearly of the unique and personal love God has for each soul on earth.

In that sense, his ministry of letter writing was a special vocation. He was faithful to it up to the time he died. He had almost finished his whole Christmas card list at the time of his death—over 1000 cards—in spite of crippling arthritis, great physical exhaustion, and daily, continuous pain. He struggled to the end, even though he knew the time was almost running out.[43]

After the official diocesan cause for Father Ciszek's canonization was formally opened, the Father Walter Ciszek Prayer League obtained testimonies and correspondence from many of Father's spiritual directees and friends. From the testimonies of these people we know that Father was a tireless communicator who always kept track of his correspondents and always made sure to respond to their letters. While the Prayer League has preserved in excess of five hundred letters from various points in Father's life, we know that this is but a fraction of what he actually wrote.

The letters presented here were chosen because they are representative of the spiritual issues with which Walter Ciszek dealt, and because they represent a cross section of the different types of people he counseled. The themes were chosen because they are perennial issues in the life of any Christian: prayer, turmoil in the Church, marriage and family life, suffering, gratitude, and faith amidst difficulties. The sequence in which the letters are presented is not dictated by the grade of importance of the themes but by the chronology of the letters within each theme. Occasionally, names of correspondents and of people mentioned in the letters have been changed to preserve their privacy.

20

Prayer

In helping souls, probably the most oft-asked and sought-for advice was on how to pray. One correspondent who asked this advice of Father Ciszek was a young girl, Mary, who was sixteen when she began writing to him in 1966. Moved by his story in *With God in Russia*, Mary wrote to Father often, asking how she could grow closer to Christ. As seen by this selection, he not only gave her sound advice but was also concerned for this young girl in her desire for holiness—tenderly helping her avoid extremes in the spiritual life.

Letter Written July 10, 1966
Dear Mary, P.C.

I know you are waiting for an answer to your three letters, written July 4, 5 and 6. Writing to you thus far, and receiving your letters, gave me a good insight into your character. Though your letters are something I expect from you and appreciate more and more with time, yet answers to them—at this stage—will take on a character of normal correspondence rather than the necessary urgent type of answer required before. Why this attitude? It is clear to me—and should be clear to you by now—that in this spiritual matter of soul perfection progress has been attained by you, so important for sanctification. These initial steps, basic and fundamental, must be passed through by everyone and consciously recorded as such, for further progress. No matter what your feelings or desires may prove to you, we must center our attention on the truth in itself. I will continue to answer your letters as I go along—and emphasize some of the thoughts you expressed in them that attracted my attention.

In the beginning of your first letter (July 4th), you mentioned that certain things I wrote to you in my two last letters amazed, angered or puzzled you. The question at stake is the vow of chastity you desired to make after consulting me. I answered and denied you permission. You did not particularly care for my answer but accepted it as a manifestation of God's will towards you.

I wrote back to you and said that even if you accept my decisions as coming from a person used by God as his instrument, yet the acceptance of God's will in this case should be a perfectly free act of yours, independent of the instrument. What I'm trying to make you realize is that the spiritual things discussed in our letters—better, your sincere desire to be a saint—are strictly personal matters between you and God. I know my role in this delicate matter of the supernatural. I lead you—or rather try to lead you—with all my powers and interior experiences, to the threshold of God and leave you there, that you may communicate directly with him, making the final step yourself [and, therefore,] so significant of a full, free act of the will. Here, in the closeness of a soul seeking God and finding him, your decisions made—inspired by the grace of God and his divine life by which you will be touched—will have maximum value for the sanctity God intends you to have, in the degree and manner he desires. This is the intimacy we yearn to have, resulting in peace of mind and habit, bringing new life into one's own being. It's a foretaste of the eternal had by a creature. This will never be realized in your life, unless you—accepting my decisions—forget me and the natural, to enter the realm of the heavenly, where in full freedom you may elicit an act of perfect surrender to God, sharing his divine life and the gifts he has in store for you, so effective in building gradually in you the true reality of sainthood. Of course, my efforts to explain are hazy, but that is the best I can do for the present.

The special graces God has given to saints to understand the malice of mortal sin and the wrong of a venial sin led them to acts of mortification and penance. These, in turn, kept them always conscious of their own sinfulness and the possibility of falling into mortal sin from venial sin. Hence, that deep sensitivity and aversion to all sin. These are the special souls, chosen by God to be a living example to others. Theirs was a special mission, which they manifested in an utter distrust of self because of the possibility of sin. Their constant fear was a safeguard for their sanctity. This strictness of judgment was practiced against themselves. Regarding others, they distinguish well the difference between mortal and venial sin.

My intention is not to wreck you in your efforts to be a saint; it's just the opposite: to help you as much as possible along these lines, in spite of the fact that you seem to be full of contradictions. Your contradictions are not real because you do not accept them as such. They are the extreme opposites of what you are called to and your rebelling nature. The struggle that is going on continuously in your mind is a serious task for you to solve. This you must do with patience, courage, and prudence. All your contradictions are clear to me; your way of expressing yourself also. I have read your letters with special attention. They show me who you are. Even the secrets of your life you have written to me in such a vivid way. I see this as an effort to be a saint in spite of all the difficulties that arise. To confide as you did to me is in itself an act of humility whether you see this or not.

You ask me to teach you how to meditate. It's not an easy thing. They taught us two years in the novitiate, the method of meditative prayer, which in time became familiar and easy. The beginning was something mechanical. Experience later became a great help.

In meditation, you must remember, above all, that it is not a mere intellectual process of reflection upon the history of Christ's life, as had in the Gospels. If taken in such a way, we acquire merely an increase of knowledge and data upon the topic we meditate. In meditating upon the Gospels, no matter what the event—it may be directly or indirectly connected with Christ—the grace of a definite mystery or truth is revealed and offered to the one praying.

Do not consider meditations on the life of Christ an excellent opportunity to draw moral lessons. Rather, when meditating on Christ we should have a real relationship to the events of his life as a remembrance of bringing us salvation. This relationship will bring the grace necessary to follow Christ. Otherwise meditations can become boring and useless.

The structure and process of meditation is as follows:

Make an act of faith before God, offering all your actions to him during the period of the meditation. Then, turn to Christ in a petition, asking him for the grace to be ready to accept fully what he wants from you during the time of prayer. The attitude to have is "Speak Lord, Thy servant heareth." This message will come from inspiration, enlightenment of the intellect, desire and will to do good, or from any interior movement of the soul, understanding, etc.

These are the fruits of meditations; they should be accepted and introduced in your personal life. This means building your spiritual life on concrete acts by doing what God reveals to you in prayer. All these distractions that you write about, even in church, before the Holy Eucharist, in prayer, [and in] confession will come. It's up to you to find ways to control these; here, mortification can help and will. When you get a light or movement of soul, you will feel attracted. Do not pass from this point to another thought, but remain on this point till your soul profits fully from it. The great difficulties in meditative prayer are distractions, restlessness, etc. When you find it easy to pray, remain in this state, praising, loving God, following the good inclinations inspired in you, making proper resolutions that God wants you to make. . . . Always end with a prayer of thanksgiving to our Lord—or to the Father or the Holy Spirit or our Blessed Mother, as the spirit prompts you. This is your way to be a saint. In meditation God will give you strength to combat against yourself—rather, against the rebellious part of yourself. God will slowly bring out concretely what he wants from you and give you a definite peace in the great work of saving souls. That's your job. Not easy at all. You have received great graces, for a definite purpose, from God. Be faithful and responsive further, to the end.

Let this be all for the time being. You are in my daily prayers. My best to you with blessing.

In the Lord,

W. Ciszek S.J.

Letter Written July 20, 1966
Dear Mary, P.C.

Your letter of July 14th impressed me very much. You write that it is written before the Blessed Sacrament. I'm glad that you follow the inspirations given you. A true devotion to the Blessed Sacrament means a special calling—to contact Christ in the tabernacle, the Holy of Holies. Cultivate that devotion as much as possible, because it will be a source of your sanctity. Prayer in his presence takes on a different form. It strikes deep and leaves the soul affected with the deep touches of grace, the true formation of holiness.

Mary, I'm going to dwell a little upon the other forms of prayer you should consider. Most important is the most Holy Sacrifice of the Mass. Realize what is happening upon the altar, our own participation in the sacrifice, which means the sharing with Christ in his sufferings. That will explain your own sufferings, borne daily, interior and exterior, whatever they may be, in union with Christ. You have been blessed and know what great grace God has given you. You already realize what this means. The question of suffering even startles you in this early stage of your life. Can you bear it? you ask yourself. Here, prayer is needed to assure you God's help. I approve your efforts in regard to the Holy Sacrifice of the Mass—a daily attendance, if that is possible; devotion to the Blessed Sacrament; daily communion; and frequent confession. Besides your morning and evening prayers, the rosary said daily, spiritual reading—chiefly the bible and other spiritual books you choose to read. Let me know your reactions in regard to this suggested plan. Slowly, you shall progress in deepening your spiritual life, what is desirable and a task of your whole life.

You are right that a priest or nun who is dedicated to God entirely has his good and bad days. I would put it more specific: he is always on the alert, struggling to do the better and, as a result, goes through many trials daily. This is good, for it always keeps him close to God, ever conscious of his dependence on him.

You are experiencing the same in your efforts to serve God. You experience frequent distractions; as you put it yourself, your mind wanders.

The word "hazy" seems to still bother you. Please, Mary, take the excerpt from my letter and send it to me, and only then can I explain truly what I meant when writing the word "hazy." I cannot right now recall in what sense I used the word. And I do not want you to remain bothered by the word any longer.

All my letters are directed to one end: to help you as much as possible. It's a work entrusted to me by God and requires a great amount of prayer on my part to do the work well. It's a mutual effort to sanctity, on your part as well as on mine. The difficulties encountered must be shared by us both, and the suffering must also be shared together. Little misunderstandings are inevitable; that will cause you pain. But God is blessing our work and is always with us, this is the consoling thought. Just to clarify what I mean by causing pain.

In your last letter, you wrote about having a sixth sense. You could feel what was happening to certain persons you knew. I, too, can say the same about myself. My last letter, Mary, has caused you much pain, and I still feel you are not over it yet. Am I right?

I am also enclosing a sheet of a few reflections had July 15th.

Please write as often as you can now. August 6 to the 15th I will be making my retreat. So all mail shall not be answered during this period.

Do not overtire yourself, Mary, nor exaggerate in any way. Build your spiritual life now, from the beginning, solidly and prudently. You have my very best wishes, prayers, thoughts and blessing. Write soon.

In the Lord,

W. Ciszek S.J.

P.S. The last report I got on *With God in Russia*—Hard cover sold for 1½ yrs.: 42,126; paperback for 3 months: 20,000. Do write all the questions in your next letter I have not answered so far. In me, Mary, you have a friend truly devoted to your spiritual life. Perhaps you will not have another such in your life.

Letter Written July 25, 1966

Dear Mary, P.C.

First, I will give a short answer to your letter of July 19th, then to your letter of July 18th.

You write that you feel worse than ever after reading the book *Heaven and Earth*. Having such reactions of depression are experiences common in spiritual life, especially for beginners. But remember the general principles in such cases to guide yourself properly. The principles are: if a person makes progress from good to better, the Evil One will set difficulties before such a person and tempt him to discourage any attempt at spiritual progress. He will cause him to exaggerate his sinfulness, that he is a hypocrite for making his goal sanctity, a presumption, etc. There are so many other [illegible] he suggests that will tend [illegible] hearten, depress, and even change one entirely. The response, Mary, is every good desire, action, etc. comes from God and must be referred to him as a gift. Hence, your desire to be a saint was genuine in the very beginning and will be to the end. It's God operating in you in this general, initial way. If you pay attention to temptations, you will see that they do not lead to good but divert one from it.

Hence, your reaction should be one of decision to follow the good desire to be a saint to the end, no matter what your feelings are. For all desolation and consolation come from God and are given by him for a definite purpose: desolation—to try how much a person is worth in desolation. To remind him that desolation and consolation come and go as God wants and that the one and the other are graces under different aspects. Finally, God takes away from a person the special graces he endowed him with and shows how difficult it is to make spiritual progress only having salvific, not actual [specific] grace. Hence, motives for prayer, humility as you had it when you considered yourself worst of all sinners. Also for faith, believing firmly that God is leading you to sanctity through these special ways of desolation and consolation, as God sees fit; he sends the one and the other for the good of the soul.

Remember, Mary, whatever happens in your life, whatever be the situation, center your attention, foremost and above all, on God and, in him and around him, go solving your problem, not for a moment losing sight of him. This is the constant attitude to be had by you, and the only way to acquire it is to go through trials that will teach you to get this attitude. God is providing for that at every moment of your life. Just follow him. I know, it is terribly hard when a trial comes; one's whole mentality changes, and with it, one's sentiments. I [illegible] these reactions continuously [illegible] never change, rather they strengthen my belief in God. The suffering, the dejected spirit is something one must accept, bear with patience, and live with until God brings about a change.

I am so glad that you write me everything that happens to you, good or bad. This does not make you worse. It only shows the way along which God is leading you. Your mind, so practical, will always give you trouble; but you do not succumb to its every judgment. Seek the truth, teach yourself how to find it, then you will make your mind serve you. Remember, Mary, between the desire of being a saint and becoming one there is a lifetime to go. Just imagine what you must go through before being a saint. Without suffering, this is impossible; suffering only makes you a participant in the divine life. Millions of saints are in heaven because of suffering that was caused by their faithfulness to the will of God. We must pay the price first—not once, not twice, but to the end—to receive the reward of sanctity. Do not be bitter when you feel depressed. In humility, seek God and remain firm in your decisions.

The description of the St. Matthias Church—with all its details—gave me a good picture of what it looks like. The statues, decorations, and other minor things did not slip your eye. It is good you occupied your mind with other things when, interiorly, you felt dry. You have my prayers daily. You are getting the best my soul can give you, in Mass especially and other spiritual practices.

I will consider your letter of July 19th answered. In a few days you will receive an answer to your long letter of July 18th. There is so much in it to answer that I decided to write separately. Not to keep you waiting, I'm closing and sending this letter immediately. I know how much you must expect an answer. To tell you the truth, I, too, await your letters with impatience. To me it is only natural, after writing to each other so often.

My blessing. In the Lord,

W. Ciszek S.J.

From your letters, I got a good picture of your home, your daily activities, the church, and your interior. This is a good background for further progress.

Letter Written August 20, 1966

Dear Mary, P.C.

This is still an answer to your letter of 8/11/66. You ask me to explain the Orthodox Church. Well, the Orthodox Church, as well as the Greek Orthodox (of Greece), are not in union with Rome. But the Catholic Greek Orthodox, or Uniate church of Ukraine, are united with Rome. It is always specified when a Church belongs to the Catholic (Roman) Church by the word "Catholic." If I find a good book explaining all this, I will send it to you.

I took my profession only two years ago because I was in Russia [prior to that]. Usually, the Jesuits make the profession after they are ordained and spend some years in the ministry. This will take from three to five years after leaving the theologate. Yes, you must know what a vocation is to appreciate it properly.

I understand your free-nature tendencies. I was the same in those years. To control yourself is a good thing, but do it out of higher motives. Simple natural motives won't make you the person you should be. But if you bring God into all your life, then your life will be developed and patterned on his. There is nothing better for us to expect in life than this. The blessing of God will always be with you.

Prayer, Mary, is the basis of spiritual life. Without prayer do not even attempt to begin living for God. You ask how much time you should spend praying. Well, you say the Morning Offering in the morning after getting up. Then, going to church, you can say the rosary. When in church, say some prayers you are used to saying. Hear one or two Masses as you feel inclined. Make a thanksgiving, and after that, leave for home. At noon you can say the Angelus; then for five minutes make an examination of conscience, recalling how you spent the morning—see the good you did or, perhaps, the wrong. Thank the Lord for his graces he has given you during that time; ask him to bless you and those whom you pray for, for the rest of the day. Make an act of contrition even for past sins. Renew your Spirit, then live the afternoon only for God, finishing with some prayer you like. In the afternoon you can read the Bible for 15 minutes; then, after you have done all your work, finished recreation, read some spiritual book or life of a saint for twenty minutes to half an hour. After that, it's all your time. During the day, the idea of God's presence and his will should be recalled when making reflections. Before going to bed, make an examination of conscience again for a period of 5 minutes in the same way suggested above; then a Sign of the Cross and off to bed. If you feel God wants more from you, consider this yourself, or, better, let me know, and we both will decide. Prayer should become your second nature; it should be the motivating force of your life. When you find ease in prayer and feel its necessity, and make all your actions, life, and existence a continuous act of prayer, then you have the gift of prayer given to you by God. Will continue tomorrow. Avoid exaggeration.

Now to your two letters received yesterday. Your happy mood just pleases me to the utmost. If you can be serious and happy as occasion requires, I have little fear for you. Your plan to send pamphlets to Donna and Karen is a good idea in itself but not a prudent one; you cannot force religion or views on someone—religion is not meant for that. Donna and Karen are in good faith (perhaps); let them alone. If they get the grace, they will turn to you for advice, and then you can give them the pamphlets, and only then. So I ask and suggest that you not send them the pamphlets.

The notes I sent you—taken by myself during the retreat in the form of reflections—will give you an idea of how God leads a soul in communion with him. His grace creates all these reactions and gives inspirations at the same time.

Your note of last night made me like you the more. For it dispersed certain fears I had regarding you, namely, that the spiritual in you would distort your character and make you morose and overly serious. I like to see you as you are, fully developing your natural qualities under the influence of the supernatural. You will then be a beautiful soul, reflecting your beauty in your whole person.

You prayed for me during my retreat, and I prayed more than ever for you. I did so much for you during that period of grace and intimate life with God. I prayed for other persons who are under my direction, but not so willingly and spontaneously as for you. Why? Perhaps it's your innocence and holy desires that attract me.

When at El Segundo, I'll hear confessions as usual.

My retreat was new in this sense: I listened throughout the retreat more to what God had to reveal and give me, than to try by my own efforts intellectually to penetrate into the mysteries of revealed truths. The method I tried for the first time this year gave far better results than I expected. The notes I sent you will reveal to you partially the interior movements I had. In Los Angeles area, I will try not to give talks but do what is necessary, and that's all.

I would suggest not to cut your hair now. You managed to handle it so far, you will succeed to do as well in the future. Keep it long.

Mary, keep me in your prayers especially now. I began to write my second book—my reflections and reactions. Daily, I write an hour and a half and that at 5 a.m.

[Russian words]

Letter Written August 30, 1966
Dear Mary, P.C.

I'm going to tell you first, what I received from you yesterday: your Russian letter, your two-page letter of August 25th, a letter with nine photos in it, and, finally, my retreat notes. I called yesterday "Mary's day" because of the many letters I received from you. Let me comment now.

The pictures came out very well; the two of you, I like best. Thanks for sending them. Having pictures of your Dad and mother, your house, and other snapshots of the vicinity gives me a good idea of your life. There is nothing better for detailed knowledge than pictures.

I'm leaving in two hours' time for Baltimore and will return Saturday. On the 1st of September I shall participate in a centennial parade at my home town, Shenandoah, PA, as honorary grand marshal—will write you about it later.

The Carmelites sent me a nice letter. They are expecting me on the 5th of September. One of the nuns wrote she was praying for me for a whole year, that the retreat go well. I, too, am looking forward to meeting the sisters. There are 25 of them in the community. It will give me an opportunity to contact people who are wholly devoted to God. It will be an encounter with sanctity and closeness with God. They want me to give them a ten-day retreat instead of an eight-day retreat. We decided to settle this question when I get there. I will keep you informed about the retreat, when time permits. Now to your letter of August 25th. I shall correct your Russian letter and send it back to you.

The examination of conscience is done in the following way:

1) Thanksgiving: to Father—Son—Holy Spirit. Consider shortly the small blessings God has given you from the period of morning to noon, also, past blessings: your baptism, Mass, Holy Comm., gift of prayer, all material blessings, all that makes up your life within and without.

2) Examen proper: what little sins you have committed, faults, negligences, little graces received that you did not profit from—make it short.

3) Sorrow for sins, present and past. Recall the Lord on the Cross. Sorrow requires interior perception of the malice of sin. Ask that God give it to you. Sorrow should come from the heart. It's God's gift, a great blessing.

4) Resolution: to make amends, in little things; ask for grace of perseverance. Don't exceed 10 minutes. Examen time is a willingness to meet God in humble prayer, get his message, renew your love for him. It's a very salutary practice because it's communing with God—nothing better, nothing so satisfying and strengthening. It's knowing where you stand with God every moment of your life. It's a . . . good preparation for confession. Confession should be made regularly, at a set time as you decide. By confessing frequently, we continue the work of redemption in us, brought to the world by the Incarnate Word.

Your letter from Mother Mary Magdalene is very encouraging. Your openness, rare in girls and women, fascinates her. Your strong desire to be a Poor Clare convinces her of your serious will to serve God at all costs, as he wants.

This is a good start, an approval of which you and I can be very happy. But do expect the contrary to happen to you, where suffering, pain, and anxiety will sometimes upset you. You will not be able to do good without the Cross. Our Lord is the best example.

Plenary Indulgence offered for the souls in Purgatory has the power to liberate a soul from her pains, and assure Heaven to such soul. This is the teaching of the Church.

When saying the rosary, think about the mysteries. If some thought strikes you, continue thinking about it as it develops in you of itself. This you will be doing when inspiration is given you. As soon as inspiration vanishes, it is useless to force yourself to prolong the uplifting reflections. That can be done only when God's grace is present and manifest under the form of an inspiration. You cannot have inspiration at your own will. It comes and goes independent of you. The simple thing is to be thankful to God for it after it is gone. Proceed saying the rosary in the ordinary way with the special inspiration already had. This experience enriches your interior life, shows you concretely what is yours and what is God's in your prayer.

Priests cannot bear arms in war, but can defend themselves if attacked. If unjustly attacked, everybody has a right of self-preservation.

I know seven languages. I can read, write, talk Polish, English, Russian, and Italian. I can speak and read German, French, and Latin. I easily understand Slav languages, read them but do not speak them, such as White Russian, Slovenian, Ukrainian, etc.

Our Lady's promise was given conditionally—if people pray, do penance, adore the Blessed Sacrament. There are many who fulfill these required conditions. The fulfillment depends entirely on God as regards time, way, etc. I believe this. More people have to be involved in this devotion. Russia is as dear to the Sacred Heart and to the Immaculate Heart of Mary; as with any other nation, the price was paid.

There are so many reasons for which people in the world do mortify themselves other than God; losing of weight is a common reason. Actors, athletes, trainers, sportsmen, beauticians all have their specific reasons, which exclude God entirely. That is why I underlined the importance of the God-element in every act of mortification or self control.

I will continue answering your letter tomorrow. There is half an hour left before leaving for Baltimore. [Russian words.]

21

Turmoil in the Church

In the immediate aftermath of the Second Vatican Council, there was no little amount of confusion in many areas of the Catholic world. For those whose faith was wavering, Father Ciszek was a rock of faith. In 1968 (arguably the height of these trying times), a young nurse, Antoinette Rienzi, met Father Ciszek. She became his spiritual daughter and remained close to him until his death in 1984. She recalls well his devotion to the Church:

> He loved the Church and was faithful to the teaching of the Magisterium. He was troubled by some of the practices and changes taking place in the Church in America, but he was also confident in the belief that Our Lord was in charge. He was also a witness of the love of God for his suffering people, whether in the cold mines of Siberia, or those that came to him in the Bronx.[44]

Bill Sockey recalls how Father confirmed his own faith during these difficult times:

> He gave me a piece of advice that has been very useful. Because I was working as Executive Director and later Vice President of *Catholics United for the Faith*, I was dealing with the turmoil within the Church. Father told me, at the end of every day, before I went to sleep, to meditate on the fact that whatever evil people do, whether alone or in company with others, they do with some good in their minds that they wish to achieve. That was a tremendously helpful meditation, because I was dealing with "bad people" all the time; and that kept me spiritually balanced to remember that all these people thought they were working for the good. This advice was given when I asked him for spiritual direction and what sort of advice he could give me. He also told me the usual Jesuit things: ending the day by going through in my mind what good things God had given me during the day—a powerful

meditation—think about the stars and weather and my friends and everything that I could think of that was good during the day; and then, reflect
upon my sins and unworthiness and make a good act of contrition.[45]

Father Ciszek gave similar advice in his correspondence. Reproduced here are
several letters from Father Ciszek to Denise, a correspondent from Germany.
In these letters, one sees a Catholic woman and mother struggling to understand the situation of the Church in the late 1960s. Father Ciszek encourages
her and confirms her in the faith, reassuring her of the truth of the Church
and the message of Christ.

Letter Written November 2, 1967
Dear Denise, P.C.

Your letter indeed did bring me pleasure and satisfaction. Even though I'm
busy, you will always receive an answer. God wants it so. You, yourself, feel
indisposed sometimes; this is so natural. A little overwork means: take
some rest and rearrange your plan of work. That's what I did, and I feel fine.
Please, keep on writing to me as you did, without restrictions. Our spiritual
relationship demands that.

The theological seminar is doing you much good. I'm glad of that.
Theology, as you have well noticed yourself, now is an academic study. It
must depend on the intellect to penetrate the facts it deals with. It is a
system, and, as such, cannot be applied to life; but it can help to a certain
degree. Enough of this.

Now let us look at life as it is. You have already noticed the difference.
Faith is a 100% gift of God—freely given, infused. It does not depend on
man for its origin. Once given, however, it must be accepted as such. The
intellect's role is to see what faith demands of us and, knowing this, to do
as it requires. This process continues to the end of one's life. Faith is not
intellect, but the consciousness of it comes through intellect. Take yourself,
as you are, not separating spirit and body. That is unreal. All that we
experience and do comes from our being. Hence, the feelings, intuition,
inspiration, desires, heart, and all bodily reactions, belong to our nature.
Being conscious of faith, all these are realities, which help to develop our
whole personality.

Love your body as well as your soul—both are gifts of God. Exaggerating
one or the other leads to wrong. My studies helped me in my hardships,
but the courage to bear them came from faith, which was infused. I did not
merit a bit of it. It was God's gift. Slowly, I learned by reflection this divine
truth. In my spiritual life, theology plays hardly any role at all. It's God's
power that does the interior wonders experienced in the soul. Yet, all the

knowledge you have, God can use in you by making you more efficient in his work. Faith infused in one's soul will always influence others because it's God's operation affecting both its possessor and all others with whom there is contact.

Your reflection on faith is so true; it's a work of God's providence. To understand the mysterious workings of God's power in us is a right especially given us by God. Sufficient is our faith for salvation. To know all will not save you. Faith, however, is rational. It accepts God. And what can be lacking if one confides in God entirely? We freely choose from the things that occur in daily life as related to all else. In this is our freedom, choosing good as we understand it, directed by faith. That means never forgetting the God element in our life, which is ours through habitual faith. If we exclude this order—by rationalizing and setting aside faith—we are carving out our own destiny without God. That means [we are making] a deliberate choice to spend eternity without him. It's horrible, yet people and systems of education propagate this human error. You either accept your faith and in a simple way live it, or you reject it and build your own life. But this [would make no sense] to a human who looks into himself and realizes what the world is. Living in faith gives conviction, satisfaction, peace, and the realization of possessing consciously God's power. If this becomes the principal attraction for man, all else is put in the second place seriously to promote the God-conscious quality in man.

Many thanks for your faithful prayers. I ask you to continue praying for me. I'm accepting you in my special list of spiritual children for whom I pray especially. Your family also will benefit. My book is coming along nicely. I do not feel concerned about it. I know he helps me the moment I begin writing. He inspires. What he wants, I write. With warmest wishes and God's blessing. In him. Many thanks for the icon.

W. Ciszek S.J.

Letter Written May 15, 1969
Dear Denise, P.C.

Your letter of May 5th arrived. It made me happy. The long silence made me imagine some mishap in your family, but not your unfaithfulness in writing. I knew a letter from you would come.

Many thanks for writing the way you did, also for the two nice pictures; I like them both. You have such a fine family. Now, I realize who Denise is, from your letter. I had a different picture of you. I hope your wish to visit the USA comes true sometime.

The Church, along with the world, is undergoing a trying period. It must [undergo such trials] if the advancement expected is to come. The readjustment in the Church is what is causing most trouble. No one person is able to give the full answer to the Church's problems, nor can what individuals write or say be accepted by all. The spirit of the age has affected the thinking in the Church. Too much rationalizing on matters of faith has clouded many fundamental truths of our revealed religion; as a result, many are confused. Why? Those at the higher level in the Church are confused themselves; or others—theologians, philosophers, and intellectuals—attempt a too-narrow explanation of revealed truths.

Faith, as a divine gift, stands beyond the capacity of reason and human understanding. Faith must be accepted as given us by God; that is the only role of reason in this field. The Church is undergoing a period of humiliation and purification. A renewal of the spirit of faith must take place through humble prayer; otherwise, the risk of error is inevitable. The basis of that prayer consists in this: God is. That's the wisdom of life for all of us. Remember that your faith in darkness, discouragement, and doubts is God's gift to you, and your blessing. Accept it, and God will show you gradually what to do. Now, since I know your family, I have the privilege of wishing you all good and blessings. You and yours are always in my prayers.

Fr. Ciszek

Letter Written October 28, 1969
Dear Denise, P.C.

I don't have to mention to you the joy and satisfaction your letter gave me. I looked forward to receiving news from you after the long, silent months. Deep in my heart, I felt you would write. Sincere and grateful thanks for your timely postal card, for your long and informative letter, and also for your thoughtful and expressive souvenir on my birthday. All these I deeply appreciate and treasure. It's good to be in contact with you again and to enjoy sharing the intimate thoughts that concern us both in religion.

You ask for an example of how the truths of religion are being rationalized at present by our theological experts, or, people posing as such. Take the Holy Eucharist [for example]; how much rationalizing has been done concerning this Sacrament of Sacraments: first of all, the removing of the consecrated species to a side altar, the [attempted] scientific explanation of the particles as not being the Body of Christ, the emphasis put on the sacrifice, to the exclusion of the [real] presence. To me, all this is strained, ignoring the foremost issue, that is, trying to bring to our human level a truth which can find its full answer only in a simple act of faith, given to us as a gift. Attending lectures and hearing scholars speak of these religious truths in scientific and rational terms makes me think how easily these people cloud and muddle truths accepted by all. If only they stated the question properly, by asserting first the unquestionable truth of faith in this mystery, then people who are not spiritually strong, upon hearing them, would better understand their cleverly theological, scientific, or rational explanation and see that it adds nothing to the religious truth, nor does it take anything away from it.

But as you mentioned in your letter, faith must be lived first, then intellectually explained to the extent that grace enlightens one. This is the root of the questions pertaining to all religious truths.

I'm glad to hear you are all well at home. The physical work you do will profit you all around. I have a bit of news to share with you, Denise. My second book is finished; soon parts of it will be published. I'm so happy; I know that you too will be glad to learn of this. Religion [i.e., the gift of faith] increases with time; it's something given to each of us in an entirely personal way.

I'm making my eight-day retreat at present. I cannot marvel enough at God's wondrous internal workings in the soul, as I consider the presence of the Most Blessed Sacrament in our churches. With warmest and best wishes to you, your husband, children, and parents. Blessings.

Fr. Ciszek

Letter Written September 17, 1971
My dear Denise, PC.

I received your letter of September 4th yesterday. I've been away giving a ten-day retreat to Carmelite nuns. It's always good to hear from you, no matter what you write. I understand your difficulties with faith, your search for God, your restless soul trying to live grace without questioning it or trying to prove it.

Unless God himself gives you this gift of prayer in your life as it is—that is, with all that is happening (events, movements within and without you)—to see all of it in, through, and with him, nothing can give you faith. [Remember what Jesus said]: "Unless you become like a little child you shall not enter the Kingdom of heaven." Faith on our part is needed to accept Christ as he is and as he daily manifests himself to us in all things. We then have no reason for questioning in the least the gift of God within us, which truly is leading us to our creator, if we believe that and live humbly and hopefully the experiences we daily have to go through. It's God living in me and slowly changing me into the person he wants me to be by his power, if only I go along with him, not resisting or rejecting his inspirations. This I call matter-of-fact, down-to-earth spirituality. Living, eating, drinking, resting, working, doing something each moment of your existence [while remaining] conscious of God in all things. This includes thoughts, doubts, feelings, intuitions, sensations, and all possible reactions one might have, be they passionate, sinful, or good, finding in them God as he is, and yourself, rightly or wrongly reflected, in your being with him somehow in grace. Let grace affect and remake you; that is the attitude of a believer.

God is leading you through a unique experience. I'm always with you in prayer and spirit. After these years of friendship, we are learning a lot from each other and see better the need of continuing to share what God gives us. I see the great spiritual and human good we render each other. Always with much love and affection. Blessings.

Fr. Ciszek

P.S. Best wishes to husband and children. I'm sending you my event photo taken three weeks ago.

22

Marriage

Many of Father Ciszek's spiritual directees and correspondents were married couples. One such couple was Bill and Daria Sockey. They had the unique privilege of having him officiate at their wedding as well as having him direct them on a retreat at the very beginning of their life together:

Mr. Sockey: We were married on April 18, 1980 at a Polish Church, and the pastor was astonished that we were bringing in Father Ciszek to perform our wedding. (He gladly accepted our invitation to come to our reception and sit next to Father Ciszek!) As a wedding present after the wedding, Father invited us to come back to the John XXIII Center so that he could give us a private retreat on Catholic married life. So, after the wedding but before the honeymoon, we spent two days with Father on this private retreat. That's where we met the man who was exchanged out of Russia with him. Father cooked us dinner and introduced us to his friend. This would have been April 19 or 20, 1980. Father cooked our meals and gave us meditations and sent us across the street to the Bronx Botanical Garden to walk around and think about the Church's teaching on marriage.

Mrs. Sockey: What I recall, mostly, is that he gave us the Second Vatican Council's document on marriage [*Gaudium et Spes*, part II, ch. 1]. He continued to be our spiritual director and confessor after our wedding as well. In terms of the direction, we would visit him at the John XXIII Center and we would have small talk for a while and then he would hear our confessions and give us any advice, if we had any questions, and that would be the end of it. We saw him just about every other month, maybe. Once we had our first child, we would bring the baby, Theresa, along. She was a quiet, serious, good little girl and, as a toddler, would just walk around Father's apartment, quietly examining this and that. Father Ciszek commented that he especially liked Theresa and commented to us that he was rather uncomfortable around very small children, but that Theresa was the exception. He felt very comfortable around her. Father Ciszek was always giving us stuff. People from the streets of the Bronx and others were always giving him things—food especially—so every time we came, he would grab another box of cookies or candy and be pushing food on us! I think that's why little Theresa liked him. One day he sent us home with a great big inflatable plastic Easter Bunny with an Easter basket full of stuff. So that's why I think Theresa liked getting stuff from Father Ciszek. One item Father Ciszek gave us was of a more permanent nature. It was a small wooden figurine of a hand, representing the hand of God, with a small child leaning into it. This was a popular image in those days; you saw many versions of it in Christian gift shops. Someone had given this to Father at one time, and he passed it on to us. We treasure this little carving greatly because the idea depicted by the image—complete trust and surrender to God's loving care—summarizes so much Father's spirituality.[46]

In the letters that follow, one sees the attention Father Ciszek gave to married couples. From words of encouragement to promises of prayers, these letters demonstrate the personalized attention he gave to each of these correspondents, especially those experiencing the difficulties of family life.

Letter Written May 31, 1972

Dear John and Annie, P.C.

It's my pleasure to greet you on your wedding anniversary. June 3rd will be a day forcing you to reflect on the years lived together in the married state. In spite of all the anxieties, difficulties, and discouraging moments, God's grace has kept you together, ever teaching you to make the best of God's gift given you in the wedded life. Why has everything turned out favorably thus far for you in the family circle? The answer is simple: God is above all human deficiency, ever lifting us up to a higher level of spiritual growth in him, at the same time deepening our humility as we recognize more and more our dependency on him. Even if we fail him seriously, he manages to gain us back to himself and infuse in us a deeper knowledge, making us ever conscious of his presence in our daily actions. In this way, we develop a need for him, which surpasses our human concerns and renders us faithful to him no matter what happens to us—good or bad.

Let these simple thoughts be a sign of my willingness to share the riches God's grace poured out in every one of us. You will have my special prayers on June 3rd. With very best wishes and his blessing to you both and all the boys. Hoping all is well at home.

Fr. Ciszek

Letter Written July 8, 1972

Dear Annie, P.C.

Your long, twelve-page letter has been received. It told me a lot. Thanks deeply for sharing your life so generously with me.

First of all, let me assure you that I'm always with you and your family in prayer. Praying for you all makes me feel secure and confident that God is not failing you, nor ever will. This thought and truth should be at the bottom of all your actions and the core of your inner life. It seems you react too strongly to the shortcomings of your children. The lack of a vital spirit of religion in them concerns you to the point of being overly anxious. As a result, you force the issue and try to get things done at once, when the situation calls for unlimited time, much prayer, humility, and faith in God. You are not saving yourself, nor are your children saving themselves. God, in his wisdom, is preparing you and your children for that gift of faith, which will carry us safely to the end of life, the eternal salvation in God. It's all his work, dear Annie; whatever we do—the good we try to achieve—is his grace disposing us that way. As a result, we feel close to him, inspired, we want all others to be as happy and therefore insist on them to do good as [we do it] ourselves, full of good will and intention. You are a perfect example of a soul deeply zealous for the greater good of others. It's a gift from God to be so dedicated in spreading his Kingdom. I'm with you in this fervor to the end.

However, in being all wrapped up in doing good for others, we should not forget God for one moment in our prayer. Praying, we feel God in us; we see his power saving you, me, and all others, not in any vague or idealistic way but as we really are: full of limitations, weakness, and faults. Even when we seemingly reject him or show little interest in him. A child denying God, or denying revealed truth because he or she read or heard it from some popular activists, is so far away from the truth. The young like to reject—be revolutionary—because of excessive energy and a shallow mindset. They have to exert themselves—even to sweat—for years, to come to the understanding of spiritual truths. Gratification in the material world is more attractive, and they follow it easily without serious reflection. All this however for a time; for God runs the sometimes rotten world, and he alone can inspire one to conquer it. It takes humility, prayer, and faith again in him; being filled in this manner by his grace, we can act and be effective.

Never be afraid of professing the truth before your children or others. You have to be a witness to others who do not yet know the truth. Be kind, do good, love and respect your children as they are, while remaining firm about your own belief in God. With just such a disposition, we must spread the spirit of Christ amongst others. Once [we are] touched [by him], God takes over. God uses us to aid in the work of salvation, but it is by his power alone that he conducts all [of his] operations in others and in ourselves.

Materialism, objects of the senses, are the forces that impress the youthful age. Next, intellectual ideas start their influence on the minds of the young. Here is where the young become sophisticated and make statements that are so immature and insincere about religion and the eternal God. Finally, comes the stage of the spiritual. Once the young have been humbled by a crisis in life and degraded by the evil power, they then listen to God's inspiration. Salvation starts from here on for them. So you see, Annie, how much the young must experience to arrive at the gospel truth—through suffering. Be sympathetic with them, forgiving, accepting always, but never weaken in your love for God and your faith. With his blessing to you, John, and boys.

With Love,

Fr. Ciszek

Letter Written May 26, 1975
Dear Joseph and Mary, P.C.

I have a letter before me received from you exactly a year ago. For this letter and for the Xmas card, please receive my most sincere thanks.

For many months in a row, I've been engaged in lecturing and retreat work. This occupation took up all my time. There was no time left for correspondence or contacting people. So the mail accumulated and created a new problem for me, that is, the hundreds of letters I'm trying to answer now, [which I] received months ago. Somehow I feel confident at present and undertook the impossible task of answering all the back mail I received; slowly, I'm making progress.

Your family does cause you both much anxiety. You feel a deep responsibility for your children for whom you must provide fully. Well! There is so much for a mother and father to do in the family. Doing what one can, and leaving the rest to God, is a sound policy to follow. Prayer will greatly help you satisfy your obligation towards your children, where human effort in no way can. Have faith and you will feel better. In this way, your balanced behavior will influence the children also. What seems simple to the eye becomes a formidable challenge to the soul, where things must be realized at the deepest level of our being. You as well as your children are in my prayers. The Lord is always with us; there is no true life or salvation without him. Warmest regards and his blessing to you both and to your children. In his love.

Fr. Ciszek

Letter Written August 12, 1975

Dear Caroline, P.C.

This is a short note for your anniversary. Let me wish you a happy and pleasant birthday, rich in his blessings. This will be my prayer for you at Mass on August 15th.

It was nice talking to you when I visited Anna August 2nd. It was a short visit, but rewarding. In four hours, I got to see and visit a few people and spent some time with my own.

You must be quite busy with the two youngsters requiring your constant attention. You do not mind the sacrifice as a mother. This is expected of you and so essential to your calling. When we are devoted to our life as a gift from God, we experience so many deep changes within us. The ordinary things that happen daily take on a deeper meaning and open the way to God, who is so totally involved in our personal life. In prayer all this becomes more clear.

Warmest regards and the Lord's blessing to you Caroline, Peter, and boys.

Love in him, Fr. Walter

23

Suffering

Certainly, Walter Ciszek was no stranger to suffering. Because he suffered so much himself, he could empathize with those who did suffer and offer them encouragement in their times of trial. Marianne Bogunovich went to Father Ciszek for spiritual direction from 1978 to his death in 1984. She recalls that she felt very comfortable in telling him anything about herself because he was so compassionate.[47] Another spiritual directee, Dolores Hartnett, recalls his great compassion for her in the midst of pronounced suffering:

> I had a lot of difficulties with my children, and also with my family, including a painful divorce. Father was a good listener. He had a great deal of respect and was sensitive to my suffering and what I was experiencing, probably because he himself had come through the unthinkable. He was an extraordinary priest and an unbelievable man, with a fatherly presence so filled with love, an inspiration to so many who knew him.[48]

In the following letters to Lilly, Father shows a great compassion for her in her battles with anxiety and offers sound advice for laying her problems in the hands of God.

Letter Written February 20, 1974
Dear Lilly, P.C.

I'm so sorry to be answering your letter received August 23, 1973, so late. It just happened that the letter, set aside to be answered promptly, had been forgotten. I hope you forgive my absent-mindedness. You know well how much I appreciate your letters, your friendship, and your confidence. God makes it possible for us to communicate. He blesses all your efforts, as well as mine, as we seek to share between ourselves whatever good we possess. Letter writing for me has become a daily occupation. So much has to be done to keep up; the correspondence increased considerably in the past years. I'm managing somehow, with God's help.

Sorry to hear of Charlotte's brother suffering a fatal accident. Also, to hear of your alcoholic brother. I do keep you, Leo, Eileen, and Suzy in my prayers, together with the members of your family. Your feeling low from time to time is something you will have to put up with, till you learn how to handle periods of depression with discretion. Your experience should give you much insight into what the nature of these bouts of depression are. Slowly you should be able to eliminate the causes and lessen the fears that frequent lapses into depression bring. There is so much to be said about these interior changes that come and go independently of us. Leo is such a balanced person. With his help, Lilly, you could slowly overcome your fears and depression. I'll be seeing you in the summer. My best to you Lilly, Leo, Eileen, and Suzy. His blessing to you four. Love in him.

Your friend always—

Fr. Walter

Letter Written April 4, 1974
Dear Lilly, P.C.

Your letter of March 11 has been received together with the two Mass stipends ($4). The Masses for the deceased mentioned in your letter have been taken care of. Thanks sincerely for sending the Mass intentions and donation. God bless you for them.

I will be in Shenandoah, August 16th to perform the wedding of Frank Flannery; that's more than four months away, but time flies as you know. Soon I will be seeing you when in Shenandoah, for the wedding; how could I miss seeing you when in Shenandoah!

From what you write about yourself, little change is noticeable in you; that is always the case with people like you—a change can take place, but in time. In fact, you are changing slowly but not in a manner you might detect. Life, in general people you contact, things you do, hear, and observe must affect you somehow. The impression once made continues to grow and deepen. Grace especially is having its influence on you, Lilly. I pray for you, Leo, and children daily and know God is reaching out to you in the manner suited to your character and disposition. You have a definite purpose in life and a responsibility that must be met; for God is seeing to it. You must be yourself, your true self; only as such you will function best as a person, mother, and woman. To me, you are a dear person and a close friend whom I cherish and wish the greatest good possible. You know that.

Eileen is your favorite; so is Suzy at her age. As Eileen grows, she will be your great consolation. You will not have anybody as close to you as she will be. Her character is so different from yours. She will be a positive influence in your life. Tell Eileen "P.C." means "peace of Christ." I love her.

You're right about Catholic education, Lilly. It does not give all, but it does give the necessary religious training, which you cannot neglect; it's essential in life.

The Exorcist is a controversial book and movie, not important in the message it tries to convey.

Keep well my dear Lilly. I'm feeling fine, thank God. My best to you, Leo, Eileen, Suzy, with his blessing. Happy Easter wishes. Regards to the Faber family. Also to your sister and Rose (Aunt). Bye. Much Love.

Father Walter

Easter greetings to Patricia, James and Helen.

Letter Written September 3, 1974
Dear Lilly, P.C.

Let me thank you sincerely for the Mass stipends ($6) three in all. The Masses you requested were taken care of already. Most sincere thanks for the offering and remembrance. Let the Lord be your full reward for your kindness.

It was good to see you and spend some time together in conversation. God is taking care of you in the many difficulties you experience. Yet, you seem not to realize this truth in all its spiritual meaning; it takes time to do so. From your frequent contacts with God in prayer, you should slowly become more enlightened in the ways of God, which are hidden and difficult to understand until prayer removes the shades from our darkened mind. I'm always with you in prayer, feeling confident God will overpower your fears and fill you with courage and trust in his love for you. You're not alone in your anxieties. Leo, Suzy, and Eileen and I do have concern for you in our respect and love for you. Such are the sentiments his grace inspires in us for you. His blessing to you Lilly, Leo, Eileen, and Suzy.

Love in him—

Fr. Walter

Letter Written February 16, 1976
My dear Lilly, P.C.

This will be an answer to your two letters received September 7th. and February 11th. It's always good to hear from you. You are never forgotten by me, be it in prayer or in thought. I myself would like to see you and visit with the children and Leo. Deepest thanks, Lilly, for writing and for your prayers; in prayer we give each other what is impossible on a human level.

I'm glad Leo has recovered from his illness. Thank God he is on his own, working in his own shop. The political world is one we must put up with. So much injustice comes with it. God however does not forsake us. This is important to know and never forget.

Your last letter made me happy. You write so openly. This is a good sign that you prove to be a true friend to me, sincere and full of confidence in our friendship. I accept you as a God-sent trusting person and know his blessing is with us. I've been busy and so taxed with work. People come to spend time with me. I put no limit to such visits, because problems cannot be fit into a pattern but understood in open dialogue. Only in such an atmosphere can God's grace operate best.

Your fears have deeper a root than you think. The possibility of living normally is in you, just as in any human being. But your psychic life has obscured this possibility and excluded its function as you experience its detrimental influence at present. I wish I could be close to you and counsel you for some time. Correspondence will have to suffice for the time being when personal encounter is excluded. I'll try to get to see you when in or near the Shenandoah area. I'll hear your confession and give you communion, and, of course, spend time with you.

I'd suggest you don't permit yourself to be passive in regard to your fears. Work at them from within. When they come, just counter them in a positive way. That is, not by trying to do things as fully as if you were in self-control, but by internally asserting yourself so that you may not succumb to such an inclination of fear altogether; instead, you want to do what is right. Such internal efforts will help you begin doing small but positive things, which counter your exaggerated fears. Pray God for help frequently. Little by little, initiative from within will prompt you to act rightly when the occasion requires.

You can write to me as often as you wish; I'll find time to answer. I'm with you in prayer, spirit and thought. Look at your pregnancy in faith as God's work. Once he permitted it, he must have planned it for your spiritual and human good. Rise above your fears, trusting in him. This is mainly what he is teaching you by your pregnancy.

I'll send you the book *Problems of Every Day Living* by Eugene Kennedy once I find it. Kindest regards and abundant blessings from the Lord to you Lilly, Leo and Eileen and Suzy. All my love and peace in him.

Fr. Walter

Letter Written May 21, 1976
Dear Lilly, P.C.

Your letter of March 12th and the two Mass stipends ($7) have been received. The Masses for the soul of Edward Jones were celebrated already. Please thank Bernard Hall and Peter O'Connell for their offerings. May God bless them for their kindness.

It was so good to hear from you. Sorry! This answer had to be put off till now. You know that it takes time for me to answer all the letters received; but somehow the Lord helps me to manage with the mail.

I see from what you wrote how much your early days have affected your whole life. You would like to be like others, yet you cannot overcome your fears. The fear of crowds must be the remnant of past experiences. With time you developed other internal difficulties, emotional by nature, which aggravated your fears the more. Being an introvert yourself, and constantly in the same family environment, does not help much to overcome your sensitivity to fear. Your dwelling on the past is another factor, which intensifies your problems. You reached the point where fear is blown out of proportion in you. To normalize this exaggerated fear, you must counteract this ever-present fear in you. If you feel capable yourself, it would be fine for you to start doing something about it. If you feel incapable, seek someone who can help you in this regard. Don't let yourself be affected any deeper by your problems; the least you do that is positive will help, not only your inner life, but also your relations with Leo. Learn to do things, not on emotional impulse, but willingly; it's going to be hard, however not impossible. I do help you in prayer daily; also, if you wish, I can help by means of correspondence. It's up to you.

I hope to be in Shenandoah July 3rd; you'll hear from me then, God willing. Keep well, Lilly, my very best wishes to you, Leo and the girls. With many blessings from the Lord to you all, and much love and his peace always, in his loving care.

Fr. Walter

Letter Written April 12, 1977
Dear Lilly, P.C.

Your Christmas letter and card, and Easter letter and card together with stipend $3 and gift $2 have been received; deepest thanks for these, for your prayers and love. The Mass for the soul of Mary Jameson will be taken care of by me soon. Please thank her friends of the 500 club for the donation. The Lord will repay them for it.

I miss seeing you too, so much time has passed since we saw each other. I hope things have changed for you. Time is a good healer; God's grace in us is always healing us from within and from without, if we accept it and do what it requires of us. We all come to this realization sooner or later in life, otherwise, the adversities we meet everywhere would overcome us completely. Such a disaster would be fatal, but God's mercy and love are on our side, always preventing evil from hurting us spiritually, if only we obey and listen.

April 24th I'll return to New York and remain at the John XXIII center as before. Only if necessary will I go to Wernersville, Pennsylvania. When able, I hope to be in the Hazleton area later in summer. So, there is hope of seeing you. I'm with you in prayer every day. You are not forgotten. His abundant blessings to you, Leo, Eileen and Suzy. Much, much love.

Fr. Walter

I too miss you. Thank God my health is better.

Letter Written April 29, 1979
Dear Lilly, P.C.

I'm so pleased that the opportunity offered itself to write to you. You are not forgotten by me in prayers and thought. If it were possible for me to travel, I certainly would visit you and Leo while in Shenandoah. Please receive my sincere thanks for your Christmas gift of three dollars and your card. It's always good to hear from you.

Our human contacts are limited by time, space, and opportunity. However, in prayer we can always do what sometimes is impossible in actual life and practice. God wants it to be so, but our very makeup as human beings limits us. Whenever I call Patricia, I mention you to her and ask her to call you. You must be more concerned about Eileen and Suzy as they get older. Family life has its many demands for sacrifice. I hope you are feeling well and able to enjoy God's gifts given us in life.

My very best to you Lilly, Leo, Eileen, and Suzy, with God's ceaseless blessings, and much love, Yours humbly in the Lord.

Fr. Walter

24

Gratitude

One of Father Ciszek's key teachings was humility. Gratitude is the mark of a humble man. As we have seen in the recollections of Jesuit Father Joseph Lingan, it was apparent Walter Ciszek "was moved by the fact that people took the time to write to him, and he wanted to show them the same consideration." In fact, for some people Father's signs of sincere gratitude are among their dearest memories of him. Carol Caraluzzi, a spiritual daughter of Father Ciszek's from 1981 onward, recalled, "I always brought him a good homemade apple pie, and he enjoyed it so much that his eyes would light up and a huge grin would appear on his face. Then he would say, 'It couldn't be sweeter.'" But even the innocent pleasures of visits and meals together were always related to God. Carol continued:

> So many times I invited him to come and stay at my home to rest for a weekend, and he would only smile. Then one day when I invited him, he replied, "I'll wait until God tells me I can go." That was Father Ciszek.
>
> Finally a day came when Father did stop to meet my family. He ate with us, and found much enjoyment in pleasing my grandmother, because she had made him a lemon meringue pie.[49]

In this series of letters to Jake (Jacob), we see a very humble Father Ciszek, who takes great pains to show his gratitude to his correspondent and likewise help him in his own life to have gratitude to God for many blessings received.

Letter Written August 2, 1978
Dear Jake, P.C.

Your spiritual bouquet of July 27th has been received. Most sincere thanks for having remembered me on the Feast of St. Ignatius. It certainly was a memorable day for me. I attended Mass at the Fordham Chapel; at least

150 priests concelebrated. Fr. [Vincent G.] Potter (Superior) preached an exceptional sermon on St. Ignatius, which must have impressed everybody hearing it. After that, we had cocktails, followed by dinner. It was good to meet many of the Fathers on the occasion. It's the only time we get to see each other—when celebrating Mass together. So God's good, even though we don't deserve it. I'm fine, spending the month of August in a parish in Port Chester, New York. There's not much to do, but I'm kept busy as ever with my own work. All best wishes to you, Jake, with his countless blessings.

Fr. Ciszek

Letter Written after September 7, 1978
To dear Jake

My heartfelt thanks and deep appreciation for the jubilee gift[50] of $50 and the spiritual bouquet, also for your spiritual bouquet sent me on July 31 for the Feast of St. Ignatius and for your long letter of August 24th. May the Lord reward you for all your generous kindness. I do not forget the good you show and do for me. The Lord works in hidden ways but in a manner that makes us conscious of his loving concern. I'm doing well and feel fine. With endless gratitude and his choice blessings.

In him,

Fr. Ciszek

Letter Written August 3, 1979
Dear Jake, P.C.

Your generous gift of $20 and spiritual gift for July 31 have been received. Both gifts are precious to me, as is the one who inspired you to show such generosity. In all that happens everywhere, I am impressed mostly by how God works in all things and especially in human nature. This to me is the best proof that God lives with us and constantly manifests himself everywhere, if only we are willing to find him in moments of our spiritual and human needs. Endless thanks for your remembrance of me on July 31st and for your spiritual support. I appreciate deeply your friendly and meaningful concern. May he repay you in the best way possible for your kindness. Know I'm profoundly grateful for your being so genuinely good to me. Again, my best and the Lord's all to you, Jake. Humbly yours in him,

Fr. Ciszek, S.J.

Would you believe it—I have 3 eight-day retreats in August and two trips to Pennsylvania—one to Shenandoah, the other to Wernersville. Will keep in touch.

Letter Written October 31, 1979

Dear Jake, P.C.

Your visit finished, it left me with many thoughts for reflection. Your generosity and kindness impress me deeply, even to the point of questioning my own worthiness. To avoid further complications, I leave everything as it happened and commend to God you, myself, and the benefit received by me from the visit; let him repay you a hundredfold for your unselfish spirit. Deign, also, to receive my profoundest expression of gratitude and thanks for your gifts, Jake, and his blessing I received in them. Your spiritual bouquet, birthday greetings and $20, your brandy, marmalade and Mass stipend make me appreciate even more your remembrance of me on my anniversary. All I can give you in return is my prayers and a daily mention in my Masses. May his infinite blessings enrich your life and make you happy in the Lord. Humbly yours in him—

Fr. Ciszek

P.S. The books were sent to you already, 10 books in all. Also the books to Paul Davis were sent out and Mass card to Mrs. Dawson.

Letter Written January 1, 1980

Dear Jacob, P.C.

It was good to read the letters you received from Sister Frances of Rome. We cannot appreciate fully the intense joy the elderly experience when those whom they once taught show them gratitude. It's all God's work in us human beings. He inspires us to noble deeds and sustains us to the end, in whatever we undertake for the good of others. That is why such deeds of ours, though simple, become so effective. God never ceases to increase the good in us even when he punishes us. Who can explain the works of God in human beings and their relationships with one another? For good, when touching the human heart, becomes a simultaneous experience for many—does not exhaust its power in doing so but continues to affect others as time passes and as the plan of God determines. We are elevated by such infused favors and are humbled at the same time. For, in our unworthiness, we realize how much God's loving concern works for our greater good. You're welcome to come and visit any time. With prayer and kindest wishes, devotedly yours in him—

Fr. W. Ciszek, S.J.

Letter Written February 18, 1980

Dear Jacob, P.C.

This is to thank you most sincerely for your Christmas gift of $20 and spiritual bouquet, also to notify you that your Mass stipend of ten dollars, as well as your check of fifteen dollars for the books have been received. For all this and for your phone calls, accept my deep gratitude and appreciation.

The good we do is nothing else than a sharing in divine goodness. To do good there must always be the giver and the receiver. Being the receiver so often makes me feel concerned about myself. It's like being on welfare all the time; and, you know what people think about such bravados [sic] who never refuse a handout! Human actions or behavior are such that they can be questioned if merely looked upon from the outside. The story changes when looking at the same from the inside. Submission to God's power and will plays the main role here; who dares to question his ways?

Thank God all is working out slowly at the Center. God is good even when we do not deserve his goodness. So you keep on believing and trying no matter how things turn out. His blessings and my best wishes with prayer in him—devotedly—

Fr. Ciszek, S.J.

Letter Written June 11, 1980

Dear Jacob, P.C.

This is to thank you most sincerely for your visit of March 19th, your spiritual bouquet, gift of $20, the brandy, marmalade, and cake your wife baked.

I deeply appreciate your kind generosity, for it reflects God's goodness and favor to me. His blessing touches us both—you as a giver by his grace and I as a receiver by his mercy. No good is done without this mutual exchange. Each good, if analyzed, has this dual element; the giver and receiver are his choice, and only because he wills it and in the manner he wills it, does good have meaning. It's a personal obligation to evaluate things in the light of the source from which they come that profits soul and body. If only body or only the soul is considered, it is not enough; both must be referred together to the Supreme Giver who is our life and our hope. So my faint efforts to thank you for your favors bring me closer to him whom I can never forget, because in his power I am what I am, a living being with capacities reaching far beyond what we see, experience, and strive after in our daily routine. That's the nature of gratitude, which St. Ignatius so wonderfully expresses in his *Spiritual Exercises*.

Yesterday and today I'm in good spirits; a few days ago it was just the opposite. Who knows the secret of life but he who created it? So, limited as I am, there is only one choice left for me to make—to hold on to the Creator and not fear the rest. Such is life in him, full of peace and hope. Let's enjoy it and be happy. Eternally yours in him—

Fr. Ciszek, S.J.

Letter Written July 17, 1980
Dear Jacob, P.C.

This is a short answer to your letter of 6/16/80, and a note of sincere thanks for your gifts of brandy, marmalade, and $10 reimbursement.

Our visits are usually short but quite inspired. We must admit fully that God makes his presence felt whenever the sacrament of reconciliation takes place. He unravels to the human mind, in such instances, the secrets of our nature and the mystery of our being. We get glimpses of these truths, not to make us experts of the eternal truth but to make us believe more firmly in the Almighty. All this happens so ordinarily that only through his revealing power do we become conscious of the process of our salvation. It's so consoling to learn of our own salvation being worked out under divine protection amidst the frustrations of this world. Our hope, then, becomes a reality that will not forsake us in the most challenging situation of appearing before the judge of all creation and hearing his verdict.

Many thanks for all your calls and for the invitation [. . .] by your son Robert. His blessings and my prayers always. With gratitude in him. Yours sincerely—

Fr. Ciszek, S.J.

Letter Written August 24, 1980
Dear Jacob, P.C.

Your letter of 8.20.80 and check for books was received. Let me thank you for these, for the brandy, and for the visit. I enjoyed every moment being with you, your wife, and your sons. It was a relaxing encounter for me. Your health caused you some trouble. To me, this is understandable; for my illness interferes at times [. . .] prevents me from giving full expression to the joys an occasion may create, such as meeting people and being impressed by them; but the deeper appreciation of any meaningful meeting of people always leaves its profound effect on the soul and mind, in spite of the physical pains and aches that may interfere at such moments. I'm deeply grateful for the pleasant surprise you gave me, in your willingness to come and visit me when you were hardly able to do so. Your oldest son Joe is always welcome to come and visit me. The Lord has his ways of influencing whomever he wants and in whatever manner he chooses.

There are no limits to God's creative power to inspire us. From the time I knew you, it amazed me very much to notice how you planned your trips to the Bronx—just for a short encounter with me and a more serious one with the Lord—with such dedication. It strikes me very much to see also how grace operates in the hearts of others and in my own soul—to what great extent it inspires people to sacrifice themselves in order to please the Lord and gain his favor. This same power, called grace, will continue to operate at the deepest level within you in your critical condition, achieving even greater heights in your spiritual life than ever before, notwithstanding your illness and the concern it causes you, because this is so pleasing to God. I'm fully united to you, Jacob, in prayer, hopeful that, for you, the best is yet to come [. . .] because such is the order and will of his infinite love. My very best to you and the Lord's every blessing. Devotedly in him—

Fr. W. Ciszek, S.J.

Kindest regards to the rest of the family.

Letter Written September 23, 1980
Dear Jacob, P.C.

Your two letters of 9/1/80 and 9/9/80 have been received. Your report on the diagnosis of your lungs is not so good. Perhaps, with the help of God, the doctors will be able to help in this matter. We are blessed and spared much suffering by the various medications available for alleviating human pains. All in all, we are not alone, and that's consoling if we truly believe it. We are never abandoned if we never cease praying.

In the human and natural order of things, there is always too much that is lacking to give us full assurance. But this obvious lack prompts us to look and seek for help right at its very source. There, we are never disappointed, discouraged, or at a loss, because in this fullness there is always something for everyone to receive (even if it be the least bit), which will have its very special spiritual effect on our whole being and, because of this, whatever our problem, this tiny "crumb" given to us becomes the power leading us to our ultimate good, no matter what our sufferings, pains, and aches. For that tiny bit of power in us, appearing to come from nowhere, is nothing less than the gift to us of persevering in faith, and thus makes, concerning us all, an eternal difference. So the mystery of both lives, here and there, is revealed to us, not as something we deserved or merited, but as an infused gift we've shared all the time through our belief in him who died for us. All this will come and be given in its time because that is the nature of his mercy and love for us. And that is the nature of my conviction and joy, which I come to share with you as inspired, as I am, in writing this letter.

His endless blessings and my humble and faithful prayers to you, Jacob.

Fr. Ciszek, S.J.

I'll be away and in Pennsylvania, from September 27 to October 4. I'm thrilled you still want to visit the lousy Bronx.

Letter Written October 27, 1980

Dear Jacob, P.C.

Your last letter of 10/14/80 has given me ample information about your illness and its effect on your disposition. There is no comparison between your illness and mine. However, I could classify your illness as belonging to the major league and mine as belonging to the minor league. But the direct relationship between our illnesses is real, and mine is surely going to develop so as to finally qualify me to enter the major league from the minor, and then I'll be a fully qualified person in the league I'll belong to soon enough. Whatever sympathy I try to express to you in my writing is simply, then, the result of my experience, which resembles yours to a great extent; so bear with me and with whatever I write you in the course of this letter.

Giving the *Spiritual Exercises* to various people over and over, my knowledge of them deepens and grows considerably. This is what my latest insight into the exercises has been: I never look at anything in life, be it the smallest or most insignificant thing, without relating it to the infinite love of God; God's infinite love constantly operates in creation and especially in man. Here is the way I see it operating: we receive in baptism the gift of faith and prayer, and with these, humility—which means the humble realization of our absolute need of God (our total dependence on him). This is the triangle from which our spiritual life develops [...].[51]

From this triangle comes the grace to serve God and others, but never without obedience to the will of God. From all this we learn to have gratitude, and, once we have gratitude, our salvation is being worked out. Therefore, having faith, prayer, humility, service, obedience, and gratitude, we become assured of our salvation through hope in God's infinite love. The following diagram gives you a full picture of what I said above [...].[52]

So what is the consequence: all that happens in life, good or bad, I accept in gratitude and in the spirit described in the circle, as God's gift. In good things it's easy to be grateful; in suffering, I offer up the pain and hardships as an act of reparation to God, pay my own debts and those of others. So in gratitude I have joy, for I see [...] God's will being perfected in me in this way.

Sorry to burden you with my thoughts and ideas. But I wanted to share, and this is why I'm so insistent. His every blessing and my best to you, Jacob and Sarah and all, all children. Yours devotedly in him—

Fr. Ciszek

25

Faith amidst Difficulties

Many people sought out Father Ciszek's counsel in other personal difficulties. Father John Catoir recounts, "In a counseling situation, or in spiritual direction, he had a rare patience. On the other hand, he would not let you excuse yourself. He would allow no rationalizing."[53] Maureen O'Brien, another spiritual daughter of Father Ciszek, echoes this:

> For Father Ciszek, it was always the work of companioning others, first by prayer, which was his life's blood, then through the slow, patient response of listening, to assist others in discerning God's presence and His will. What animated Father Ciszek was his passion for people and his unconditional acceptance of them. He had a shepherd's love for people. He was always giving retreats and always on the go! He took so much time providing spiritual direction through writing letters to many people.[54]

In a series of very tender letters to a twenty-something young woman, Sheila, in the early 1980s, Walter Ciszek demonstrated this "passion for people" and "unconditional acceptance." Sheila had struggled in living out her Catholic faith and in various challenges in the spiritual life. When Sheila faced an unintended pregnancy, Father Ciszek neither condemned nor shunned her but, rather, helped her along the path of forgiveness and reconciliation.

Letter Written January 24, 1980
Dear Sheila, P.C.

Your letter arrived today. It's good to hear from you. I'm still taking care of you spiritually as before, so dispel all doubts to the contrary. Do write twice a month; this will keep you aware of your obligation to write and give me information as to how you are progressing. You have an intense character that needs to be guided; otherwise, the different reactions that you experience can easily confuse you. Feelings or emotions are difficult to handle, no matter how much you advance in spirituality. Usually, when you strive after greater perfection, the least negligence can make you feel distracted or bad. Dryness can come from superficial fulfillment of your duties, or it can come from a trial that is preparing you for a deeper test of faith. God permits dryness to happen. He always has in mind your greater good, when dryness appears. When it comes, however, do not change; continue doing spiritually what you have been doing—even with greater devotion—and it will normally pass.

Go to confession every month; no less than once in two months. You may send your love notes, if you need spiritual advice in these matters. Remember, as for now, your calling is the married life. It has different obligations than the religious life. Make a five-minute examination of conscience before retiring, read the scriptures as you have been doing, and make a fifteen-minute meditation daily. This will bring discipline into your life. It's going to cost you effort, but without it you'll not accomplish anything worthwhile. You have to learn how to do things with the talents, capacities, and willingness at your disposal. This is the way you learn spirituality, as God gives you his grace. Do not overdo it, for you also have other obligations to fulfill. God's power is in you to help develop your natural talents; more in the next letter.

My very best to you Sheila and his many blessings. Yours devotedly in him.

Fr. Ciszek

Sheila, I'll be privileged to say Mass and perform the wedding ceremonies July 26.

Letter Written March 26, 1980
My dear Sheila, P.C.

Your letter of March 15th has been received. As always, it's good to hear from you. Your concern to do the will of God is indeed a blessing. To find and do his will, however, is never easy, taking into consideration our unstable nature and our strong inborn tendencies to self-will. So far, you are doing fine, Sheila, and your frustrations and lack of full peace are the result of grace leading and teaching you to evaluate the things of life and the world in the light of faith and eternity. You are here to live normally; enjoy the natural things God has given while using them properly—always with gratitude and thanksgiving. Now to your letter.

You and Luke know best what is good for you. You have sufficient knowledge of one another to decide your future. The years you had [together] had their influence, so if you finally decide to separate, be prepared for reactions afterwards; they can be disturbing. But the peace of heart that you enjoy coming from the decision of not going through with the marriage will be your best sign of being in the right.

Now, to seek something else in life besides marriage will feel strange and difficult, as does everything in life that is new.

Lent is a time of deeper penetration into the spiritual life; it's a time of sacrifice. But that does not mean you are going to do all that seems to be lacking in your life. Lent has the power to make us conscious of our need to be more centered on God and Christ—that is, to be purified, first in desire, and then to recognize and admit our shortcomings and lack of self-denial, which means how easily we fail partially or wholly to do what is right. The purpose of grace, at this point, is to teach one to accept oneself as inadequate and to start relying more on God and praying more earnestly. The conflict of nature with grace never ceases; it will take a long time before you respond to grace fully, Sheila. You have to go through all these interior changes, challenges, frustrations, weaknesses, failures, sins, and imperfections to know and learn how deeply grace touches our sinful nature. For, at the very depth of our being, we are purified and made true children of God. Because of this conversion or transformation in you, you will experience a new love surging within you; a love of God ever growing in intensity. This love is in you, but it must be brought out by all the experiences you are undergoing now. So you see, Sheila, you are a normal girl, with a great deal of energy to live, and live fully; but God wants your love first, not to deny you everything else, but rather, to have you enjoy to the full all things in this world through him.

You have strong passions, Sheila, especially your sexual drive. We all have them. To neglect oneself by not curbing them, while being aware of their presence, can easily lead to unjustified pleasures. That's why we have marriage in which these tendencies to sex can be gratified rightly. If God wants marriage for you, he will make it possible for you to marry, by sending someone as your partner and friend for life; until then, just live from day to day. Do as others do, always trying to perform your duties as each day makes that possible; then offer all to God and be grateful for the good you've received and sorry for the bad you've done. In this way, you will learn best God's will as to a choice of life.

In regard to your staying to teach for another year in Kansas, pray over it. Grace is never given beforehand, that is, the special grace, but the sufficient grace never is missing. So, it is in the moment God chooses to give it that things happen. Be assured, he knows how to take care of you and to take care of all people. About getting involved with some fellow and giving in, try to overcome the natural urge by asking God to prevent such a thing from happening. If this really becomes a threat, then you can think of coming home. You're on your own, Sheila, and you must learn how to live, being responsible for your own self. Hope you have a wonderful Easter. Lots of love in him.

Yours devotedly—

Fr. Ciszek S.J.

Letter Written October 7, 1980
My dear Sheila, P.C.

Your letters of August 21 and September 22 were received. Thanks sincerely for the letters and the $25 offering sent me after the retreat. Your August letter made me feel good, because writing it you expressed such enthusiasm and confidence in yourself.

Then, behold, came your letter of September 22, and what a change you underwent in a month's time, Sheila! I feel deeply for you and know what it means to be in the trouble bothering you now. Every day at Mass and in my examens, I pray confidently to God that he spare you the consequences of your misdemeanor. You can call me when you feel up to it, or write when you can. I'm with you to the end, no matter what happens. My hope is all will turn out well. Even if you suffer the inevitable, the problem will suggest a proper solution that will spare you the feelings of helplessness you are experiencing now. God never forsakes us because we are his. He permits us, however, to suffer the pains due to our errors and sins. It is necessary that should come first, so that when the heart is purified, humbled, and justified by grief and sorrow, God may manifest his infinite, merciful love to his repentant child. If I have endless compassion for you Sheila, what about the Almighty?

You did not hear from me sooner because I was away for a week, then, when I returned, I could not easily find time for writing letters.

His all and my best to you Sheila. Yours devotedly in him,

Love, Fr. W. Ciszek S.J.

Letter Written October 28, 1980
My dear Sheila, P.C.

Your letter of October 9th had so much sincerity in it—the result, [no doubt,] of a deep purification you are going through. Sheila, never even permit yourself to think that I will ever give you up—no matter what happens in your life. You are going through a unique experience that is causing you to feel the humiliation, hurt, suffering, and the terrible loneliness every infidelity creates. But, in this way, you are learning your utter weakness and are being taught the absolute need for God in your life.

You have to go through what is happening to you now, to reach the height of spiritual freedom. God's grace operating in you is above your sins, and the Blessed Mother's protection over you will shield you from succumbing to any total turning away from God that would be detrimental to your soul.

You are a person with an almost uncontrollable drive and craving for love, which easily leads you to the sensual and makes you fall, no matter how cautious you may be. Prayer and turning to God, asking for his special help, is the spiritual option that will help you in your weakness. Also, avoid occasions that inevitably lead you to deep emotional arousal; they must be a constant reminder, warning you not to take risks beyond your capacity. God loves you, Sheila, and he will make you the person he wants you to be by teaching you the lesson of your own weakness, so that, being aware of it at all times, you may slowly begin to follow his directives. In this way, you will have peace and confidence and come to rely on his loving goodness to teach you how to live in the calling you will soon choose to follow.

Just keep being faithful to your prayer life and fulfill well your obligations each day, and your life will develop normally and strongly. Life—and all that is in it—is a gift from God. Take life as it comes, doing what it demands, and leave the rest to God; then, happiness will be yours.

My best and His all to you, Sheila. One with you in prayer and united with you in His love,

Yours devotedly.

Fr. Ciszek

Letter Written January 21, 1981
My dear Sheila, P.C.

Your letters of November and December have been received, both are full of the topic that concerns you and Ted at present in a most challenging way. What happened to you and Ted was in God's eternal plan. This is his way of speaking to you, Sheila—a way he chose—for he knows best what to do in order to win your heart and your whole self. I have no doubt whatsoever that, in all this, there is concealed an even greater blessing. But to realize this and be convinced of it in faith, much exterior suffering has to be borne in humility. So take things as they come, from now on, and do your best, Sheila. I, your mother, Ted, and others are fully with you in this unique and unwanted experience. The answer, as to what to do in your situation, will come and become clearer as things develop. The real answer to our prayers, needs, and expectations comes normally in the development and growth of events, as they happen, generating a deeper discernment of God's will, which includes human action, reason, and especially, faith. So that, in this process, the will of man and woman, finally, becomes properly disposed to receive and accept God's will in its basic elements; once this decision is made, the following of God's will and its directives becomes the way to that growth in which peace, joy, justification, and strength are given and found.

So, Sheila, you are learning in this way, as things are happening to you at present, to belong to God and to be his favorite child (in spite of your weakness and mistakes), bringing you into the responsible situation of becoming a mother. There is a great deal you will have to hear that lies ahead, but slowly you will be able to handle each new experience, before the delivery [of your child], in a more balanced way, because grace will enlighten you more and more each day, and lead you safely to where you will become fully yourself, a beautiful person, tried, but not broken.

I'm returning to New York to stay on January 24th. His every blessing and my deepest best to you, Sheila. Yours to the very end—being one with you in his love.

Fr. Ciszek

You and Ted are very much in my prayers.

Letter Written March 28, 1981
My dear Sheila, P.C.

Your letters of February 10th and March 24th have been received. Both were interesting because you are in a situation of decision making, a task neither easy nor pleasant. The fears we normally have in life can be helpful, if they are not exaggerated; yet, they become powerful and frightening when it comes to making a decision. But this does not mean that these fears are a sign of our guilt. Rather, they are restraints helping us make better and truer judgments. They make us reflect more seriously on spiritual matters, rather than allowing us to become totally self-centered and rely only on human strength and ideas. It's God's grace that leads us to feel such difficulties when taking a serious step in life, reminding us, over and over, to seek and find the will of God in what we decide to follow in life, rather than to be overly concerned with our own little selves.

In your first letter, you explained very well your attitude towards Ted, and rightly so. Now, you have to see for yourself, and be convinced, what it is God wants from you in the present situation of your pregnancy. As for your future, your best decision and strength will lie in accepting first, the grace offered you by God, and, then, living it out to the best of your ability. This grace, or God's power, should be your principal motive for decision making, for it will give you the balance, peace, and blessings needed for facing the future, which depends essentially on God's favor.

Now, let's consider the contents of your second letter. You wrote, after reflecting on the pros and cons, that you are still scared (i.e., full of disturbing fear), and see God's will as favoring marriage, but that you do not have the strength to follow it, as you see it.

So, Sheila, what does St. Ignatius say to one who must make a decision, while being in a state of mind as full of fear as you are? Here is what he says: "After pondering every aspect of the matter in question, I will consider which alternative appears more reasonable, and come to a decision because of weightier motives presented to my reason, and not because of any sensual inclination."

After the choice or decision is made, one must turn with great diligence to prayer in the presence of God and offer him the choice that his Divine Majesty may deign to accept and then to confirm it, if it is for his greater service and purposes. From that point on, faith must be your guide and your strength.

Isaiah 30:15–18 says: "By waiting and by calm you shall be saved, in quiet and in trust your strength lies. Yet the Lord is waiting to show you favor and he rises to pity you, for the Lord is a God of justice; blessed are all who wait for him!"

So, Sheila, his plan is slowly being revealed to you. His ways are not our ways; they are sound and full of wisdom. In prayer, your faith will grow and become your great strength in life, but things will continue to happen in just the way you are experiencing them. He will take care of you in the way that is best; that's for certain—just rely on him, and do as best you can and know.

Your love for Luke will be only a pleasant memory, a reminder that we are not the creators of truth but simply its followers. As creatures we are weak and dependent. As believers, our weakness is complemented by God's fullness, becoming thereby a source of new hope and vision.

I'm with you, Sheila, and share your secret joy, soon to be realized for us all to see and admire. His every blessing to you both and Ted.

Love you three in him—

Fr. W. Ciszek S.J.

Part Five

THE LOVER OF
GOD'S WORD

26

Walter Ciszek's Biblical Reflections

In August 1976, Walter Ciszek suffered a massive heart attack. Before that, he was accustomed to traveling a great deal, giving conferences and retreats. Afterward, however, he had to stay closer to home and was limited to counseling people through letters and phone calls. However, there were others, mostly lay and religious women, who would visit him in the Bronx and make a day of recollection with him, or even an eight-day retreat, in the apartment above his in the John XXIII Center. Their memories of the time they spent with Father have many common elements, whether they date from the early 1970s or from the mid-1980s.[55]

Often, people would write to him after having read *With God in Russia* or *He Leadeth Me*. One of them observed,

> While reading his books, I formed an image of Father Ciszek in my mind as a tall and emaciated man whose face was serious and sullen from his years of suffering in Siberia. I was drawn to his spirituality of trust in divine Providence and to the fact that Father Ciszek had actually lived this spirituality under the most oppressive terms and for many years. I rang the bell of Father Ciszek's residence. A short barrel of a man opened the outer door of the building. He made me think of Santa Claus with his white hair and smiling blue eyes. The man exuded joy. Having a different image of him, I asked for Father Ciszek. The priest said, "I am Father Ciszek." I was really taken aback. His joy proved to me the words he had written about his experience with God in Russia, ongoing even then in his ordinary life in the Bronx, still with God at each moment.

The food he served was basic. On arrival, there were cookies and milk at his kitchen table, then, for breakfast, a crusty piece of bread with a cup of coffee. What he shared spiritually was equally basic: following St. Ignatius's *Spiritual*

Exercises, he selected Scripture passages for the retreatant to read and reflect on, and then met with him or her twice a day to share their thoughts and discuss the passages.

One of the retreatants later recalled, "At the end of the retreat I felt refreshed and felt an increase of faith and hope and that I had grown spiritually within my soul." They observed that his message was always simple: the place where you are now is where God wants you to be; stay in the present moment, trust God in every circumstance, let yourself be carried by Him, and rest in his love. They saw the strength of his words flowing from the fact they were the fruit of his own life, and when he talked about Russia and his sufferings in the camps, it was only to share what he had learned there. When Father Ciszek celebrated Mass with his retreatants, they were always deeply impressed, as is obvious from the comments of one of them: "It was a delight to participate. I did the first reading and offered some personal prayers. The Mass was about the Mass, not about Father Ciszek. He didn't say Mass, he prayed it." Another noted that he showed the same reverence in his listening. "He had a great deal of respect and was sensitive to my suffering and what I was experiencing, probably because he himself had gone through the unthinkable."

Around 1980 Father Ciszek received as retreatants Dr. James Schaller and then his wife, Marianne.[56] They were both in their forties and the parents of six children. They had been introduced to him by the war hero Lt. General William S. Lawton (1900–1993), then retired and vice president of Catholics United for the Faith. At the time of a visit to their home by General Lawton, the Schallers had mentioned the book *He Leadeth Me*, and he told them that if they wanted to meet the author, he would arrange it because Father Ciszek was giving private retreats at the John XXIII Center. They replied that they would love to meet him. Dr. Schaller later described that meeting as follows:

My retreat began early Friday and lasted until late Sunday afternoon. The retreat was one-on-one; I was his only person on retreat in the whole building. Father Ciszek was really tough on me. He told me to pull the shades because he didn't even want me to be distracted by looking out the window. It was a very intense thing, although it was very relaxed, very serene, and very peaceful. I was a practicing obstetrician-gynecologist at the time, and so the idea of not having a phone, not having TV, not having any connection with anything, was very alien. We had our retreat in his room where he actually lived, where he cooked and ate. The only time we were in the chapel was when he said Mass. All the rest of the time, I would just go to his room, and he would talk for an hour, and then I would go back and think about what he said for an hour—the insights—and then I would fix myself something to eat and then go back and visit Father, and we would do that all day long, both Saturday and Sunday.

When I went out there to Fordham, I felt rather sad, like, "What do I want to be when I grow up?" I didn't think I had achieved my potential; and boy, Father Ciszek put that attitude to rest right away. He said that what I was doing was exactly what Jesus wanted me to do. Exactly what he wanted me to do. So I never thought again about being a failure; I just resolved to be a better obstetrician and gynecologist. It was very relaxed. Like him I tend to do things "all out." I don't tend to prosper under such circumstances, but with him, I could have gone on for a week! He wasn't threatening, he wasn't judgmental, and he was so kind.

It was such a wonderful weekend with him that when I came home, Marianne said it was like I was walking around in heaven. I was so happy, so serene, and so peaceful. She was so impressed that she said she wanted to do the same thing. So she made a retreat a few months later.

Recalling her retreat, made some time later, Mrs. Schaller related the following:

Father Ciszek had dancing eyes. He didn't make me stay quite as long at Fordham as he made others. He told me to stay at the retreat house; I said, "You're really tough!" Father responded, "Ok, I'll let you walk down to the campus, but don't go further than there." During the retreat, he would sit at the table with me and talk for forty-five minutes—all about Our Lord—and at a Sunday Mass he would talk for about thirty-five or forty minutes, like he was talking to a full church, only I was the only one there. I think the other thing he got across to me was how much God loved me. It was almost to the point of tears that I realized that, and that has stuck with me ever since, that Christ would have died for me even if I were the only one.

Spontaneous as they seemed, the contacts that Walter Ciszek had with his spiritual sons and daughters were always the result of prayer. God let him know—as he was fond of saying—what mail he should open, to whom he should respond, whom he should receive or visit at home. And as he was always obedient to the movements of the Spirit, so, also, did he expect obedience from the persons he guided, as the Schallers earlier testified.

The same observation was made by two women who, from 1980 onward, together with two other women, visited Father Ciszek on a monthly basis for a day of recollection, usually on a Friday, sometimes on the first Friday of the month.[57] They would arrive at nine o'clock in the morning and, in turn, each of them would briefly meet with him, "to get his instructions and to receive his spiritual wisdom concerning how to interpret Scripture, how to meditate and understand all that God was saying to us through the Bible, never to rush as we read." He said that if some particular sentence seemed to "jump out at us, we were to stop and meditate as to the meanings of the words or sentence." After some prayer time in one of the apartments upstairs, the women would take turns returning downstairs to spend some time with Father, discussing the ideas upon which they had meditated. At the end of the morning they would celebrate Mass together. Speaking of those masses, they said, "When Father Walter elevated the consecrated Host, his eyes showed that he was totally engrossed in Jesus." Afterward they would have lunch in his room, listening to the stories he shared with them. Following lunch, they would go back upstairs to read and reflect some more, and, then again, they would come down to talk with Father and share what they had learned from their meditation.

Sometimes they made their confession to him. For their penance they would receive a psalm or some other Scripture reading, which they always found to be very appropriate, thinking, ". . . . exactly what I needed to read in regard to what I had told him." In fact, they came to believe that Father Ciszek had the gift of reading people's hearts and knowing their needs, as is clear from the following incident recounted by one of them:

> As we journeyed to Father's residence in the Bronx for our day of recollection, all four women would be chatting about something or other. But as soon as we met Father and he greeted us, he would continue the same conversation that we were previously having in the car! Also, when I was having a particularly trying day at home, Father never failed to telephone to see how I was.

Another recalled, "He opened my soul to the knowledge, understanding, and wisdom of learning God's will in every aspect of my life. The intimacy with the Most Holy Trinity was a great grace bestowed on me through the times I had spent with Father."

Another person who became acquainted with Father Ciszek around 1980 was Gerald R. Lilore, a man in his early fifties who worked as marketing director and was active in the Cursillo movement, which focuses on showing Christian laypeople how to become effective Christian leaders. His own marital difficulties led him to begin support groups for the separated and divorced at several parishes. His witness follows:[58]

I was working in New York at the time, in the textile business. I had my secretary locate Father Ciszek. I met Father for the first time in July 1981. I called him and went over to see him, taking along a good friend, my public relations man. He had read Father's books, too, and was spellbound. When I told Father that the man was Jewish, he laughingly said, "I thought you were a Methodist." Father had a great sense of humor. We spent a whole afternoon at a restaurant in the Bronx with him. Father was a man who always had a sparkle in his blue eyes and a generous and open smile on his face.

I used to go over to his apartment on Sunday morning, and he would say Mass. I would do a reading, and he would give a little talk. I noticed his simplicity at Mass—no drama, he was very humble. We were in the little chapel in the apartment building for Mass, and later we'd go back to his room for a cup of coffee and talk.

After I had first met him, we set a date for a directed retreat in September. He would give me different excerpts from Scripture to read and reflect on. Later we'd discuss them and he'd answer my questions. Father Ciszek never spoke sensationally when discussing his life experiences, but only from a point of spiritual reference. One of the most interesting things was that he lived totally in the moment. He said, "Remember, your past is the present, and the future is where you are now."

One thing I gained from him was an understanding of God's will. Rather than become embittered or view his years in Russia as a waste, Walter Ciszek had a clear and strong sense of the meaning of his life. He said that while he was struggling to find God's will in the mistakes he had made—for example, signing papers in the prison—he came to realize that God's will was in the mistake. In other words, the situation you are in *is* God's will, the very circumstance itself. Sometimes I'd say, "I can't believe I did such and such a thing." He'd say, "Jerry, you can only do with the grace of God you have at the time." These truths sustained him through the long years of darkness and suffering. "God is a very patient teacher, and I was a most stubborn pupil," he would say.

He really knew human nature. For example, in business matters or conflicts where I had problems finding solutions, he would understand and get right to the "core" of it for a solution. His approach to anybody's problems was about coming to a rightful moral conclusion. In regard to his contribution to the Church, I believe that God allowed him to go through all that he experienced so that he could come back and relate to us the simplicity of God's message. One time at a dinner at Fordham, he commented to me, "It's not that complicated; the theologians and philosophers complicate it. For example, it doesn't matter if you're Protestant, Catholic, or Jewish. You're going to be judged on how you affected other people, either for the good or for the bad."

Father Ciszek was simple. He said, "Jerry, just try your lousy best, and if that isn't good enough, then try your lousy, lousy best, then leave the rest to God." His definition for "humiliation" was taking the negative out of it, and going forth with it; his definition for "humility" was "the truth." He used to say, "Jerry, do you know what resurrection is? It's nothing else but having to go through life slowly dying." He was one with Christ on a continual basis, just as close as when we receive the Eucharist. His prayer to Jesus was, "Help me to accept whatever your Father chooses for me and to respond in your spirit of love, forgiveness, kindness, total alms-giving, compassion, and mercy."

Just before he died, I said to him, "You're going to leave me soon." "Don't worry," he replied, "I'll whisper in God's ear for you. Has anyone ever trusted in the Lord and been disappointed? God is infallibly (sic) reliable."

"His love of Scripture was so encompassing that it became his own conversation," Gerald Lilore said. Sister Mary of Jesus, one of the Discalced Carmelite Sisters who made a retreat with Father Ciszek in February 1984, confirmed this impression:

Rereading the notes I took after each meeting with Father Walter, I am struck by his tremendous love for the Holy Scriptures. He told me that he read his breviary "with great gusto," and often, in the course of our retreat, he would take a psalm, verse by verse, word by word, and explain it to me. Scriptures were alive to him in a degree I've not seen in others. Father encouraged me to study the Scriptures and use them for prayer, saying that they will mold my personality in God's Spirit, and that I would then be able to nourish others. It seems to me that Father was describing what he knew to be true in his own life. He told me in the course of my retreat that the Bible should be used as a theological basis, not "he said, I said." "This approach," he said, "would ground a person in mystical and ascetical theology, giving one the 'big ideas,' the basic truths, which God imparts as wisdom to the simple." During my retreat in 1984, Father Ciszek said of his love for the Scriptures, "It's a virus I have!" When I replied that I hoped it was a contagious virus, he laughed and said, "It's not contagious; it's an infused virus."[59]

Others have commented on how Father Ciszek really helped them reflect and meditate on the Word of God, and how much he liked to preach on it at Mass, even when there was only one person present. These homilies were sometimes rather long, not because Walter Ciszek liked to hear his own voice but because he was constantly trying to hear God's voice; the right words did not always come to him easily. As Sister Rosemary Stets, O.S.F., who knew him for fifteen years, wrote in her recollection of him three years after his death,[60]

Someone once asked me if Father Walter was a charismatic. I told them that there wasn't anyone I knew more Spirit-filled, open, and sensitive to the divine indwelling of God. Of course he was charismatic, in the best and truest sense of the word.

I remember how carefully he picked up on the words of Scripture, or a special prayer, or a line from a spiritual book. He was like a child, just filled with amazement and delight at what he had discovered. These "inspirations" would come to him at any time, but mostly in prayer or at Mass. He would read something and then spend the next few weeks totally absorbed by the depth and power of this statement. In his phone conversations and letters it became the central object.

If any visitors came, he would spend the greater portion of the visit explaining the beautiful meaning in this line, as if the visitors had come just for that purpose. And in Father's mind, with his sense of trust and spiritual direction, perhaps they had.

Father Walter was alive with the Spirit of God, and what he shared was a result of the fullness of grace and wisdom that flowed into his heart. He longed to share all he had received, and he never neglected or took lightly the profound effect these graces had for others.

Three weeks earlier Sister Rosemary had written,

He was a perfect conversationalist, but not just light talk, his talk was very heavy. Instantly he was absorbed in the message he had to convey. He went right to the heart of the matter in every encounter. The small, superficial, pleasant actions that surround and decorate a conversation were utterly useless for him. His style was absolutely basic and superbly authentic. He could entertain you and make you laugh and keep you enthralled with the stories of his experiences, and he could talk in circles about something that was completely in the dark to your mind. And all the while, in every word and glance and gesture, you felt surrounded by his love, his true affection, his wisdom.

He was always so sure of what he said; he did not expound about theories or ideas or mysteries that could not be understood. When he spoke, he spoke of God, the Trinity, Scripture, Mary, with authority and much conviction. He had an answer or explanation for every argument, and yet he never "had all the answers." His speech was so humble, so unassuming. He made fun of his littleness, his poor health, his simple ways, in such a way that he invited you to share the fun of this poor, sorry condition and see in yourself a shadow of the same. He could pass from fun to serious business in the blink of an eye. He assessed every situation with divinely infused wisdom and intuition. He had the gift of discernment, especially in the Sacrament of Reconciliation, and the gift to read hearts.

Walter Ciszek was not in the habit of writing out the conferences or homilies he gave on Scripture. However, there do remain two collections of his biblical reflections. The first was written between February 24, 1964, and July 1, 1965; these reflections are probably the fruit of his daily meditations. The days he did not write anything were the days he was away from home. The notes show us that in that period he meditated on the Gospels of Matthew, Luke, and John, successively and from beginning to the end, rather than follow the liturgical readings of the day. The first entry is on Matthew 13:3–9; presumably, the earlier notes, begun after his return from Russia, have been lost. In spite of the private character of those notes, Father Ciszek hardly ever uses the first person singular, but it is not difficult to detect an exhortation to himself when he writes about "you" or "us," as in "Our care should be to help others"; "If you fear and become timid, there is nothing you will do worthwhile for God and others"; "Your vocation requires sacrifice on your part by leading the sheep that went astray from the fold"; "Learn from Christ, he is the Good Shepherd."

In December 1977, word had it that Father Ciszek was preparing a new book with reflections on the Gospels. He may have started working on it a couple of months earlier when he returned to the John XXIII Center after a long absence because of his convalescence from a major heart attack. Again, he started with the Gospel of Matthew, and then in January 1978, he turned to the Gospel of Luke, which he seems to have studied simultaneously with the Gospel of Mark. In November of that year, he stopped at Luke 15 and continued exclusively with Mark, from chapter 6 onward, up until January 1979, when he had reached chapter 13. Instead of beginning Mark's Passion narrative, he went on to Jesus' "farewell discourse" in John 16—19, most probably for reasons of chronology. However, these reflections were soon interrupted, first in March 1979 by health problems and then by his decision to meditate on the "suffering servant" chapters in the prophet Isaiah (52—53). It was not until July 1979 that he again took up his commentary on the Gospel of Luke, studying its Passion narrative, together with parallel or otherwise relevant scriptural passages, followed, in October 1979, by the farewell discourse in John. In February—March 1980, Walter Ciszek finished the first drafts of his book on the Gospels but, presumably for reasons of age and declining health, he never edited the reflections in a more readable format.

From the remaining hundreds of manuscript pages,[61] which are rather varied in form, quality, and style, we can deduce that, with some interruptions because of the liturgical season and activities elsewhere, Walter Ciszek wrote more or less one reflection a day, one or one-half page in length, beginning with a summary of the biblical passage and finishing with a "colloquy" or short prayer. As for his exegetical methods, one does not get the impression that he consulted academic commentaries much or cared about the history, the structure, and other meta-aspects of the text; he took Scripture as he found it, in the English translation, and settled for the so-called literal sense and its moral interpretation. The Word of God and the teaching of the Church were one and the same for him, supreme and authoritative guides helping us follow Jesus Christ to the end, which is nothing less than seeing and being with God in heaven. "Christ's teaching is full of examples directly or indirectly teaching the truth needed for salvation," he wrote somewhere in the beginning of the project, and the following day he added that the love, humility, and faith that Christ teaches, morally and satisfactorily take care of all the problems of the intellect in the world, and, in general, existing everywhere. "Humbly contemplate the Word of God, and with his grace, i.e., divine faith, hope and love, you will find the answer to all your problems." That seems to have been the exegetical method that Walter Ciszek followed, while continuously reflecting on his past spiritual experiences and on his aspirations for the future. He had no doubt that the God who spoke to all ages through Scripture was the same God who acts now in our daily life.

The biblical reflections that now follow were selected because they represent so well Father Ciszek's thoughts on some fundamental aspects of the Christian life and/or because the theme—Our Lady, for example—had not yet been developed by him in either of his two books.[62]

27

Human Living and Loving

Biblical reflections by Fr. Ciszek

The Human Body Reflecting God's Beauty (Luke 3:23–28; May 13, 1964)
Our Lord chose a body for himself. His ancestors, according to the flesh, came from the house of David.

Man's body is a wonderful production of God's handiwork. Just look at the newborn child—what natural processes it had to undergo in order to develop to the moment of birth. Man merely fulfills the demands required for conception, but the process of the body's formation begins independently of his will, following the strict workings of nature's laws. The work, done all by itself, is so perfect that, in normal conditions, all mistakes are excluded, and the body, after nine months in the womb is ready for independent existence.

Every new body is, in general outline, the same in construction, yet it is so different as to its continuing development. The beauty of its development through the years is astounding. Men do not always see it because they are engrossed in their work and distracted by their daily occupation. They are not always reflective enough to notice this wonderful product of God's handiwork with all its beauty, the essence of which, though exteriorly changing, retains the attraction of its interior splendor throughout the whole of life. Apart from the exterior beauty, as men may classify it, there is that essential inner beauty in every body reflecting God in itself, no matter whether the body is perceived by our mind as beautiful or not.

This reflection of God's beauty in the human body is of maximum importance. Man, realizing this and recognizing that beauty, elaborates a spiritual estimation of his own body and the bodies of others and thus develops a special moral respect for them in every circumstance of life. This interior spiritual appreciation of man's body is the principle necessary for the proper care, respect, and treatment of the body. Always remember that the person in question is a true reflection of God. The body looked upon in this way becomes a holy and valuable object. When one estimates it in this way, any lustful desires that might arise lose their force, and their evil is seen in all its hideousness.

This sanctifying attitude of respect for all people is something desirable and should be fostered amongst all, because it gives man a true conception, a positive appreciation, which is a true incentive to acquire this Christlike ideal in regard to one's own body and the bodies of other people. A deep appreciation and understanding of the principle that every human body is a direct production of God himself, and remains so to the end, is the best safeguard for us all—especially for our young people—against all sexual liberties and excesses in vogue at present. It ennobles the mind, soul, and the body itself, to remember that man is God's creation and cannot be changed in spite of his (deliberate) sins.

Practicing Poverty (Luke 12:13–21; Autumn 1978)

Our Lord reacts strongly when the question touches upon riches. Jesus himself loved poverty. He wanted to teach us that poverty is a necessary requirement for all those who want to follow him. Jesus understood poverty in its basic meaning; he knew we were born poor, and we will die poor, for to create means to bring something into existence from nothing. That is true of our human nature. When we were born we had nothing; when we die we must leave everything we had. This implies that from the very beginning—which takes us back to the eternal plans of God—we depended on God for our very existence, our birth and life. When life on this earth ends, all that still remains to come will also depend on God. So, on our part, we have nothing to say about how our life begins or how it will end, except to acknowledge we are totally dependent on God. This is true not only in regard to our birth and death but even more so to life, as it is given to us here on earth to enjoy, to make use of, and to explore. Christ wants us to be aware of God's concern that we might live and act as life itself teaches us through reason and the inspiration of grace—always aware of our beginning and our end and of what awaits us afterwards.

Our Lord wisely warns us of the danger riches pose for us. One who is attracted to them can easily lose a sense of reality concerning his life and destiny, and get so involved in hoarding riches all his life that he forgets what is most important: his purpose in life and his salvation in the life which is to come. That is why Our Lord warned all of us in the scripture reading (cited above) and also said, "Watch, and be on your guard against avarice of any kind, for a man's life is not made secure by what he owns, even when he has more than he needs." We must heed Christ's wisdom (accept, understand, and love it) in order to avoid evil and its sinful consequences. For all human beings seek security in life, but our sinful human nature falsely sees the attainment of this security in having many possessions. Once avarice affects the mind of man, then his material, physical, moral, intellectual, and spiritual life are also affected. Our Lord warns us to be on our guard against avarice of any kind.

How? By practicing poverty and loving it as the most secure means for living a God-fearing life here on earth, and leading to a peaceful death in the end.

Poverty does not exclude possessions, nor does it prohibit the amassing of goods; what it really demands is a total detachment from all earthly goods and a full attachment to God. It means that we live, enjoy and love life in all its beauty and splendor, but we must never forget God. This of course implies freedom from sin and the fulfillment of God's will in everything we do; that is the spirit of poverty. It makes us seek things, not for themselves, but for the end they were given—that is, to praise, reverence, and serve God—to use them in as much as they help us attain our end, and abstain from them in so far as they impede our reaching that end. It is in the first place the poverty of the intellect and will; for from these faculties our whole life is either properly ordered or it is not. If mere spiritual poverty is not enough in a certain set of circumstances, then actual poverty has to be accepted and practiced. The readiness of our will regarding poverty must be such that spiritual or actual poverty can be readily embraced and practiced, as the occasion demands.

The Parable of the Talents (Matthew 25:14–30; April 1, 1964)
In this parable, Christ teaches us the truth that everyone must make a return to God as a result of his actions, and according to his ability.

The less talented have no excuse for being lazy or inactive; their serious obligation is to do as much good as possible, even at the cost of much effort, because the Lord is going to ask an accounting from every one of us when he comes. The fearsome truth, "I reap where I sow not, and gather where I have not strewed," gives the assurance that everyone can rely upon God's grace and help. Even in hard circumstances, where, humanly speaking, very little good can be done with the limited amount of talent had, the Lord lets us know that it remains perfectly possible to do good. If we rely, as he wants us to, both upon his grace and our sincere effort, with prayer and good will, we can expect full success. Hence, there is no ground for excuses, even for the most untalented person.

If you are more talented, however, more is expected from you. You must apply more serious effort in your works, and your deeds should manifest greater perfection; not that you sow yourself before men but that you praise the Lord more by so doing. Hence, all fear, false humility, excuses, and shunning of difficulties are only signs of [spiritual] weakness and pride, fearing to humble yourself because self is put before God. Pray to God, in such cases, purify your intention, be humble, act and use fully the talents you have, and by that you will give God the highest praise. You are not to seek to appear grand or brilliant in your actions but simply to present more clearly the truth in all its fullness.

Try to find the will of God in your actions and do not impede God from having his way. You will do this if peace of conscience and mind accompany your actions. It's false to pretend to depend on God if you have not first properly prepared yourself for something you are about to do, and then expect God to do everything for you. Be always alert before beginning something, to find out first exactly what God wants you to do. In general, reason itself will already tell you what the right thing to do is [without a special light from God].

Human Relationships (Luke 8:19–21; Summer 1978)

Jesus' Mother and brothers—his relatives—came to see him. They no doubt had something to communicate to him. But Jesus used this occasion to teach the bystanders a new meaning of mother and brother in the new law. He emphasized the universal law of love found in the love of the Father for all mankind. The Father's love for us all is the source of all love. Therefore, the natural love found in family, in friendship, marriage, etc., must be ordered to the love of the Father. From this infinite love of the Father all human relationships take their meaning.

Christ wants to emphasize the eternal significance of all human relationships so that we may find in our human communications the everlasting truth underlying them. This truth should not be forgotten or ever allowed to escape our mind and consciousness. That is, when we are truly related to one another—whether mother and father to the family and to their children, whether friends united amongst themselves by love, or spiritual persons bound with one another by spiritual ties—we must never forget the will of God in these relationships. For we are, first and foremost, mother, brother, friend, relative, wife, husband, spiritual persons brought together by spiritual love, when we fulfill the will of the Father in all our relationships with one another, because they have their origin in God from all eternity. We are called to have such relationships with others by the eternal Author of all life and all being; for it so pleases him who is all powerful, the Lord and God of all creation. Hence, all that is and exists on the natural level becomes truly what it should and must be, only then when expressing the will of the eternal Father in thought and deed.

O Lord Jesus, how wonderful is your teaching, so otherworldly, yet so rewarding and fulfilling. Show us, your brothers and children, the way to learn the eternal truth as you teach it, through the revealed word, so that living it we may be one with you here on earth and for all eternity. Amen.

Love Is Sacred (John 13:31 ff.; January 10, 1979)

Before leaving the disciples, Christ poured out his love for them in all he had said about his relationship with the Father—that is, he and the Father are one. Christ revealed the eternal secret of God's plan of salvation now in the first part of his last discourse to the disciples. He spoke to them as someone who knew, possessed, and lived in full what he said, as he made known to them the eternal plan of God's love and salvation. What depth of spirit is revealed in the simple words Christ used to communicate the Father's message to the disciples—and, through them, to all mankind.

Love is boundless, without barriers. It transcends time, for time is a created reality while love is itself uncreated; it is the reality of all that is and the source of untold and incomprehensible mysteries. How much of his love the Father will reveal and show to each and every human being created in his likeness only he knows. Even all that will be revealed to every saved human being in the beatific vision is as nothing compared to what God is in himself. Yet, what we human beings have received in Christ is of maximum importance. For Christ himself said, "Greater love than this nobody has, to lay down his life for others." It's a mutual love for all mankind expressed by the Father in the Son, and by the Son for the Father. And the realization of that love of the Father and the Son is God's greatest gift to mankind in the person of Jesus.

So love is sacred; it's the source of all being and the cause of all existence. Its sacredness touches the core of our being. It tends to purify and make holy what is unholy in us. All of us born into this world have that spark of divine love in us. There are no words to express the depth, the purity, and the infinity underlying simple human love. This love projected into us human beings from God's love is demanding, causing excruciating pains in the human heart. For even though the intensity and depth of human love, experienced at its profoundest level, gives us the most exquisite joy and happiness and a sense of liberation, it does so only for a short time. For soon after, something happens to the human heart, takes away the beauty of the elevated experience of love, leaving it to experience the depths of frustration and futility. The wounded heart, torn and tormented by untold pangs of pain and suffering, feels a dejection even greater than the elevation sensed a short while before. Why? This is the process all human nature must go through while being prepared and made worthy to have part with the Holy of Holies, united finally in the infinite love of God.

Love, though spiritual by nature because it comes from the infinite love of God, does include also the physical and bodily love of man and woman. This human love has its strong attractions, gives man and woman much pleasure, and disposes them to acts of heroic sacrifice and patient suffering. Yet it is only when human love reaches the point of saturation that the spiritual craving in man and woman begins to awaken. There is a continuity in love hardly discernible to the soul that is undeveloped in matters spiritual. Most important in human love is the divine element, ever elevating, purifying, and disposing the human love to true spiritual experiences. So that man and woman sense in

themselves a new craving to become spiritual in their most intimate relationships as husband and wife, to become new creatures seeking a fuller and more
perfect union with God.

Every human being has the favor of God's love operating in him. The mystery of personal salvation is not for us to explore but, like Christ, to be faithful
to what the Father's love working in us exacts from us. Being faithful, then, to
God's grace in fulfilling our daily duties to the best of our abilities assures us of
God's blessing in all our efforts. And to the extent God wants, and in the manner he wants it, we will be able to help others on their way to salvation. All this
is developed in an atmosphere of love—a love that never stops challenging us
but is always giving us the peace Christ promised to all who show their love for
him by keeping his word and living according to it.

Father of us all, from you alone we expect all that is necessary to help us
reach our final destination, our union with thee for all eternity. Do not forsake us when we err or sin, but have pity on us whenever we show ourselves
unfaithful. In Christ Our Lord. Amen.

28

The Eucharist

Biblical reflections by Fr. Ciszek

His Great Act of Love for Mankind (Matthew 14:13–21; February 28, 1964)
Christ showed how tender was his heart toward the multitude in the multiplication of the loaves. He pitied them and did not want them to leave hungry; their journey home would be long.

At that time, they did not understand the significance of the miracle Christ performed. The multiplication of loaves showed Christ's supernatural power. He satisfied the hunger of a great multitude by multiplying the loaves they brought to him.

Christ used that same power to multiply the bread of life, his most precious Body, which he gives to the faithful for nourishment, to satisfy their spiritual hunger. Christ felt pity for us when he was about to leave this earth. He showed that pity by continuing to remain with us sacramentally in the Holy Eucharist, always giving us what we spiritually need, providing that we come to him. This miracle is his great act of love for mankind; it is for us a source of constant joy and strength.

Visit the Lord in the Blessed Sacrament as frequently as possible. Enter into an intimate friendship with him, and you will be happy and blessed.

Humility in the New Covenant (March 1978)
These last days of Lent, including Easter Sunday, had a strong influence on me.

On Holy Thursday, Our Lord instituted the Holy Eucharist. This happened during the Last Supper. After observing the ritual ceremonies of the Passover feast, Our Lord went on to prepare the apostles and disciples for the new Covenant, which he was about to introduce and give to the world. He prepared them by washing their feet, showing them by this act that they should have the humility to be the servants of one another.

To serve and not to be served is what Our Lord taught his disciples and all his followers. Why? Because sin had corrupted human nature so deeply that man became self-centered and domineering and unconcerned about the good of others. The sin of pride entered man and made him feel as if he were self-sufficient and independent. To counterbalance man's proud and arrogant attitude, Christ taught his disciples the virtue and value of humility, making it something basic and essential in the new Covenant he was entering into with mankind. He washed their feet and commanded them to wash one another's feet—to serve and not to be served; for only in humility can true love flourish. Christ knew this better than anyone else; to have part with him, man had to dispose himself, through humility, to the greatest acts of love, sacrifice, and service. Mankind lacked this basic virtue of humility and was now being taught to acquire it in the very same manner Christ taught us to acquire it, by washing the feet of others; in other words, by performing humble acts of service—menial acts, which people everywhere and at all times resented.

Only after Christ performed this great act of humility did he then proceed to show his disciples, and all mankind, how great is his love for all of us. He took the bread, blessed and broke it, and said, "Take and eat, this is my Body." Likewise, he took the cup of wine, blessed it, and said, "Take and drink of it all of you, this is the Blood of the New Testament, shed for you and for all, for the remission of sin. Do this in memory of me."

Did the disciples understand what they were doing, eating the flesh of Our Lord and drinking the cup of his blood? They did not understand. However, all that Christ was requiring of them was that they believe in him and accept what he was doing for them as something very important. Christ performed an act of supreme love for man at the Last Supper, instituting the Holy Eucharist. By doing this, he gave us an example whereby we must do good to others no matter how they may react, or whether or not they appreciate the good done to them. One must have a deep sense of discernment—deep faith and courage—to be a true witness to Christ in such cases; all of which is possible, but only with the help of God's grace and power.

How far is man from practicing his faith publicly, from fearing nothing except to sin and fail in professing his faith! Our weakness, cowardice, and helplessness prevent us from being like Christ in his love. We must constantly pray for help in all humility, and never be too frustrated when we fail to show love for others, in spite of our best efforts. That's what we are, all by ourselves: living examples of sinful creatures, not capable of spiritual progress, except with the help of God's grace and his favor. In this way we work out our salvation, and the salvation of others, through continuous, humble prayers and sacrifice.

Lord, how wonderful you are in the Sacrament of love and in the power of your Cross! Praise be to you forever.

A Mystery Never Fully to Be Understood (Luke 22:19–20; September 23, 1979)

In the course of the Passover supper, Christ instituted the new Passover supper, the Holy Eucharist; as he did, the observance of the old Passover ended.

Christ and the apostles were very deeply moved by their participation in the old ritual meal. Their deepest religious feelings were so intensified and ennobled by the ceremony that these simple men were now ready to receive the most precious gift of God's love in his Son; Christ then confirmed forever his infinite love for us sinners by instituting the Holy Eucharist.

What an intense and profound spiritual experience was manifested at the Last Supper! The apostles were moved very deeply by the power of the old Law, which touched them through and through as they ate the Passover meal. Now, the power of the God of love, residing in the Son, touched these same simple apostles in an infinite way. At the Last Supper they experienced for the first time the full significance of being with Christ, when he, fulfilling a mystical desire, transformed the old into the new by giving us his own Body and Blood as nourishment. Who will ever understand fully this mystery of God's greatest love shown to us sinners in the institution of the Holy Eucharist? Only faith can satisfy the cravings of the soul once it has experienced this august mystery of love.

The Eucharist makes possible, in the measure God permits, an understanding and a spiritual perception of the wonder of God's wisdom in revealing his love for us through his Son under the species of bread and wine. It has the power to convert, purify, elevate, and make us truly spiritual persons, to become God's children in exactly the way he planned it from all eternity.

Praise, glory, and adoration to the mighty God, who rules and governs all that exists. To him we bow down in reverence and exalt him forever. Amen.

29

Called and Chosen in the Church

Biblical reflections by Fr. Ciszek

Take the Risk, and Persevere (Luke 5:1–11; March 1978)
In the beginning of his public ministry, Jesus was alone. Crowds followed him because he taught with authority. Soon afterwards, he found some simple fishermen whom he intended to call to follow him.

First, he asked to use one of their boats; then, moving away from the shore a little, he could speak freely to the crowds, which gathered to hear him speak. When finished, he told Simon to cast out his nets for a catch. But Peter, reluctant to do so, told Jesus they had fished all night and caught nothing. However, Peter obeyed and was rewarded with a huge catch of fish. Peter understood at once who Jesus was after the miraculous catch of fish. "I'm a sinner," Peter said, "Leave me, Lord." James and John were present at the scene. Jesus then said to Simon Peter, "Do not be afraid, from now on it is men you will catch." They left everything and followed Jesus.

Our Lord's personality and the miraculous catch of fish opened Peter's eyes. He understood at once who our Lord was and, at the same time, sensed his own sinfulness. It was this interior experience that caused Peter, James, and John to leave everything and follow Christ.

The first impact of a calling disposes the one touched by God to obey the voice of his conscience without questioning it. One thing matters at the moment when a calling comes—that is, to leave everything and to follow: in religion, to embrace the religious life; in marriage, to embrace the state of matrimony; in other callings, to follow what attracts the soul. The motivation may be mere material or natural advantage, or it may be spiritual and ideal. Whatever the motivation, the person, moved by any of the reasons mentioned, forsakes everything and follows the objective to which he is attracted and tries to find fulfillment in it.

Who can foresee or foretell what each calling has in store? Nobody! Every calling has in it the element of risk. Of course, the risk is always viewed as worthwhile, but it does not exclude the possibility of failure or painful change.

191

The principal factor in every calling is the deliberate effort to persevere—to be willing to meet every situation as it comes, to the best of one's abilities, and not to be overcome by the difficulties encountered. Rather, to direct everything in such a way that it helps strengthen one's resolve to persevere, and it excludes the possibility of being discouraged or inclined to give up the struggle found in every calling. To acquire such an attitude, the spirit, mind, and body must work together. Prayer, faith, reflective reason, and physical effort are indispensable. The grace of God we have been given, if followed, will express in us all these tendencies in their truest light. We need God's grace to become genuine human beings and the children of God.

Unusual Powers (Mark 6:7–13; Autumn 1978)
Jesus chose the twelve apostles, gave them authority over unclean spirits, and sent them to preach repentance. He told them to take nothing with them. They were to live on what people gave them. Whoever received them would receive a blessing, if they were worthy. Those who did not receive them would be found responsible. The apostles cast out many devils, anointed many sick with oil and cured them.

When one is called to any state of life, he is given the grace to live that life as it should be lived. The apostles received special spiritual powers to help people in their spiritual needs. The married receive the graces needed to live their family life, bring up their children in the fear of God, and sanctify their own souls as parents. The apostles, the religious—priests and sisters—the faithful are given the grace to know the mysteries of the kingdom and to order their lives according to them. It is most important, however, to stress the truth that the apostles were participants in God's power. Using it properly, in faithful prayer and humility, they would lead souls to God through repentance and acceptance of the word of God. The power they were given over the evil spirits showed how much the evil one had possession of the people living without God.

In deep humility, every priest who is a faithful follower of Christ should be conscious of this power given him over the evil spirits, and, at least in prayer and as the opportunity arises, he should use this power to help people overcome by the evil one, who is keeping them in sin.

Lord! How unworthy is man, called to such high dignity as the priesthood, in which state he receives unusual powers over evil spirits and over sin—to forgive and absolve. Lord! Don't hold my sins and unfaithfulness against me.

Women Missionaries (Luke 8:1–3; Spring 1978)
Jesus permitted women to accompany him in his mission. They provided for Jesus and his apostles out of their own resources.

These women must have assisted in other ways also, in the work for souls. They took care of the sick, the aged, and the needy. They organized prayer groups to teach the simple and ignorant the truths of the good news. They visited the lonely, received sinners, the abandoned, the hungry, and the desolate. They were living examples of the truths Jesus taught them and witnesses of their faith in Christ and his teaching in their own lives and, in so far as possible, in the lives of others—making Christ known to the families, to the public living in towns, villages, and far off in the country. They helped the apostles be messengers of the good news to all people—good, bad, or sinners—in the places accessible to them at that time. They preached by their example what the love of God meant; also, love of neighbor and of enemy. All this needed time, energy, sacrifice, and the willingness to be Christ's disciple in spreading the good news. These women were the first missionaries who were converted to God, called to follow Christ and dedicate themselves to serve God in the salvation of mankind. So they were inspired by Christ and his teaching and responded to the interior call in all generosity.

The small group of women accompanying Jesus in this mission were the forerunners of religious orders, organizations and congregations formed throughout the ages until the present day in the Church. So from the time of Christ, women, by associating with Christ, were assigned apostolic work that, by their calling, would help the Church of Christ to promote most effectively the kingdom of God here on earth. They were not chosen to be apostles as the Twelve were, but were chosen as companions to render their service to the Church and to God for the salvation of souls.

Lord, in your wisdom you arrange all things to serve man in his efforts to attain his destiny and to be with you forever. Amen.

Fools of Christ (Matthew 28:1–8; March 12, 1980)

What should the empty tomb mean to us who believe? It should mean all that Christ himself foretold while teaching the truths of the heavenly kingdom to the poor, to his disciples, and to all who were willing to listen; that is, after suffering and dying on the Cross, he would rise from the dead by the power of God.

This is what the women witnessed when early in the morning they went to the tomb to anoint Jesus. In arriving, they found the tomb empty, to their great surprise and bewilderment. But God in his divine plan chose those simple and devoted women to be the first, not only to see the empty tomb but also to receive the message (directly from the angel sitting on the stone rolled away from the entrance of the tomb) that Christ was no more among the dead but had risen from the dead as he foretold on several occasions before going to his passion. The angel's message confirmed what the Scriptures foretold, and the Scriptures were fulfilled on Easter morning when Christ had indeed risen.

To one who has the gift of faith, the resurrection is an indisputable fact. The person of faith feels no difficulty in accepting and believing in the resurrection. In the gift of faith, the understanding of the Scriptures is given together with the understanding of this unique mystery of our Christian faith. The simple childlike attitude of one who has received the gift of faith gives him or her the ability to discern the truth of God's wisdom reflected in the event of the resurrection and to penetrate ever and ever deeper into the mystery, while being led and inspired by God's power operating in his or her soul. The gift of the Holy Spirit given to the chosen ones is such that it makes them spiritual beings; with the facility of a child they approach the things of God in a direct manner. They do so because that is the nature of the inspiration enabling them to see the mysteries of God as they are, in a personal infused vision, or in a revelation communicated to them by the power and pleasure of God.

Such chosen people are thus favored to become witnesses and objects of God's love and glory. For the gift they received is spiritual in nature, bereft of all human insights and abilities. Because the spiritual gift, received in grace, is above the natural, the human, and the acquired, operating independently of these, and only when inspired by the Holy Spirit. For no person having faith is in command of the grace operating in his soul. It's all the work of the Holy Spirit. So in deep humility, in deep realization of one's nothingness and unworthiness, one experiences God in his gifts bestowed on him.

In the eyes of the world and in the minds of the intellectuals or worldly minded people, the one experiencing God in simple and humble faith, in moments when affected by grace, while totally surrendered to God's will and power, is considered: queer, deluded, and visionary, not in tune with reality; in contradiction with the findings of science and of the academic experts; a person not worth bothering with and even looked upon as dangerous to society, to progress, and to education. In other words, God's grace in the chosen ones exposes them to unique experiences in the world, such as being looked upon as foolish, not normal, and even as a psychopath because of a seeming lack of intellectual acumen and the absence of certain standards accepted as academic norms of thinking and behavior.

Such are the fools of Christ, the nobodies of this world, who are looked upon with scorn and passed over as simpletons; yet these "rejects" live a full life—simple, humble, silent, and hidden in God, constantly doing good unnoticed, while helping others without discrimination and never tiring in their efforts. They pass their life in this way, abounding in spiritual riches, and they end their earthly journey peacefully, without glamour, obscure as becomes the insignificant person, the mere nothing one appears to be.

30

Our Lady

Biblical reflections by Fr. Ciszek

The Immaculate Conception (December 8, 1978)

Mary had a central role in the recreated world because of Jesus Christ, the Son she bore. Mary, his Mother, chosen by God from all creatures, was involved, as no one else was, in her Son's redemptive work; all that happened according to the Father's divine plan.

The human mind cannot fathom God's wisdom manifested in Christ Jesus and in his Blessed Mother. For in this world, all God wants from us human beings is that we should have faith in his power recreating all human nature and all creatures—as the mysteries connected with his divine Son reveal. God's infinite love, power, wisdom, and mercy have been revealed to us in his incarnate divine Son, the greatest of all mysteries. And it was Mary who was chosen as his Mother to bring about the birth of Christ into this world.

She was blessed amongst all women because she was full of grace. That is, already being with God while living in this world and enjoying the heavenly vision of God while experiencing fully at the same time both the earthly and heavenly life.[63] This was given her simply because God willed it so. Becoming the Mother of God's Son, she became also the Mother of all mankind through the fullness of grace operating in her. She became Heaven's choice gift to us, and our boast.

Merely by acknowledging the gifts and graces without number given to her through divine love, we can never exhaust the treasure she possesses, for such is the nature of God's infinite depth permeating Our Lady's whole being. Following step by step, with the Blessed Mother, the continuity of this incomprehensible intimacy and union of God's being, we exhaust our limited powers and can no longer penetrate or follow the thoughts and concepts of this mystery, except by a simple act of faith that leads us to acknowledge what Mary's true place is in God's divine plan.

In practice, this means not seeking the extraordinary in her but "Those who trust in Him shall understand truth" (Wisdom 3:9).

The Annunciation (John 17:1–26; December 29, 1979)

If we look at Mary and observe how she responded to the angel, we will see how perfectly one she was with God. She was always one with God in prayer. For she prayed continuously, not by spending every moment of her life in formal prayer, nor by remaining in seclusion and contemplating the mysteries of God, but by spending time in contemplative prayer and then living and doing all she had to by virtue of the spirit of God's power operating in her and affecting her behavior and actions throughout the day.

The peace of God's presence inspired her at all times, for prayer is a gift received from God by means of which a soul, favored by such gift, is quietly disposed to all communications from God in every situation of life. Such union or oneness with God is primarily the work of God entering into the soul of one gifted with the power of prayer and enabling such a favored person to listen continuously to the promptings of God's Spirit communicating to the soul in the way his divine will chooses.

The soul having the gift of prayer is able to listen to the messages received from the Holy Spirit habitually and receive those messages and promptings and movements in faith and respond to them in simple acquiescence or doing what one can and how one knows. In this atmosphere and readiness of humble obedience, a oneness of deepest intimacy is elaborated between God and the soul, ever increasing in holiness, in an unending surrender to the mysterious influence of God's power working in the soul for its greater good.

Being one with God, as Mary was, every soul blessed by God tends to extend that oneness with God to every fellow human being in the spirit of charity and love. For oneness with God is the result of God's love working in the soul and converting it into a new being of love, after the manner of God's infinite love. As God unceasingly affects the universe and all creation by his infinite love (while sustaining it and providing it with all that is necessary, in spite of all the opposition, disobedience, and malice of evil and sin found in every human being), so also, in the measure it is given, the soul is affected by God's love, inevitably tending to do good to others, in spite of all the difficulties and hardships that might oppose such God-inspired love in the human soul. Such outpouring of love by the soul for others in sacrifice, obedience, and total dedication to God's service, while fulfilling the Father's will, is a manifestation of God's love uniting all creation—especially all human beings—with his divine nature. So it is, that true and real oneness comes to creation from the Creator in whom unity and oneness are the very traits of his divine being and nature.

How do we acquire this oneness in God and with our neighbor? Only through the source of all being, that is, through God. First, by means of simple prayer. Then, by infused prayer, which is an added gift from God. In prayer, then, we will dispose ourselves to be made one with God and, slowly, with one another in this world.

Mary is an excellent example of a person involved in humble prayer. Through faith, Mary became the favored one in God's sight to be chosen to be the Mother of the Word Incarnate. When the mystery of the incarnation was revealed to Mary by the Angel Gabriel, she immediately responded to God's will in humble obedience because God's power working in her was unobstructed. Only in this way could Mary prove herself faithful, worthy, totally disposed to accept and fulfill the demands of the graced calling she received to be the Mother of God.

In prayer we learn the eternal truth of God's infinite love. As we become affected by the infinite love of God, we are prompted in turn to affect others with God's love in us. Only in this way are charity and love of neighbor developed and promoted. For God's love reaches beyond the personal. It tends to reach all else with its power of goodness and thus enrich all creation with its bounty. We observe this in the world around us. We find this especially to be true in the human soul and person, where God works wonders so that all inanimate and animate beings could give him praise and glory as his divine nature demands and deserves.

The Visitation (Luke 1:39–56; May 5, 1964)

The Holy Ghost led Mary to visit Elizabeth. Both of them were blessed by God. Elizabeth, hearing Mary's words of salutation, rejoiced. The child leaped in her womb and was sanctified, and she praised Mary for her belief, and Mary praised God.

Here we have an example of the wonderful workings of the Holy Spirit in these two women blessed by God. The Lord chooses the simple heart and does great things through the simple because only such as they are able to cooperate fully with him. They seek not themselves but the Lord who found them worthy of his grace. Here the humility of Our Lady was most significant. She knew perfectly well that God was working in her, and she cooperated with him as completely as possible. She entirely forgot about herself and sang his praises, pondering in her heart the great things the Lord did for her. This was a meditation on her life, because throughout her entire life, she sensed the fullness of grace in her soul. God was her full possession. She did not seek friends in the world because she enjoyed continuously the friendship of God himself. That was her life, to pour out all her love upon her divine Son. In her great love, she forgot the world with all its riches and attractions, living as every mortal but not feeling herself of this world. She was all holy, full of grace as God wanted her to be—the only creature existing so privileged by God. Her mission as the Mother of God and our Mother is to render us her help.

We should profit from her help and love for us. She will lead us to her son and protect us from all that is evil and thus make us ever happier by uniting us with Jesus and teaching us how to be like her Son in everything, especially in soul and mind, abounding in the powerful virtues, which he had in abundance.

The Magnificat (Luke 1:46–56; December 1977)

Mary realized the significance of her divine Motherhood. She was full of grace. She was affected through and through by the mystery of the incarnation. Because of this, her very being felt God's greatness and her own nothingness, being a servant and a nothing, yet chosen to give birth to the son of God. What a privilege! She sensed her unique calling as God's greatest gift to her in the most profound way and fully rejoiced in God, as no human being ever had or will.

She was a simple, humble girl. Mary considered herself a lowly person; in no way did she ever do, think, or desire anything whereby she would be putting herself before God. She simply expressed what she really was when, full of the Spirit of God and this lowliness, she won favor for herself in God's sight, for God had chosen her as the object of his special love. She reached out to the divine love unreservedly, as a child does to her parents. In those highly favored moments, Mary responded to God's grace perfectly. That is why every generation, to the very last generation, will praise and bless Mary. They see in her an ideal for all people to follow. She always had armies of devout followers whom nobody could take away from her.

Even in our own times (when devotion towards Mary cooled considerably and many sought a higher form of devotion centered on Christ) devotion to Mary, though less emphasized, became more significant because it flowed out of the mystery of Christ's act of redemption and salvation. Many who neglected devotion to Mary saw their mistake and slowly resumed it, as they realized how much their devotion to Our Lord lacked that deep spiritual unction and force when it no longer had the support of a devotion to Our Lady. The simple logic is not the fruit of human reason or understanding but of God's eternal will having arranged that close unity of Our Lord's person and the person of Our Lady, making them almost inseparable, for she was honored and chosen by God to be the Mother of the Incarnate Word by the eternal decree of the Blessed Trinity.

And yet the human mind knowingly or unknowingly strives to elaborate something that it has not the power to accomplish. This is what we call pride: the curse of sin weighing heavily on all human beings. Over and over, people commit the same mistakes, errors, sins, and stupidities because human nature has almost uncontrollable tendencies to independence, self-assertion, and dominance. Is this ignorance, freedom, creativity, or self-sufficiency within human nature, or is it a simple illusion with a strong admixture of the pride of life distorting the inborn qualities of human nature to revere, praise, and serve God, which can never be destroyed in man? That is why Mary in her humility shines as a beacon on the narrow way that leads to Christ. Sin distorts the true image of God in man, hurting the human race seriously, making it foolishly and stupidly seek its own destruction in ignorance rather than the truth of God leading to eternal happiness.

How willingly men and women, young and old, hold on tenaciously to their own false gods with words and deeds of conviction rather than to the true God, whom they have rejected and forsaken for that corruption in human nature called sin, independence, and pride. In such followers of Christ and believers in God something is basically and essentially wrong. Why judge and spend time on such people in discussion and persuasion, while the kingdom of God must be spread and made known for people to accept and enter?

Father, in humility we turn to you, as Mary did in the Magnificat; we pledge our faithfulness to your Holy Will by humbly following thy Son as Mary did in the Church he established and promised to protect to the end. Amen.

His Mother, Our Mother (John 19:25–27; February 17, 1980)
The scene under the Cross of Jesus, with his Mother and John the evangelist standing there, has deep meaning for the Church and for all its members. Christ, seeing his Mother standing under the Cross, spoke to her, in the presence of John, Salome, the other Mary, Mary of Magdala, and the few other women who were with him till his death. He spoke, with authority, words honoring and expressing the role of Mary in the Church he instituted when he said, "Woman, this is your son," and to John, "This is your mother."

To the members of the true Church, Mary has been given as their spiritual mother while at the same time becoming the Mother of the Church that Christ instituted, for this was the wish and will of Jesus before his death. The significance of Mary, as the Mother of the Church and the mother of each member of the Church, was something taught to us by Christ, who had the utmost concern for those he had chosen to be his followers. He was the head of the Church. The Father had given him a mother when he assumed a body like ours. The great love Jesus had for his Mother prompted him before leaving this world to recommend her to our love also. As he loved her, so, also does he want us to love her in the same manner. We do not deserve a gift as unique as Mary is for us. But having loved us so much (even unto death), Jesus wanted to pour out his love for us, in that last moment of his life on the Cross, by giving us his Mother, just as he gave himself to us in that act of supreme love confirmed by his death on the Cross.

If we contemplate the mystery of the Cross, we will appreciate how important a role Mary played in the act of redemption. Jesus brought us to this awareness when he spoke to her, "Woman, this is your son," and to John, "This is your mother." In the order of nature, Jesus had a mother, just as we do. What Mary was to Jesus, Jesus wanted her to be to all of us who believe in him: a mother in the spiritual order. For she had been chosen by God to be not only a natural mother, as happened in the incarnation, but also to be a spiritual mother by virtue of the merits of her Son's redemptive death on the Cross. Through this very redemptive act salvation is attained, but, as has been revealed to us, Mary, as spiritual Mother of the Church and mother of all mankind called to salvation, becomes mysteriously involved in the salvation of every individual belonging to the true Church.

Loving Christ, then, we must love Mary, because that is the nature of the gift of salvation revealed to us in the grace of the Cross. It's the power of God and his wisdom working for our greater good and eternal salvation through Jesus and Mary. We acknowledge Mary as our mother because Jesus himself revealed this to us when, addressing his mother standing under the Cross, he said, "Woman, this is your son; son, this is your mother."

Eternal thanks to the Father, Son, and Holy Spirit for the unprecedented gift we have received in Mary as Jesus revealed that gift, suspended from the Cross, addressing his Mother.

Part Six

THE LEGACY

31

Fr. Ciszek's Final Words

In February 1984, several young Sisters of the Holy Annunciation Monastery in Sugarloaf, Pennsylvania, made a retreat directed by Father Ciszek at the John XXIII Center, followed by a day of recollection on Easter Wednesday, April 25. Recalling their experience, what most frequently came to their minds was his way of dealing with interruptions from doorbells and phone calls.[64] Father never disregarded anyone out of impatience or annoyance, no matter how busy he was. When the interruptions were numerous, he would laughingly remark that in Russia and in the United States he was like an old milk cow and everyone wants a full bucket, and he gave that full bucket. He did always keep the phone within reach and answered immediately, because he felt that those who were appealing to him in an emergency needed his help more than anything else that was going on at the moment. He called those people the "intensive care ward." "Christ was waiting for him in that person, and Father did not want to ever keep Christ waiting," explained Sister Mary of Jesus. He once said to Antoinette Rienzi, who first met him in 1968 and continued to see him as her spiritual director, that no matter what you are doing, even when you are tired, when a person comes to you or calls, God wants this person there at that moment, for you to respond to them. He himself was the first to put that advice into practice. Any person who came by or called enjoyed his full attention at that moment. Sister Andreja Vladia would recall later,

> Father did not ask me to leave but simply redirected his full concentration from me to the one whose difficulty was extreme that moment. When the suffering person had been helped, Father's attention returned to our conversation, and we took up where we had left off without any loss of understanding about the matter we had been addressing.

An example of such a person in need was given by one of Walter Ciszek's nephews, Joseph Barinas. One Christmas Eve in the mid-1970s, one of his wife's relatives was in deep distress; her husband had thrown her out, and the shock caused a severe attack of paranoia. They had taken her into their home, but after a few days the paranoia returned and they did not know what to do with her. Called for advice, Father Walter asked some questions and then wanted to talk to her personally. Joseph told of how they spoke for well over an hour and how then she was admitted to the hospital, from which she was released the next day. She has not had a problem since.[65]

Another religious, Sister Rosemary Stets, O.S.F., who met Father Ciszek for the first time shortly after his return from Russia, noted, "His voice was entirely too soft for a man—as if someone had altered his ability to speak. He had a great laugh, and when he smiled, he lit up the room."[66] In the ensuing years, during her early twenties she met with him several times to ask his advice; she also had written to him once or twice a year. In 1973, however, he became her spiritual director, and their contact intensified. She said,

> It seems to me that there was no end to the people who flowed into Father Walter's life, in a constant, steady flow. I am reminded of Christ in Mark's Gospel, always being hemmed in by crowds. In Father's case, the crowds were smaller but always present. There was never a time that I visited him that he did not have visitors. Somebody was always knocking on his door, or the phone never failed to ring. Sometimes, I know, he was tired, but he never let anyone see it. You had to know him well, the condition of his health, to realize that he had to be fatigued.
>
> I only remember one time that he let the phone ring or did not answer. He said he knew who was calling: an old, slightly confused man who kept talking in circles and never was coherent. He would call in the middle of the night and keep Father on the line for an hour. Sometimes he made sense, but most times he just argued about ridiculous things and failed to grasp a single point. Father never hung up on him or put him off. He responded as if the man were perfectly lucid and had every right to be treated with seriousness and dignity. This particular time we had just begun my retreat, and it was a little late in the evening, and Father knew it was prudent not to answer the phone.

This may have been the same man with whom Father Ciszek had been working for thirteen years, a man who suffered in many ways—spiritually, psychologically, and otherwise. Father admitted that this was very trying for him, but he would not give him up; he just kept on trying. In fact, in the autumn of 1984 he got permission from the bishop to exorcise the person, and apparently that helped the man.[67] The day Father decided not to answer the phone, Sister Rosemary was struck by his discretion in correcting or dealing with the difficult people in life. He was so accommodating that one hardly noticed that he could be upset, or grow angry, or annoyed, just as any man. She concluded that the human side of him was very strong but was under control, and that was what made him different.

About her own phone calls to him, she remembered that it was usually Father Ciszek who did the talking. "It was always easier for me to talk to him in person, but on the phone I just liked to listen." She explained how he would tell her about a trip he had made or how many visitors he was having, and then how he would pick up on a theme, such as faith or suffering, and then begin to explain what this meant to him. She spoke of how he used examples or sometimes events from his own life and of how it was a kind of rambling affair; she felt that he was always seeking to refine the idea, to express it better, more accurately. Later she added,

> Often his best explanations eluded my grasp, but that didn't matter, to him or to me. He knew what he wanted to say, and I understood the basic idea, even if I didn't quite follow the exact meaning. He would laugh at these efforts and make jokes about his own deficiencies. And I would laugh with him, sharing a joy that went beyond humor. It was a peace and fulfilled contentment just to be in touch with him and know he was, at that moment, sharing my life.

The joy of just being with Father Ciszek led several people, willingly and generously, to dedicate their time to helping him with various tasks.[68] In his later years, he was suffering much from emphysema and arthritic pain as the result of the cold weather and hard labor in Russia. It took him an hour to put on his socks and shoes, two hours—in his final days—to take a shower, and sometimes forty-five minutes simply to get from his table to his bed; nevertheless, he maintained a joyful disposition. "I never heard him complain, nor did the physical suffering keep him from doing God's work," Antoinette Rienzi said. Periodically, she—a registered nurse in her thirties—and several other ladies would spend a day at the Center tidying up his apartment, where retreatants were coming and going all the time. "We took pleasure in doing things for him; he was so grateful and appreciative."

Among these ladies were Sister Santa Priolo, M.P.F., and Mary Zentkovich, a former Benedictine nun, both in their fifties, and Lucille Cutrone, who was still in her thirties and would enter religious life sometime later, in 1988; they had all met him in the period between 1980–1981. He was spiritual director to Sister Santa ("At times I would contradict him and he would say in response, 'Santa, you don't know what you're talking about.'") and to Lucille, but when Mary asked him to become her director as well, he declined. "I felt Father Ciszek was my mission," she said later, explaining how she took care of the chapel at John XXIII Center, went shopping for him ("He would tell me what he'd like to eat"), took care of his clothing, and helped him do his mail, especially at Christmas, because by that time he could no longer write very well. Mary Zentkovich told of one occasion when Father sent her to get stamps, [and the Post Office worker] didn't take the money for some reason. She mentioned this to Father Walter, and he sent her right back to give the money to them. Lucille Cutrone, too, assisted Father with his correspondence and any other needs he might have. She said,

> I witnessed the great love he would have for the people who visited the Center, whether it was a bishop or the elderly lady who lived up the block. All were received with joy and reverence, as if they were the most special persons in the world. [. . .] Even in times of illness, when he was resting, he would get up immediately to receive visitors who came at a moment's notice. He did so with graciousness and joy and heroic patience.

The Christmas greetings he sent came close to one thousand cards. Father would begin writing them around Thanksgiving or even late October, together with a network of helpers who would work for three or four hours at a time, writing cards and then addressing envelopes. As years went by, he would just add his signature; he had a message written for his "secretaries," and they would just copy it. "It was the most organized process I ever saw," Antoinette Rienzi said. And Lucille Cutrone remembered,

> The last time I was with him, we were writing his Christmas cards, and I was crying the whole time because I thought the Lord would be taking him any day. I asked him, "Father, when you die and you have a tombstone, what do you think should be written there?" And with the most radiant, beaming face, he said, "Just write, 'I am so glad that God is.'" He really knew what it was all about. He lived this truth; he radiated this truth.

In fact, as early as 1983, he had told those who were helping him with the Christmas cards that he would not be there in 1984 to send out the cards. "I was in all honesty amazed that he was with us until December 8, 1984," Mary Zentkovich later said.

In 1984, the weekend of December 8, the feast of the Immaculate Conception, would have been the time Walter Ciszek and his "secretaries" were to finish the Christmas mail. Antoinette Rienzi knew he was not feeling well so she called him on the evening of December 7 to find out how he was doing. She could hear in his voice how exhausted he was. He told her, "Toni, I have been in the emergency room all day, and I am so tired. I am going to say my prayers and then I'm going to rest." Mary Zentkovich, too, having seen Father exhausted, called him later that evening. He told her also that he was very tired and that she had better not come to Mass the next morning but should go rather to the nearby parish church. A bit worried, she phoned his superior, Fr. John Long, and asked him to go downstairs and look in on Father. "Mary, he's going to be all right," Father Long said. "Don't worry, he's going to be OK, I was just there."

One of the last persons to speak with Father Ciszek was Mother Marija of the Holy Annunciation Monastery, which he had helped found.[69]

I spoke with him on the evening of December 7 at about seven-thirty. A mutual friend had told me he was ill. It took him so long to answer the phone that I wondered why I waited. But this night, although he was literally at death's door, after telling me of his inability to move, he perked up and gave, as usual, his all and more. He said to me, "Tell the kids (that's what he called the young Sisters) if they want to have peace at the end of their life, strive always and only to do God's will. It may be your lousy best, but try to do God's will." Then he added, "I have that peace tonight. If people only realized the blessing that confession is."[70] His advice to me was: "Stay with God—keep away from evil. Leave it to God."

I then mentioned to Father that I wanted him to come to a "clothing" of one of the Sisters. He seemed very pained and said, "You know I would if I could." I believe he knew he was going to God. The Jesuits were planning on his going to Wernersville where the Jesuit infirmary was located. Next morning at about seven I phoned Father John Levko [a member of Father Ciszek's community] to tell him that they had better hurry up if they wanted Father Ciszek in Wernersville, for he seemed to be walking off to God—not because of illness but the *joy* in his heart, soul, and voice as I perceived it in this last conversation. What I did not know until ten that morning was that he was already dead. Father Ciszek died in the early hours of December 8, some seven hours after our conversation.

That Sister's profession took place on January 6, a month after Father Ciszek died. She received a letter from Father Ciszek on that very day; it was a Christmas card. He had written it probably in late November. It had first gone to the wrong address and then finally arrived at the monastery on that very special day of her profession.

On the morning of December 8, a Saturday, Mary Zentkovich, while going to Mass, looked across the street and saw an ambulance parked in front of the Center. She thought, "I'm so glad they are taking Father to the hospital, they'll be good to him." When she rushed over and went into his apartment, Leo the janitor and Father Long were standing in front of Father Ciszek, who was sitting in his chair with his pajamas on; he had been getting ready to go to bed. She recalled later, "Leo looked at Father Long, and Father Long just indicated it was OK, and so then Leo stepped aside and told me that Father had died. The tears came. Then I knew they didn't take him to the hospital." She went on to tell of how the janitor, who had always been a great help to Father, had gone over early that morning to help him out and had found him dead, and of how the day before, Father Ciszek, with some kind of premonition, had told Father Long to thank everybody who had helped him. When Antoinette Rienzi later that morning tried to call him, one of his fellow Jesuits answered the phone and told her, "Father passed away saying his prayers, with rosary in hand."

Sister Santa Priolo arrived a bit later by car from Brooklyn, ready to help Father finish the Christmas mail. Recalling the moment, she said,

The expression on the face of the maintenance man alerted me. I ran up the steps to Father Walter's apartment. The door was slightly open. I walked in, and there he was, sitting in his rocker, wearing his blue terry-cloth robe, with a brown comforter around his shoulders. He looked ever so peaceful. His head rested against the back of his chair. Around his neck was his worn-out scapular, reminding me of his special love and devotion to Our Lady. He was asleep, the eternal sleep of union with God! As his body was taken away, I went to his bedroom and noticed that his bed had not been slept in, but on top of the spread were his trousers and undergarments. He probably had been having difficulty breathing, so he slept that night in his rocker.

Later that day, after Father's body had been removed, she sat in the chair in which he had done most of his apostolate of praying, writing, and spiritual direction, and she opened his little book where he jotted down his inspirations. "There," she said, "in his clear, steady handwriting were words that summarize his whole spirit, words that showed he was ready to leave this life for the eternal one: 'With simplicity of heart, I have offered all to you my God.'"

Many people, perhaps hundreds of them, received a posthumous Christmas card from Walter Ciszek that year. One of them was Fr. Dominic Maruca, S.J., who had remained in contact with him ever since their meeting in the novitiate at Wernersville in October 1963. They had corresponded and he had visited with Walter at Fordham when he went there for his ministry. They usually talked about the ministry he was doing with religious women because Father Maruca was engaged in doing that same kind of work—giving retreats and spiritual direction. He related the following:

In 1983–1984, I was stationed in Rome; there was a Polish brother in our Gregorian Community who had great influence in Rome. I said to him, "I would love to get a beautiful papal blessing for Father Ciszek for his eightieth birthday." So the brother arranged to get the papal blessing and have a calligrapher compose it in Polish. I airmailed the parchment blessing to Father Ciszek early in October 1984—his birthday was Nov. 4—but I didn't hear anything from him in return. The next thing I heard was that he had died on December 8. I said to myself, "Oh gosh, I guess that blessing never got to him." Then I forgot all about it. But just before Christmas, I got a beautiful card from Father Ciszek. And then I remembered that he had a regular procedure: whenever he received a note in September, October, or November, he would write a Christmas card to that person and thank him for whatever it was—for me, it was that I sent the papal blessing. I got the biggest charge out of it, that after he died, I got this beautiful thank-you note from him! I've loaned it out several times to people who have wanted to invoke his intercession, as something that would be a second-class relic, as it was his handwriting and his message.[71]

Another Jesuit who received a thank-you note from Walter Ciszek, on January 4, 1985, was the Superior General of the Society of Jesus, Fr. Peter-Hans Kolvenbach, S.J., who had written him a letter of congratulations on his eightieth birthday.[72] The card read,

Dear Rev. Fr. General P. Kolvenbach, P.C.

It was my great pleasure to receive a personal letter from you on my 80th anniversary. It made me happy and grateful to God for all his blessings, and mindful of his never-ending concern for our spiritual and human well-being. All I can say in all sincerity is that to have persevered thus far in my calling never for once questioning it was and is a sign of his special favour so overwhelming and convincing. There is nothing more that I could wish in life than to be convinced of God's love for me and my love for him as given me in the grace of my calling and in all that happened to me thus far and will happen to the very end. Such is the meaning of the prayer of St. Ignatius, "Take and receive . . ." and its power.

Humbly and gratefully in the Lord,

Fr. Walter J. Ciszek S.J.[73]

The full text of the Ignatian prayer that Father Ciszek had cited is

Take, Lord, and receive all my liberty,
My memory, my understanding, and my entire will,
All I have and call my own.
You have given all to me. To you, Lord, I return it.
Everything is yours; do with it what you will.
Give me only your love and your grace, that is enough for me.

That prayer is the closing prayer of the *Spiritual Exercises* of St. Ignatius, part of the so-called "contemplation to attain love." Formal as this prayer may seem, Walter Ciszek took it very seriously, as may be seen from the following story, told by Maureen O'Brien. In 1970, when she was a young Carmelite Sister, Father Ciszek had become her spiritual director; in the ensuing years he became her friend as well, and her mentor in the spiritual direction she was doing with laity and clergy. She visited him at the John XXIII Center yearly and made several eight-day retreats there. She recalled the mutually directed retreat they made together at the Spirituality Center at Wernersville in October 1973:

We had been doing reflections with scriptural passages developed by the rector from the *Spiritual Exercises*. Individually, we spent five hours a day in prayer and reading our breviaries as well. Father celebrated Mass at the St. Denis Chapel. On the second to last day, I suggested we say the *Suscipe* prayer at the Offertory of the last Mass: "Take, Lord and receive. . . ." Father immediately said, "You can, but I can't." I sensed something but did not know what, nor did I ask him to explain. The next day during Mass, as I began to say the prayer, he stepped over and said the prayer with me. After the retreat, he shared with me that it was the first time he had said that prayer in forty-three years! After saying that prayer on a long retreat as a novice, he had never again prayed it until that October morning in 1973, ten years after his return from Russia. He explained, "God took me at my word the first time, and I could just not risk praying it again until today. Up until today I believed in God, I felt His love for me, but I never *felt* I loved God!" I was astounded by this revelation. He lived on sheer faith. In the conclusion of this retreat, the grace was felt deeply.[74]

The life of Walter Ciszek, for the readers of his two books, ends in 1963 with his return from Russia. So it is that they may well think he came back fully converted and ready to convert America as well. But there were many times in the last twenty years of his life that Father Ciszek experienced new moments of personal conversion, greater and even deeper, possibly, than that well-known moment of seeming failure in Lubianka prison. His retreat in October 1973 seems to have been just such a moment. These experiences, interwoven with the experiences of the people he guided and upon which he continuously reflected in silent prayer, in spiritual correspondence and conversation, searching for the best words to capture what he learned, eventually led to new versions of the very same *Suscipe* prayer, which he had hesitated to pray and yet managed to live to the full.

On one occasion, talking on the phone with Father Walter, Sister Rosemary Stets began to make some notations on what he was saying, just writing phrases, words, basically the general idea.[75] Later on, reading over the notes, she was deeply affected by the words she had written. Father had been speaking of a prayer he often said, a "formula."[76] He called it a prayer of surrender, and he tried to explain the significance of this prayer in our spiritual life. From the notes that Sister Rosemary copied, she put together a short text, which is really an explanation of the prayer.

Take the negative reaction, sin, disturbance of mind (or the positive feeling), and offer it up to the Will of God for those always who are in dire need of acts of compassion. Make a simple act of surrender, and then go on to what comes next in your life, in the natural order of things.

The moment you feel any disturbance, any aggravation, any break with the Lord or loss of peace, turn immediately to the Spirit of Christ and intensify your prayer. Do not dwell on the negative but allow the negative to be replaced by charity, compassion, and almsgiving. Giving in the spiritual life means giving up to God what these people need for salvation. In this is real healing. The whole secret is never to lose the contact of doing God's will.

In a spirit of sacrifice and suffering, you find your true self in living for others. Erase yourself totally; let him take over. Surrender to God, and he will do everything for you.

She shared this text with many people at different times, and they were all very grateful. "In my case," she said, "from the very first time I began to pray it, I was consciously aware of an enormous interior peace and a very powerful current of grace in my soul." She added, "This prayer, for me, is a remarkable gift. No matter what happens, however difficult the moment, the action, or the person, this prayer clothes me with Christ." And she concluded, "I think that in years to come it will draw me ever more deeply to union with God, in faith and love."

Mary Zentkovich knew the "formula" as well. Father told her that it was a very powerful prayer he was inspired to say amid his many trials and fears. Because it helped him, he taught it to many who came to him for retreats and spiritual guidance.[77] Sister Santa Priolo, M.P.F., quoted the formula thus:

In any negative situation turn to God. Offer whatever is negative for those in dire need. Offer the negative in the spirit of Christ, in charity and love, in compassion—as an almsgiving. Then do whatever follows in the order of things, without the least attention to the negative.

"To offer your will in charity, love, compassion, and almsgiving," Father explained to her, "means to be the servant, as Christ was, always having the good of others in mind, not your own good, as suggested." According to him, almsgiving signifies offering God our limitations, insufficiencies, etc., because we have nothing positive of our own to give him. Those who are servants of God as Christ was, will win God's favor, he said, as is clear from the words of God the Father at the baptism of Christ: "This is my beloved Son, on whom my favor rests." The example of almsgiving that Father Ciszek gave was that of the woman who dropped her last penny into the offering box, "She gave all she had, but received God's favor in return, which filled her with God's power."[78]

The cause of canonization of Fr. Walter J. Ciszek, S.J., was formally opened in 1990. Reading through Father's personal correspondence assembled for the cause, the co-postulator, the Rev. Monsignor Anthony D.

Muntone, came upon two or three letters in which Father Ciszek gave counsel on how to pray in times of discouragement, counsel which was quite similar to that found in Sr. Rosemary's notes. Monsignor Muntone was deeply moved by this plan for prayer because it seemed to be so clearly what Father Walter himself had learned and followed in the very difficult circumstances of his own life.

Monsignor Muntone thought that its elements should be reassembled in the traditional form of a prayer addressed to Jesus. So he set about to do so, and, after he had completed it, he presented it to the members of the board of the Father Walter Ciszek Prayer League, recommending that it be printed and made available by the Prayer League to those who might be interested in it. The board unanimously approved the suggestion, making only one revision, suggested by Fr. Daniel Flaherty, S.J., who had assisted Father Ciszek in the writing of his two books. He observed that, because Father Ciszek had not actually composed the prayer in the form in which it was to be printed, at the conclusion of the prayer, the following words should be added: "Based on the writings of Father Ciszek."

The Prayer of Surrender was printed and made available by the Prayer League. It was widely distributed and has become one of the Prayer League's most frequently requested items. The text of the prayer follows:

Prayer of Surrender

Lord, Jesus Christ, I ask the grace to accept the sadness in my heart as
   your will for me, in this moment. I offer it up, in union with
   your sufferings, for those who are in deepest need of your
   redeeming grace. I surrender myself to your Father's will, and I
   ask you to help me to move on to the next task that you have set
   for me.
Spirit of Christ, help me to enter into a deeper union with you. Lead
   me away from dwelling on the hurt I feel:
   To thoughts of charity for those who need my love,
   To thoughts of compassion for those who need my care, and
   To thoughts of giving to those who need my help.
   As I give myself to you, help me to provide for the salvation of
      those who come to me in need.
   May I find my healing in this giving.
   May I always accept God's will.

May I find my true self by living for others in a spirit of sacrifice
and suffering.

May I die more fully to myself, and live more fully in you.

As I seek to surrender to the Father's will, may I come to trust that
he will do everything for me. Amen.

32

"Father Ciszek Dies—Russian Missionary"

It[79] is one man who brings us all together this evening. It is one man who summed up in a single life the riches of religious dedication, priestly service, indomitable courage in witnessing to the faith, gentle counseling, and fatherly admonition. This one man has gathered us from so many backgrounds, with so many differing problems and concerns, with so many varied memories of the uniqueness of our individual relationships with him.

Though coming from the very rich tradition of Roman Catholic Poland, Fr. Walter Ciszek embraced the Byzantine tradition in order to be of greater service to the Christians of the immense Slav world. Whatever the circumstances of his life, he never lost his love and respect for this tradition. It fed his own personal prayer as well as his spiritual life; it was a significant element of the spiritual formation he gave to other people coming out of different religious traditions; it was a joy for him to preach, to teach, to give retreats to many of your people.

We have heard of some of the more glamorous events of Fr. Walter's life. At times we have laughed at them with him, at times stood back in awe and admiration. But what you have also been telling us by your presence and your words these days is what he achieved in the quiet of individual counseling, of personal sharing, of admonition, rebuke, yes, and even of celebration. Your words put flesh and blood on what we have heard in the Scripture readings today.

God did prove him in the furnace of Lubianka. He tried him in the frozen north of the Soviet Union and the various other places of his exile. Bodily suffering did not end when he flew into Idlewild airport. And further, God also placed on his shoulders the burdens of so many of us.

Fr. Walter wrestled with them; he continued the struggle; he grew weary, but because his hope was full of immortality, he bore them with us and helped us to bear them ourselves. He did this with a sense of urgency which came from the deep, soul-searching experiences he had had during the long period in Russia. How strong that sense of urgency was!

I think I was but the last of a number of superiors who tried to moderate his work, to get him to rest, to cut down on the number of engagements which filled his days and far into his nights. With a simple smile, but with his eyes filled with wisdom of serpents, he would say, "If God has sent these people to me, have I the right to refuse them—and Him?" You had to have pretty strong arguments to counter that.

The God whom Fr. Walter served and preached is a demanding God. He is not to be served with superficiality or half measures. Our task is to search out His ways, wherever they might lead, and to walk them to the very end. He is a God who can be silent at times when we are desperately searching for a word of comfort. He demands more from us at the very moment when we feel we have already reached the end of our endurance. In *He Leadeth Me*, Fr. Walter distilled his understanding of this: "There was but a single vision, God, who was all in all; there was but one will that directed all things, God's will. I had only to see it, to discern it in every circumstance in which I found myself, and let myself be ruled by it. God is in all things, sustains all things, directs all things" (p. 90).

This God loves each and every person He has called into existence. The gifts of this world are so many expressions of His intense love for me, the unique person that I am. Trials, sufferings, even the frustrations of my own attempts to return His love, are part of His love, are part of His loving design for me. If I will only keep that vision before my eyes, I can have confidence and trust, no matter how low I may fall.

While this confidence and trust are intensely personal, they should also enter into the life of communities and of the great community of the Church. Fr. Walter could sympathize with the fears of those who are unsettled by our swiftly changing Church in a changing world; he could speak bluntly about the abuses and excesses taking place. Yet he had a very deep trust that God was guiding His people, His Church, because of His love. Nothing we can do will shatter God's loving design for His Church.

This confidence extended to other areas. Though he never lost his sense of deep-rooted opposition to a materialistic and atheistic philosophy which, when it came to political power, used every instrument at its disposal to root out the faith and traditions of a vast nation, Fr. Walter never lost the serene certitude that the Russia he loved so much would one day bring forth a new reflection of God's love in the renewed faith and intense religious dedication of its people.

He would never admit that the atheist had triumphed, that the Soviet Union was an atheist country. Under the ashes of almost seventy years of struggle and outrage glow the coals of a thousand years of faith, of sacramental life, of intense spiritual striving. For Fr. Walter, in God's loving design, His Holy Spirit which makes us strong, loving, and wise will breathe upon those coals, and they will once more burst into flames.

The dream of the young Jesuit who set sail for Rome to begin his studies at the Russian College had become the certitude of the old man, reflecting on the significance of his experiences there as he serenely faced his passage into eternity.

Fr. Walter was a strong man. His words and his writings bore this out. In fact, I think I am being honest in saying that at times he could be a stubborn man. Many of us could tell our stories about that; we could have many a laugh. I think, however, that this very human trait was a sign of something more fundamental.

So many of us experienced the strength underlying his gentleness and the force of purpose we could detect deep within those smiling eyes. It would take us much too long to uncover and examine the many sources of that strength. May I suggest two which particularly struck me?

The first was his familiarity with, and love of Holy Scripture. To search the Scriptures was his food and his delight. I had a number of personal experiences when he would come to recount some new insight into the Word of God.

Another source of strength was his love for the holy sacrifice of the Eucharist. May I make this citation from him? "How much it meant to us to have the body and blood of Christ as the food of our spiritual lives in this sacrament of love and joy. The experience was very real; you could feel its effect upon your mind and heart, upon your daily life" (*He Leadeth Me*, p. 146).

The Eucharist was at the core of his personal, priestly spirituality. And yet, in both his writings and in his conversation, he never considered the Eucharist as merely an instrument for one's personal communion with God and personal spiritual perfection. He was a priest, commissioned to celebrate the Eucharist for others.

It is this Eucharist we celebrate together tonight in communion with him whom we commend to God. We will continue to remain in communion through the memories of his wisdom, his gentleness, his firmness which at times—we will all admit—became stubbornness. But, above all, we will remain in communion with him through our continued sharing in the sacrament of the body and blood of Christ which is, for all of us, the continued presence among us of a demanding God, a faithful God, a God who loves mankind.

33

His Continuing Story

Upon his arrival back in the United States on October 12, 1963, there was a flurry of media interest in Walter Ciszek and a desire to know more about this priest who "came back from the dead." Not only was the public at large curious about him, but his fellow Jesuits were also very interested in him. Thus, at the insistence of his Jesuit Provincial, and with the help of Father Daniel Flaherty, S.J., the young Jesuit book editor of *America* magazine, Walter Ciszek embarked, almost immediately, upon the task of writing about his many years in the Soviet Union.

The first book was his story, the day-to-day experiences of his twenty-three years in exile, and was entitled *With God in Russia*. When the book was published on December 16, 1964, it achieved immediate popularity, and the author was much sought after to give retreats, spiritual conferences, and lectures. How did Father Ciszek manage to put into words all that he had endured in the Soviet prisons and labor camps? The answer is that, although his mind was crowded with the memory of so many brutal experiences and so much suffering, Father did retain a remarkable ability to recall countless persons and events in great detail. But he still needed the considerable editorial expertise of someone like Father Flaherty to help him give coherence and clarity to his account.

"A short, stocky, pleasant man," is how Daniel Flaherty remembered Walter Ciszek; he recalled, "especially his eyes, and the twinkle in them. He laughed easily and often."[80] He described him as being "not much different than the folks you might find in the shopping malls of Shenandoah today, if it came to that." Father Flaherty and the others who came to know him saw that he was not someone who would dazzle people with his brilliance; to them he wasn't all that articulate or awe-inspiring, he was very much "just an ordinary guy." Even his message was as old as the Bible. But through the sharing of his personal experiences in the prisons and labor camps, first narrated in *With God in Russia*, he made that message very special. How the book came to be is best told by the man who helped Father Ciszek bring it to fruition, Father Flaherty:[81]

Following the media circus at Idlewild, Father Ciszek returned with the *America* magazine editors Fathers Thurston Davis and Eugene Culhane and his sisters to Campion House, home of the *America* staff, where I first met him. That very same afternoon he went to the Jesuit novitiate in Wernersville, Pennsylvania, where he would be close to his family in Shenandoah and away from the media frenzy occasioned by his return from Russia after having been presumed dead. Everyone wanted to know his story, and Father Davis arranged with the New York and Maryland provincials to have *America* magazine tell that story. To this day I have no idea why he asked me, the youngest and newest member of the staff, to write the story that was ultimately published as *With God in Russia*.

America magazine was sent each week to the printer in Philadelphia after an editorial meeting on Thursday morning. The very next week, on Thursday afternoon, I went to Newark airport for an afternoon flight to Wernersville, where I was met at the airport and taken to the novitiate to meet Father Ciszek. "Hi," I said, "I'm here to help you write your book." He looked at me with a blank stare. So I introduced myself and asked if he remembered meeting me at America House. He did not. Nor did he know anything about a book to be written; no one had said anything to him about it. We went for a short stroll about the grounds while I explained that I had been appointed by the editor of *America* to help him write his story because everyone wanted to know about his years in Russia and the labor camps. He was polite but hardly forthcoming. He said very little and answered most questions with one or two word answers. I finally just gave up and flew back to New York on Friday morning. I told Father Davis what had happened and said that if there was a story to be told, it was not going to be told by me; I might just as well have been one of Father Ciszek's NKVD interrogators.[82]

Father Davis telephoned the Maryland Provincial. No doubt the Maryland Provincial then telephoned Walter. At any rate, Father Davis told me to go back to Wernersville the following Thursday and meet with Father Ciszek again. It was an entirely different situation when I arrived at Wernersville that afternoon. Walter was waiting for me at the door with a big smile and an apology and then said, "When do we start?" We started that evening after dinner, in a visitor's parlor of the rambling novitiate building.

We started with Walter telling me about his childhood in Shenandoah, "because," he said, "you'll never understand the things I did unless you understand why I did them." Fair enough. So he talked, and I took notes. Sometimes I asked simple questions to better understand what he was telling me, but mostly I just listened and wrote furiously. We met again Friday morning and Friday afternoon and Friday evening, and, again, on Saturday morning, until I said, "Enough, Walter, I can't do any more this week."

I flew back to New York on Sunday. Of course, we had our usual weekly editorial meeting on Monday morning, and I had my usual editorial jobs to do as book editor during the week. But I was determined to finish the dictation of my Father Ciszek notes before I returned to Wernersville on Thursday afternoon, so I worked well into the night on Monday, Tuesday, and Wednesday dictating the Ciszek story.

That was the schedule we kept, with some exceptions, for the next six months. I flew to Wernersville on Thursday afternoon, met with Walter Thursday evening, Friday, and Saturday, then flew back to New York on Sunday. Once or twice, a flight was cancelled due to weather. Walter and I spent the Thanksgiving holiday weekend with our respective families, and then the Christmas holidays and the New Year holiday. But by Easter of 1964 we had pretty much completed the story that ultimately became *With God in Russia*.

It was not a hard story to write. Walter had a fantastic memory, and my only job was to get it down on paper. I would occasionally ask some specific questions, such as "What did he look like?" or "How long did that take?" or "Why did you do that?" or "What did he/you do next?" and things like that to keep the story on track and the chronology straight. But my main problem was to take good notes and dictate the text while it was still fresh in my mind.

One of the secretaries at America Press typed up every week the discs I dictated, but I didn't bother to read the typescript myself or discuss it with Walter until we had "finished" the story. After the Easter holidays, we began to review the "chapters" serially on my weekly visits to Wernersville. Walter at that time became concerned about using other peoples' real names in the story for fear the NKVD would track down those who were still alive for questioning (or something worse). So I kept a list, for my own purposes of keeping things straight, of the names we assigned to people. Walter had many corrections and additions—the narration triggered associated memories—until the "finished" manuscript was over 1500 pages.

Mr. William Holub, *America*'s business manager, had chosen McGraw-Hill to be the publisher of the Ciszek story, after receiving proposals from a number of publishers. When I told Harold McGraw the size of the manuscript, he gasped and said we'd have to cut it to something more like 500 pages of manuscript. "Here's how you do it," he said, "cut out all (or most) of the stuff about daily life in the Soviet Union—what things cost, shortages, people's attitudes—and just assume most people already know that sort of stuff from the daily papers. Just stick strictly to the Father Ciszek story."

So Walter and I went through the manuscript again with a hatchet. We had a lot of laughs (and a few serious arguments) over what to cut and what to leave, but we finally did get the manuscript down to something close to 500 pages. The original 1500-page manuscript, however, is preserved—as far as I know—in the Maryland Province archives. Finally, as Spring turned to summer in 1964, Walter came with me to America House in New York to meet with Harold McGraw and put the finishing touches on the manuscript. In the following weeks, questions were raised by Dave Scott, the editor assigned to the manuscript by McGraw-Hill, which Walter and I answered, and by July 31, the feast of St. Ignatius Loyola, the book was sent to press.

It was an instant success. Professional reviewers who saw the book in galleys told McGraw-Hill they "couldn't put it down." McGraw-Hill increased the planned press run and began to schedule author interviews—at which Walter, frankly, did not shine, but his genuineness came through to everyone. As part of the publicity for the book, he even appeared on a popular TV show of the time, *What's My Line?*, in which celebrity panelists had to determine, by asking questions of three men all wearing clerical suits and Roman collars and claiming to be Walter J. Ciszek, S.J., which of the three was actually Walter. There was no doubt in any of the panelists' minds after they heard him speak, which one was Wally.

Regarding the message Walter Ciszek wanted to communicate more than anything else, namely, his mission, Father Flaherty related the following:[83]

Father Ciszek's faith in God was absolute; it simply underlay everything he did or said. He didn't talk much about it, but it was the principle out of which he operated, and you gradually inferred it or learned of it through dealing with Walter.

His "converse" with God was easy, familiar, almost scandalously off-hand. He seemed to make up "rules for the spiritual life" as he went along, just the way he made up home remedies for colds or the aches and pains of growing old. We used to laugh about it. I was just a few years out of theology then, and I had "all the answers" with that certitude we all had before Vatican II. "Wally," I would say, "you can't say that; it's heresy." "Ha!" he'd say with a wave of the hand, "the back of my hand to you," as the Irish say, with a good-natured shrug or chuckle. "Well, you fix it up and make it sound right—but that's the way it was, that's what I did" (or said, or whatever).

I remember his telling me, the very first time we got together at Wernersville to begin working on the story that ultimately became *With God in Russia*, that he was convinced God had preserved him in Russia and arranged for his return to the States in order to tell people what he had learned. He kept saying that as we worked, and I kept waiting for the message, the punch line, the great revelation. He was on fire with the conviction he had something to tell people, to teach them about God, and about the ways of God with men. And of course he did—but it really wasn't anything new or startling at all! It was as old as the Old Testament, as the call of Abraham, "our father in faith" as the old Roman Canon says.

Faith, faith, and trust in God our Father: the faith of Abraham, the trust of Mary. *That* was the message Walter Ciszek learned through his experiences in Russia and brought back to tell us. *That* was the message he taught us by his seemingly nonchalant familiarity with God, his way of speaking, his way of acting, his way of living. If you've read his books, you know the crucible in which that faith was forged and tested, tested to the point of despair—"Like gold in the furnace God tried him." You know the misunderstandings and the heartbreaks it took to get the "I" and "me" burned out of his absolute trust in God so that his "not my will but thine be done" was unconditional and unreserved: absolutely. Totally.

While *With God in Russia* was a great success and—from the testimonies of many—great spiritual lessons were derived from Father Ciszek's Russian odyssey, the author himself wasn't satisfied. Ciszek was convinced that God had preserved his life and brought him through his many sufferings so that he could share the spiritual lessons that he learned in Russia with others. He often said to others, "*With God in Russia* is the book they wanted me to write. *He Leadeth Me* is the one I wanted to write." And so, shortly after *With God in Russia* was published, Walter Ciszek began writing down his thoughts for a new book on the spiritual lessons and insights he derived through his Russian experiences. His writing proceeded in fits and starts over the next seven years, as priestly duties called and health problems plagued him. Finally, in 1973, he published *He Leadeth Me*, a book of a concrete and earthy spirituality for everyman. Father Flaherty, again, recounts how this book came to be written:

Almost as soon as we finished *With God in Russia* at Easter 1964, and even before that book appeared in print, Walter said to me one day, "When are we going to write my book?" I was nonplussed! "Wally," I said, "we just finished your book and it's at the publisher." "No," he said, "that was the book everyone was asking for, that was the story about what happened to me, but it wasn't the book God sent me back to the States to write." He was convinced, you see, that God had arranged for him to leave the Soviet Union—where he was not allowed to function publicly as a priest or even talk to people about religion—to tell people what he had learned about "the ways of God with men," about what he had learned the hard way about "God's will" and what God expects of us.

I said to him, "Wally, I can't write that book; the experiences you had were unique to you. I didn't experience them; I can't begin to describe them or how they affected you or what you learned as a result of them, but I can tell you how to write about them." "O.K.," he said. "How?"

"Start with the presumption," I said, "that people have read *With God in Russia* after it's published. You don't have to retell that whole story. But pick out the experiences that affected you the most and from which you learned the most about 'the ways of God with men.' Going into Russia, for instance. Was that really God's will—or your will? Even at the time you left Albertyn you wondered who was going to help the people you were leaving behind and whether you were a shepherd deserting his flock, so you asked the bishop in Lvov for his permission. Or in Lubianka, during the interrogations, when you wondered over and over again why God didn't 'give you the words' to confound your persecutors as He'd promised in St. Matthew's gospel. Things like that." "O.K." he said.

Some weeks later, he brought me the first draft of a chapter about God's will; it was awful. For one thing, he didn't write anything like the way he spoke, simply and directly. He wrote as if he were imitating the great spiritual writers he had read during his days in the novitiate and other Jesuit formation. Theological treatises, the third degree of abstraction, as I used to tell him; all abstract nouns and multisyllabic adjectives and verbs in compound sentences. "Just tell it like it was," I said, "in your own words and how you felt." "O.K.," he said, and went off to try again.

Some weeks later, he was back with another draft, but it was the same thing. Maybe a little better at describing the incident or the problem, but right into the stratosphere of abstraction when he "reflected" on the incident in "theological" terms. "No, no," I said, and went over the same directions I had given him before. He tried again, producing another draft chapter, but it was no better. He was frustrated at my reaction, and I was frustrated at his concept of "spiritual writing." We went on like that. The intervals between our meetings got longer. Months would go by. He was busy giving retreats and helping out in Byzantine-rite parishes, and frankly frustrated with the process of writing. But he didn't want to give up. He knew he had something to say. He could say some of it in sermons, or talks, or the retreats he gave, but he couldn't write it! So he kept asking me to help.

I would get 3 x 5 postcards from him telling me what he was doing, how much people liked *With God in Russia*, thanking me again for helping him write it, and asking me again for help in writing "his" book. But my situation at *America* had changed; I'd been appointed executive editor, and I spent a lot of time in the business office as well as the editorial office. Walter had a heart attack, then another.[84] We kept in touch, but he gave up writing drafts.

Finally, in the fall of 1971, I had to tell him my Provincial was recalling me back to my home Province, Chicago, to work at Loyola Press rather than at *America* magazine, where I'd first met Walter upon his return from Russia and been assigned to help him tell that story. He came down to *America*'s offices from Fordham University, where he lived and taught at the Russian Institute, to see me. He was distraught. "How can I write my book without you?" he said. "Wally," I said, "we're not getting anywhere with this book; apparently you can't write it, but neither can I."

The Jesuits who worked at Loyola Press lived at Canisius House in Evanston, Illinois, a so-called "writer's house" supported by the Press, where Jesuits would live for shorter or somewhat longer periods of time while working on a manuscript. After I'd been there for a while, feeling guilty about having "deserted" Walter, I asked Father Amberg, the superior of the house and director of Loyola Press, if we could invite him to come to live at Canisius House and I could try once more to help him with "his book." Father Amberg agreed, Walter came to Chicago in September, 1971, and we began.

I asked him where he wanted to begin. He chose Albertyn, as I had suggested long ago. "All right," I said, "you spend tomorrow or the next couple days writing that, and then we'll get together again." The next night, when I came home from the Press, he was waiting for me, manuscript in hand. After dinner we went to my room to review what he'd written. The same old "third degree of abstraction" stuff and style. My heart sank. "Wally," I said, "this is awful! What are you trying to say, for God's sake?" Like a chastened schoolboy, he looked at me with pleading eyes and said nothing. "All right," I said, "tell me what you're trying to say." And it came pouring out. He talked, and I took notes as fast as I could, occasionally interrupting to ask for a clarification or further explanation. When he finally wound down and I was exhausted, I said "O.K. I'll work on this. What's next?" He thought a bit and said "our decision to go to Russia." "Fine," I said, "you work on that tomorrow or the next day, and then we'll get together again."

He went to his room, and I picked up the Dictaphone. Working from my notes, while it was all fresh in my mind, I dictated the chapter on Albertyn and took the disc to the Press with me the next day to have it transcribed. I put the typescript in a folder, filed it, and never looked at it. We did that week after week, chapter by chapter. I had made a pact with myself that I would not go to bed after each evening's session without dictating the chapter while it was fresh in my mind. His "writing" never improved, I may add, but I insisted that he had to write the chapter before we "discussed" it.

Months went by; we didn't work on the weekends, but I often took Walter with me to my parents' home for Sunday dinners and, little by little, he became a regular part of family gatherings, around the Thanksgiving table, for instance, though he did go back East to be with his own family for Christmas. The folders multiplied in the drawer, thanks to Marion O'Neill, our executive secretary at Loyola Press, who faithfully transcribed the Dictaphone discs in addition to her other duties. Once in a while she would tell Father Amberg, the director of the Press, how wonderful Father Ciszek's story was. That was encouraging to hear.

When we finally finished "the book" in early February, 1972, we started over. I gave Walter the first folder on Albertyn, told him to read it, and we would discuss it that evening. After dinner we got together and I asked him what he thought. It had been months, of course, since he'd first "written" it. "Well," he said, "it's pretty good but . . ." "But?," I said, "but . . .???" And so we started over. With the manuscript in front of me, I made notes, asked for clarifications, argued a bit over his "theology" or his "insights," and then gave him the folder of the second chapter to read and correct the next day. He went to his room, and I picked up the Dictaphone and began dictating the first chapter again. We didn't have computers in those days, so that meant the whole chapter had to be typed all over again, and filed.

We spent months going again through the twenty chapters of what would ultimately become the book, correcting or clarifying or amplifying the "buts." Again, I worked late into the evening, dictating the revised chapters for transcription before going to bed. I was also engaged full-time at the Press on the preparation of a religion textbook series for elementary schools, which was at once an additional burden but also a distraction from "the book." We took a break that summer [on July 30, 1972]; Walter went back east to see his family, to give some retreats, and to help out again at Byzantine-rite parishes in the Eparchy of Passaic for his good friend Bishop Michael Dudick.

When he returned in the fall of 1972, we started again. I gave Walter the first of the rewritten chapters all over again and said we would discuss it that evening. He liked it much better, "but . . .!" So we worked our way through all the chapters again, following a by now familiar pattern. I thought surely Marion or Father Amberg would begin to complain, but by now they were committed to seeing the book through. I had always assumed that McGraw-Hill would be the publisher of this book, as they had been of *With God in Russia*, but when I finally wrote to them about it, the leadership of the company had changed somewhat, and the answer I received was a polite "no thank you." I didn't say anything to Walter, but I did talk about it with Father Amberg. It clearly was not a book for Loyola Press, which at that time was largely a publisher of textbooks for Catholic grade schools.

After some further thought, I thought of John Delaney at Doubleday, whom I had come to know when I was book editor at *America*. It was John who had originated Doubleday's successful paperback division, Image Books. Doubleday had been one of the original bidders to publish *With God in Russia*, but when McGraw-Hill won that contract, John had negotiated with them the rights to publish a paperback Image edition. I wrote to John, therefore, and sent him a couple of folders of Walter's new book. He responded almost immediately and said he'd be "very interested" in publishing such a book.

And so I kept on with Walter, week after week. My life became even more complicated, however, when I learned in November 1972 that my name had been included on a *terna* [list of three candidates] sent to Rome for the next Provincial of the Chicago Province. I reassured both Walter and John Amberg, however, that there was very little chance I'd ever be selected for such a job.

After New Year's Day, 1973, Walter and I started on our fourth time through the folders. The "buts" were minor enough this time that corrections could be made by hand in the manuscript itself instead of dictating a new draft. And when Walter was finally satisfied that the book said what he wanted to say, we worked on the Prologue and Epilogue and sent the "completed" manuscript off to John Delaney at Doubleday. Just in time, too, because word had come back from Rome in late January that, to the consternation of everyone, I had in fact been chosen to be the next Chicago Province provincial. Soon after that, my predecessor, Father Robert F. Harvanek, S.J., who had called me back to Chicago to work at Loyola Press, had a minor heart attack—not connected with my appointment, as far as I know, but it did hasten his sense of urgency to have me take over the reins! I pleaded that I needed time to finish the religion textbook series I was working on at the

Press, as well as Walter's book, and we agreed that my transition to Provincial could be made in June.

John Delaney and his readers at Doubleday had some questions, of course, which Walter and I answered or explained or amplified. John also personally did not like the title, even though I told him it was drawn from the hymnal version of Psalm 23, The Lord Is My Shepherd, known as "Brother James' Air." Ultimately, but reluctantly, John agreed to the title and printed the relevant stanza of the hymn as the book's "frontispiece." I had told John of my new assignment, of course, so he managed to put Father Ciszek's book on a fast track, and Walter and I were able to go over the galleys and correct them together before we both left Canisius House in June, 1973—he to return to Fordham and I to report to the Provincial residence in Oak Park, Illinois.

The Byzantine Franciscan monk Philaret Littlefield was a staff and community member of the John XXIII Center between 1969 and 1973. He served as Father Ciszek's secretary during his spare time, typing his letters and also the notes for *He Leadeth Me*. He said, "I recall after reading the published edition that it was largely the work of his co-author. The notes he had dictated to me were more anecdotal."[85] But an intimate friend of Walter Ciszek from 1966 onward, Mother Marija Shields, O.C.D., who had also read the manuscript of *He Leadeth Me* before publication, gave the assurance that "although Father Flaherty helped with both books, there was no question that Father Flaherty was a faithful 'hollow reed' transmitting Father's message. It was all Father Ciszek's content with Father Flaherty's grammatical expertise."[86] A third opinion comes from someone who had only met Father Ciszek in late 1982 or early 1983, after having read his books, and had chosen him as her spiritual director for the remaining two years of his life; she wrote,

> I liked his books well enough to go and meet him. But, after meeting him I realized the voice expressed in the books was not fully his own. This deficiency would be expected in books written as they were with the assistance of another. The man was greater than his books!

She then continued on a more personal note, probably expressing the experience of not a few of Walter Ciszek's readers:

> Father is also a wonderful model for "wayward" youth, of which I was one, to allow one's energies to be used and transformed for good rather than for mischief and self-will. But for the grace of God, Father Ciszek would have

been a cruel and selfish man, and he knew that about himself. Perhaps, that is why he used the term "devious" to describe our nature. His youthful mischievousness demonstrates how much transformation he needed and, by contrast, how well he submitted himself to God's design for him.

His admissions of his own adolescent negative traits are stepping stones to healing for himself and for others. I have come to see how God can use stubbornness and willfulness to prepare one for life's later challenges and God's own goals. Father Ciszek's confession in Lubianka was the lowest point of his own weakness, which then becomes his jumping-off point to holiness of life and fervor of spirit, a spirit that had been broken at Lubianka. His natural "spiritedness" had been totally transformed by the Holy Spirit so that he acted as a guide for others in their own journeys to union with God.[87]

34

A Boyhood Remembered,
a Calling Claimed

The 1500-page manuscript of *With God in Russia* had been preserved, just as Father Flaherty presumed.[88] The following original, unabridged version of the "Introduction," as it appears in that manuscript, is the story of Walter Ciszek's youth, which had been summarized in merely seven pages of the book and entitled "An Unlikely Priest." Ciszek, however, had actually written of that period of his life in much greater detail, for, as he told Father Flaherty when they began writing the book, he wanted to be as honest as possible about his childhood, "because you'll never understand the things I did unless you understand why I did them."

An Unlikely Priest

I was born on November 4, 1904, in a small frame house on the outskirts of Shenandoah, Pennsylvania, the seventh child of Martin and Mary Ciszek. They were both of peasant stock and came to America from Poland in the early 1890s. Neither of them had much education—perhaps the equivalent of four years of grammar school—and were, therefore, determined that their children should have the best education they could afford. Martin, like many of the Polish immigrants to America, began his life in this land of opportunity as a miner. He afterwards opened a saloon and worked behind the bar for the rest of his life. I saw pictures of him as a handsome young miner, but I remember him as a medium-sized man with thick black hair and a glorious mustache, stocky, and, if not fat, at least not the trim young miner he had been. He was a wonderful man and a good father, strict with the children but always trying to help others and with a special soft spot in his heart for newly arrived immigrants. His wife, Mary, was a small light-haired woman, very religious and strict with the children. She brought up all her children (thirteen in all, of whom four boys and six girls survived) in this same religious spirit, and two of the girls entered

230

the convent. Mary died in 1932, of diabetes, after a long illness. Martin married again but lived only a few more years and died in 1936, while I was studying theology in Rome.

By the time I was in fifth grade, my reputation was pretty well established, and it had nothing to do with the priesthood. I was, in fact, the leader of what can best be described as a gang. I was thin and small, a less than ninety-pound weakling, but my idol was [the body-builder] Charles Atlas, and my passion was boxing and wrestling. Along with my collection of detective stories, I had large batches of pulp magazines on boxing and wrestling, and I had cleaned out a space in the hayloft of the barn (where we kept our one, old milk cow) to form a small ring, where I liked nothing better than to take on two or three of my friends at one time, boxing and wrestling, no holds barred. At school—and to most of the neighbors, for that matter—I was known as a ruffian and considered something of a bully in the bargain, so that, later on, when I said I wanted to be a priest, everyone simply laughed at the idea.

Small as I was, I refused to admit there was anything I could not do or anyone I couldn't lick. Our gang used to go around in the evenings, looking for other gangs on the street corners and picking fights. We would form a ring in the middle of the street, and I would take on all comers. I got my lumps that way, but I never admitted I was licked. I came by my reputation as a bully early enough because I was forever stopping other kids on the street and telling them I didn't like their hair, or their nose, or their shoes, or their shirt and, then, sneaking in the first punch in the ensuing argument.

One day I tried it with another redhead. He wore glasses and, perhaps, I called him "four eyes" or some other school-boy insult, but, in any event, he was soon asking me if I was looking for a fight. I said, "Yes," and he said, "O.K., wait right here and I'll be right back." He came back all right—with ten others. Only one other member of my gang was there that day, but I wasn't going to back away from a fight, so I smashed the redhead right on the nose, even before he took his glasses off—a cardinal sin, as any school boy knows. He came back fighting, and someone else landed a couple of good ones on my buddy, so I turned to help him, and the others jumped us. It was quite a scuffle, but we finally managed to break loose and ran down an alley with the gang in pursuit, then turned into the next street and ducked up onto the porch of the first house on the block. The gang was right behind us, so I rang the bell, and when the lady came to the door, I pretended I had come to her house by mistake. One look at the two of us, and a look at the gang down by the front gate, and I think she understood what the problem was, because she asked us to come in, and we stayed until the gang had left.

Still, odds in a fight never bothered me. One day, some of the girls in my grade at the parish school told me that some of the kids at the public school, a block away, had bothered them on their way to school. So, hero that I was, I ran over and picked the biggest kid I could find in the school and waded into him. He went down, and as I went to jump on him, he threw a handful of sand in my eyes, and the fight was over. Some of my gang, who had come running over, helped me back to school, where I got no sympathy from the nun, who simply scolded me and asked when all this was going to stop. Then she sent me home, and my mother called the doctor, who finally cleaned all the sand out of my eyes; when the doctor had gone, my mother gave me a good, sound thrashing.

Another day, I got into a scrap with a kid who called me a few names, including bully. I didn't say anything; I just hit him right in the mouth. He began to cry, so I quit and he ran away, but when he got to the corner of the street, he turned and started to call me names again. So I shouted at the top of my lungs, "Just wait, I'll get you!" At that, the people on the street began to scold me for being such a bully, so I turned on my heel, jammed my hands into my pockets, and walked away mad. I then ran into another of my enemies, just coming out of a store with a big package in his arms. I didn't say a word, just seized the golden opportunity and began to wade into him. The people on the street started to yell, and I turned to run—right into the arms of a policeman. He took me to school, where the nun scolded me again and kept me after school until almost 6 o'clock. By then, I was afraid to go home, so I hung around the streets until it got quite dark, hoping that my father would be so worried about me that it would keep me from getting a good licking. He wasn't, and it didn't.

My father, in fact, was becoming quite disgusted with me and was not quite sure what he had done to deserve to have such a hellion for a son. It didn't help matters any that I was always playing hooky from school, after he had worked so hard to be sure his children got the education he had never had an opportunity to have.

One night, after I had spent the day playing hooky, my sister came to tell me that my father was looking for me. On the spur of the moment, [...] I decided to run away from home. For three days, I didn't go near the house, and every day a buddy of mine and I would sell hot waffles for a neighborhood bakery on the street corners to get money for the movies. Once we came across an older gang in the alley and watched with fascination while they played craps. Finally, one of them flipped us a quarter and asked us to go round the corner and get some change. We went around the corner all right, but never came back with the change. A couple of days later, they caught up with us while we were selling waffles and beat us up so badly we had to go to the horse trough and wash off the blood. We didn't particularly resent it, but just figured we had gotten our money's worth. With the money we earned selling waffles, we went to the movies every day and bought peanuts and candy.

It was quite a lark for a while, but on the third day one of the gang crawled up to me at the movies and told me that my father had the police out after me. I immediately ducked down under the seats and crawled along the aisle and out the side door. Then, about midnight that night, I decided to go home and see if it was true. The house was all dark at that time of night, but I no sooner stuck my nose inside the door than I was grabbed and got the beating of my life—to the delight of my brothers, who were awakened by the noise and crowded along the stairwell to watch the fun. I made the mistake of hitting back at my father, and then the fur really flew. The next morning, my father was still so mad he announced that he was going to take me to the police station and have me sent to the House of Correction. My mother was horrified, but my father really meant it. He said I was a disgrace to the family and bringing shame to the house—an Old World expression, which quite accurately conveyed both the source and the extent of his anger. He did take me to the police station, but the police convinced him it would be more disgraceful to have a son in an institution than any disgrace I might be at home.

I do not mean to give the wrong impression of my father. The poor man was almost at his wit's end at having what almost amounted to a juvenile delinquent (although we did not use the term in those days) in the family. Talking to me did no good, and thrashings only gave me an opportunity to show how tough I could be. With his inherited pride of, and deep belief in, the family, I am sure it was shame, rather than anger, that led him to drag me off to the police station. And my father's shame and humiliation before the police that night—although at the time I would not have admitted it and certainly didn't show it—made a very deep impression on me. Still, it did not affect his deep love and concern for me as his son.

I remember another occasion, about this time, when I went to a Boy Scout outing and spent all the money my father had given me at an amusement park near the camp grounds. I had no money for the train fare home. So I hung around the station and hitched a ride on a train, hanging on to the outside of one of the cars, almost getting killed against the walls of one of the tunnels we passed through. I arrived back in Shenandoah at about 1 o'clock in the morning, very cold, very tired, and very scared, to find my very worried father still hoping and waiting for me at the station. He took me home very solicitously, lit a fire in the stove to warm me and, then, without waking my mother, cooked a meal for me with his own hands and finally saw me safely to bed. Many years later, in the Siberian prison camps, it was that episode, above all others, that I remembered when I thought of my father.

Yet, outwardly I changed very little. I was still out on the streets at night, killing cats and throwing stones at street lamps and windows, and indulging in all sorts of adolescent pranks—not all of them innocent. We once took a whole steam shovel apart at one of the mining pits and sold the brass we removed to a scrap dealer, who was later arrested by the police for dealing in stolen property. At other times, we would put dynamite caps on the railroad track along a steep grade outside of town. The object was to make the train lose traction or cause the engineer to stop on the grade, where he couldn't start again. He would then have to back the train down the hill and build up steam in order to make the grade.

I was still driven by the desire to excel among my contemporaries, to show that there was nothing anyone could do that I could not do. If we were walking in the woods after school, I would plunge into a freezing pond or river with all my clothes on, just to show how brave I was; or I would lead the group into an abandoned mine shaft until everyone else got scared and only then would I consent to turn back. Perhaps the most dangerous of these feats of youthful bravado was our custom of daring one another to crawl down sewer pipes, to see who could go down the furthest and stay the longest without choking on the gas. Still, my mother's training was not forgotten, and no matter how late I came in at night or how tired I was, I never went to bed without saying my night prayers. And, if I regretted my reputation as a bully and a ruffian at all, it was because the nuns at school would not let me be an altar boy due to my reputation, and that was an honor I coveted above all others.

Aside from that, and the opportunity to play team sports, in which I excelled, school had absolutely no interest for me. My mother used to keep me home some nights and try to make me study, but I used to trade shamelessly on the fact that the poor woman had no education herself, and give any sort of outlandish answers to convince her that I really knew the matter. My mother, too, used to worry about me very much and wonder what would become of me and, gradually, this concern of my parents began to penetrate my thick Polish skull and sober me somewhat.

Finally, at the end of the sixth-grade school year, I resolved to do better. Characteristically, the resolve had nothing to do with schoolwork, as such, but there were two brothers who graduated from the eighth grade that year, winning all sorts of scholastic honors, [for which they] were highly praised by the nuns. This praise for others rankled me, and I decided I would show the nuns, my parents, and my peers that I could do better than those two brothers. What anyone else could do, I could surely do, if I made up my mind to it. And so, all during the seventh and eighth grades, I studied hard and my marks improved, although it was something of a blow to find that I was still not winning any honors. Moreover, I was still very much the tough guy and interested in any sort of competition, although now my fighting had largely been replaced by sports. I had read in one of the sports magazines that running and swimming were great conditioners, so I used to get up early in the morning before school and run for miles; also, I swam whenever I could seize the opportunity. I have the recollection that I played sports in those days from morning until night (though of course I must have done some other things too), whatever was in season; I even played a lot of tennis, just to prove that no one could beat me at that either.

At the end of the eighth grade, almost out of a clear blue sky, I told my mother and father that I wanted to be a priest. I don't remember exactly how I came to that decision, and I only vaguely remember the occasion that prompted me to declare it, but I vividly remember my parents' reactions. My father was stunned and asked me, frankly, what sort of priest I thought I would make. Priests, in his eyes, were men of God and very holy, and I was anything but that. Perhaps it was a response to my mother's religious strictness, or the obvious piety of my sisters, but I was never outwardly pious, and although I prayed a good deal, I would never pray if anyone else were around. My father, therefore, couldn't understand my decision and thought I should, instead, be a doctor or a lawyer. My mother, who finally decided the issue, as mothers often do, at last told me that I could be what I wanted to be, but if I wanted to be a priest, I should be a good one. Again I was stubborn and insisted, and so that September [1921] I went off to Orchard Lake, Michigan, to SS. Cyril and Methodius Seminary, a high school and seminary run by secular priests, where many other Polish lads from our parish had gone before me.

Here, too, sports were my specialty, particularly football and baseball; but I was also determined that no one should be better than me in anything, so during the five years of high school and one year of college at SS. Cyril and Methodius, I ranked quite high in my class. Out of the sixty-four boys in my year, I once ranked as low as seventh, but for the most part I was third or fourth; but it galled me not to be first.

Even though I was in a seminary, I took great pains not to be thought pious, and I was openly scornful of those who were. Yet, at night, when there was no one around, I used to sneak down into the chapel to pray. The adventure section of the library shelves was still my favorite haunt, but the book that impressed me most was a life of St. Stanislaus Kostka. Biographers have done this saint a great injustice, and the plaster statue representations of him, with his sweet look and eyes turned up to heaven, is certainly an abomination, which ought to be smashed outright. Stanislaus Kostka, in fact, was a tough young Pole who walked from Warsaw to Rome, through all sorts of weather, and showed no ill effects whatsoever. He was also a very stubborn young man who stuck to his guns, despite the arguments of his family and the persecution of his brother; perhaps it was this tough-minded stubbornness that appealed to me. Although, I made no conscious effort to imitate him, I was stubborn and did make an almost conscious effort to be tough. I would, for instance, get up at 4:30 in the morning, long before the others, just to run the five or eight miles around the lakes on the seminary property, and then finish it off with a cold shower. Or I would go swimming in November, when the lakes were little better than frozen, just to prove to myself that I could take it.

In the third year of high school at SS. Cyril and Methodius, a Jesuit came to give us our annual retreat. He had such an influence on me that I wish now I could remember his name, but try as I might I cannot remember it. Yet he so appealed to me that from that time on, I knew I wanted to be a Jesuit, although I wouldn't admit it even to myself. And from that time on, too, I resolved always to do the more difficult things. I have always had, and still retain, a very strong feeling for family ties, but that summer I stayed at school during the vacation, working in the fields and around the grounds, just to do the more difficult thing and see if I could take it. I don't think it even entered my head, although I often thought of it later, that this decision of mine was a far greater imposition on my family than it was on me. At that time, I thought only of doing something that I knew would be hard, and I forced myself to bear the loneliness and the separation from family and friends.

It was all part of a pattern. For a half year, I ate no breakfast at all, just to see if I could do it. During Lent the next year, I ate nothing but bread and water for the full forty days, except for a bowl of soup at the main meal. The next year, I ate no meat at all for the whole year, just to see if I could do it. Contrary to everything I had been told, and because I was a very stubborn young man, I asked no one's permission to do all this and told no one. So when our prefect noticed what I was doing and warned me that I might hurt my health, I told him bluntly that I knew what I was doing and ignored his concern. All in all, I was very independent, and it amazes me now that anyone should have let me get away with it. All this time, I had been playing on the high-school baseball team and, at home during the summers, with the Shenandoah Indians, a local team that played against teams from other mining towns of the area. I played second base or third base and also pitched on occasion; I loved the game. Yet, in my first year of college at SS. Cyril and Methodius, I began to drop all such activities—because it was the more difficult thing. The baseball team was supposed to go to Ann Arbor, Michigan, to play, but I simply refused to go. It caused something of a crisis, but I was as stubborn as ever. I was determined to do whatever was hardest for me to do, and it was certainly very hard for me to give up the sports in which I had always excelled. I mention all this now, looking back, not with any sense of approval or boastfulness, but simply to indicate how my character was developing, and so that the reader will understand, in some small way, how I could in later years put up with the hardships demanded of me.

On the other hand, although I was to begin the study of theology and the last steps to the priesthood in the following fall, I spent that whole summer at home going to parties, dances, and dates; I was, in fact, the life of the party. My mother had simply given up trying to understand me, although I am sure she was almost convinced now that I would never be a priest, and it saddened her. In the midst of all those summer activities, I was undergoing something of a crisis myself. Characteristically, I asked no one's advice and tried to fight my own way to a decision. I had never told anyone that I wanted to be a Jesuit, and I now tried to convince myself that I did not want to be one. Despite the whirl of parties, I was at 6 o'clock Mass every morning, praying for guidance. I simply could not shake the idea of entering a religious order, and yet I did not want to make that decision. I tried to argue myself into the secular priesthood, into staying with the members of my class and going on to ordination. [I kept asking myself,] "Wouldn't they be serving God as well as I, and doing great work? Then, why do I have to be different?" I didn't want to be different, and I didn't want to become a Jesuit, but I couldn't shake the idea. That was the summer of 1928, and I was due to start my theology in the fall. It was now or never.

Three weeks before I was due to return to the seminary, my sister who had already entered the convent came to pay us a visit. While she was home, I took her aside one day and asked if she could get me a catalogue of all the religious orders. She looked at me strangely and asked why I wanted it. I told her brusquely it was none of her business, for I had still not learned to ask for help and advice. When she sent me the catalogue, I wrote a letter to the Polish Jesuits in Warsaw, telling them that I wanted to enter the Society there, but I told no one. Then, five days before I was due to leave for the seminary, with my father asking if I ought not to start packing and making final arrangements, there was still no answer from Poland. However, that same morning the answer came. It was a very gracious letter, but the gist of it was that I would probably find life and conditions in Poland much different from those I was used to in America, and it suggested that if I wanted to be a Jesuit I should contact the Polish Jesuits in New York. I showed the letter to my mother but not to my father. Early the next morning, while my father was still in bed and half asleep, I told him I needed some money. He didn't think to ask why but just told me that his wallet was in the pocket of his pants in the closet; so I took what I thought I needed and bought a ticket for New York.

Somehow I found my way to 501 Fordham Road, the office of the Jesuit Provincial. The brother who was in charge of the door told me that the Provincial was not at home. I wouldn't tell him what I wanted but asked when the Provincial would be back. He said the Provincial would return that evening, so I asked if I could see him. The brother shrugged, and I left. I hadn't eaten anything, so I found a cafeteria and got a meal, then spent the afternoon walking up and down Fordham Road in something of a daze and with a delayed attack of butterflies in my stomach. At 6 o'clock, the Provincial still was not home; I went out and walked around the grounds of the Fordham campus, feeling more nervous all the time. At 7:30 I returned to the Provincial's residence and asked if he had returned; the brother told me to take a seat in the parlor.

At 8 o'clock that evening, Father Kelly, the Provincial, came into the parlor and asked me what my visit was all about. I told him where I was from, and of my trip to New York because I wanted to be a Jesuit. He looked at me for a moment, and then sat down. He wanted to know about my parents. I told him that I had only that morning told my mother but had not yet told my father. However, because I was twenty-four years of age, the decision was mine to make. We talked for a long while after that, and I tried to explain my decision to him. I was probably not too helpful, because I simply kept insisting that I wanted to join the Society, and about the only concrete facts he could get out of me were my marks in the seminary. At length, he told me to wait a moment, and he went out and sent in another Father to talk it over with me further. He was a wonderful old man, although I have forgotten his name; [I remember that he was] quite deaf. He had some sort of hearing device and, with the aid of much shouting, we managed to get through the story again, while I insisted ceaselessly that I was determined to be a Jesuit. I also talked to another priest, and finally at about 11 o'clock that night, Father Kelly himself returned and told me that things would probably work out all right, but I should go home and wait for his answer.

When Father Kelly, the Provincial, told me that everything would probably be all right and that I would be hearing from him, I was elated. It never occurred to me that when I heard from him, the answer might be no. I was in that state which was then called "seventh heaven" and is now, so I understand, called being "on cloud nine." It was not just joy but a very deep and soul-satisfying peace, something more than the quiet and release from tension, which follows the settling of an emotional problem. It was a positive and deep-seated happiness, akin to the feeling of belonging or of having reached safe harbor, but deeper than that—it seemed to be a gift from God. I practically floated from the room, and I don't even remember saying good-bye to Father Kelly or the brother at the door. In fact, I remember very little, until I came to myself again in a bar down on the Bowery. Perhaps I walked there, but more than likely I took the old elevated train; I simply cannot remember. I do know that I had ordered a meal, and then when I realized where I was and got a good look at all the tough and odd-looking characters surrounding me, I paid my money and left hurriedly without touching a bite of the food. I was so happy I could have danced all the way home, but I did in fact take the ferry to Jersey City and caught the train for Shenandoah.

Yet, when I got home, I still could not bring myself to tell my father what I had done. I told him simply that I had gone to see a friend in New York. He didn't question me much about it, probably because he was so relieved to see me deep in the process of packing, supposing that I was getting ready, at last, for the seminary and the beginning of theology. Instead, not long after, I got a letter from the Provincial's residence in New York, telling me to report on such and such a day [Sept. 7, 1928] to the Jesuit novitiate at St. Andrew-on-the-Hudson, Poughkeepsie, New York. The die was cast, and the moment inevitably had come when I must inform my father. He looked at the letter for a long time, as if he had difficulty comprehending it, and then said quite suddenly, "Nothing doing, you're going to the seminary!" "No sir," I said, "I'm going to St. Andrew's." We then argued like father and son, each as stubborn as the other, until suddenly my father banged the letter on the table and said for the last time, "You're not going." With that I banged my fist on the table and said, "I am going! I am the one who is going, not you, and I am going to St. Andrew's!" Because I had waited until the last possible moment to tell him, and my bags were already packed, with that parting shot I simply walked out without a farewell or the traditional father's blessing, threw my trunk on the back of a neighborhood beer wagon, and asked the driver to take me to the railway station.

I caught the train to New York all right, but somehow I got mixed up in the station and missed the train for Poughkeepsie, so I finally arrived at the dark hulk of St. Andrew's, on its promontory brooding over a bend in the Hudson River, at the ungodly hour of 2 o'clock in the morning. I rang the bell for what seemed forever and could hear it echoing down the long corridors of that massive brick building. Finally, a very sleepy Brother Moran appeared to open the door. He was absolutely incredulous when I tried to convince him that I was a novice who had come a little bit late. Perhaps he thought it was some sort of prank, until he saw my luggage piled up on the doorstep and then, even though he believed me, he remained a bit confused about what to do with me at that hour of the morning. We were, both of us, rescued when Father Weber, novice master, came on the scene. He welcomed me very warmly, despite my inauspicious arrival, and, because he did not want me barging into the novices' dormitory at that hour of the night, took me to one of the large spacious guest rooms. He very solicitously offered me some cakes and hot milk, correctly surmising that I must be starved after such a long journey and a hard day, but I thought he must be already testing the sincerity of my vocation, so I stubbornly refused them.

I went to bed and slept for little more than an hour, then, shortly after four o'clock got up, went to the nearby lavatory, and began the forty-five minutes of calisthenics that had become part of my daily program. While I was twisting and jumping away, the bell rang and the community arose and Father

Donnelly came into the washroom. I will never forget the look on his face, which revealed, plainer than any words could have, the idea that there was a madman loose in the house, and he hurriedly left, slamming the door behind him. I went back to my room, where Father Weber collected me and took me to Mass and then to breakfast. Because I was a day behind the others of my class, he assigned one of the older novices especially to me to show me the ropes and acquaint me with the daily order of the house, and to see that I didn't miss any meals. After that, I settled down into the usual routine of the novitiate and began to get acquainted with my fellow novices.

Acknowledgments

The editors would like to gratefully acknowledge the following individuals for their invaluable assistance in the production of this volume:

First and foremost, to Joanne Wright, for her tireless efforts on behalf of Father Ciszek's cause. Mrs. Wright did the yeoman's work in interviewing the fellow Jesuits, friends, and spiritual sons and daughters of Father Ciszek and acquiring their recollections. These recollections have helped us to know better Father Ciszek in his "American years" and have given much-needed context to many of Father's writings contained herein.

To Patricia Extance and Sr. Doris Burkot, O.S.F., who generously helped Mrs. Wright type and edit the interviews.

To Monsignor Anthony D. Muntone and Fr. Daniel L. Flaherty, S.J., for their expert counsel and judicious proofreading.

To His Excellency Bishop John O. Barres, Monsignor Ronald C. Bocian, Elaine Cusat, and members of the Fr. Walter Ciszek Prayer League in Shenandoah, Pennsylvania, for providing us access to many of Father's unpublished writings in the League Archives, and for their prayerful support.

To all who have provided their recollections or have otherwise assisted in the production of this volume: Sr. Andreja Vladia, O.C.D.; Thomas Anton; Fr. George Aschenbrenner, S.J.; Sr. Ruth Aubrey, A.S.C.J.; Br. Edward Babinski, S.J.; Joseph Barinas; Marianne T. Breiter Bogunovich; Fr. Francis Butler, S.S.J.; Carol Caraluzzi; Lita Carlucci; Fr. John Catoir; Fr. Denis Como, S.J.; Sr. Lucille Cutrone, C.F.R.; Fr. Edward Debaney, S.J.; Fr. Robert Dorin, S.J.; Fr. George Drury, S.J.; Patricia Extance; Fr. Daniel Fitzpatrick, S.J.; Joan Gourin; Michael Harney; Dolores Hartnett; Edward Kleha; Fr. Thomas Kuller, S.J.; Fr. Brendan Lally, S.J.; Gerald Lilore; Fr. Joseph Lingan, S.J.; Fr. Philaret Littlefield; James T. Maier; Dr. Marvin

Makinen; Fr. Leo Manglaviti, S.J.; Fr. Dominic Maruca, S.J.; Sr. Mary of Jesus, O.C.D.; Cathy McCarthy; Fr. Paul McCarthy, S.J.; His Excellency Bishop Timothy McDonnell; Nick Melone; John Michalczyk; James Murphy; Br. Edward Niziolek, S.J.; Maureen O'Brien; Sr. Santa Priolo, M.P.F.; Antoinette Rienzi; Sr. Joan Roccasalvo, C.SJ; Judith Roemer; Dr. James and Marianne Schaller; Mother Marija Shields, O.C.D.; Peg Short; Carl and Marie Siriani; Fr. James Skehan, S.J.; Fr. William J. Sneck, S.J.; William and Daria Sockey; Sr. Rosemary Stets, O.S.F.; Mara St. James; John Sweeney; Fr. Robert Taft, S.J.; Fr. Brian Van Hove, S.J.; and Mary Zentkovich.

To Annie, Thomas, John, Helen, Julia, Margaret, Joseph, Anna, and Francis DeJak for their encouragement, support, and prayers for the editors especially as they toiled together.

To Fr. Paul Brian Campbell, S.J., and the staff of Loyola Press, whose enthusiasm for this volume helped bring it to fruition.

Finally, we would like to acknowledge the prayerful support of the Bernardine Sisters at St. Casimir's Convent in Shenandoah, Pennsylvania, the Byzantine Discalced Carmelite Sisters of Holy Annunciation Monastery in Sugarloaf, Pennsylvania, the priests of the Church of St. Agnes in St. Paul, Minnesota, and the countless clients of Fr. Walter Ciszek, S.J., who have prayed for the editors and their efforts. To all, you have our humble thanks and fervent prayers.

Endnotes

1. Fr. Walter J. Ciszek, S.J., interview by Fr. Silvio Chini, O.S.J, November 14 and 21, 1963, the *Catholic Light*. The weekly newspaper of the diocese of Scranton published the article shortly after Fr. Ciszek's return to the United States. The author, an assistant pastor of St. Anthony's Parish, Exeter, served on the U.S. staff of *L'Osservatore Romano* and other leading Italian Catholic periodicals. He translated the text of his article from the original Italian for a member of the *Catholic Light* staff. A few minor factual errors have been discretely corrected. On October 8, 2013, Mr. Bill Genello, editor of the *Catholic Light*, kindly gave permission to reprint the interview in this book. All rights reserved.

2. Thurston N. Davis, S.J., "Foreword," in Walter J. Ciszek, S.J., *With God in Russia* (San Francisco: Ignatius Press, 1997), 7–13, 11.

3. Walter J. Ciszek, S.J., "The Loneliness of the Long-Distance Jesuit," *America* (October 31, 1964): 513–17.

4. Dr. Marvin Makinen, interview by John M. DeJak, December 11, 2011, as is the following story of his return to the United States together with Fr. Walter Ciszek.

5. Walter Ciszek, "Father Ciszek's First Public Statement," *America* (October 26, 1963): 475.

6. The following paragraph is based on Fr. Dominic Maruca, S.J., interview by John M. DeJak, January 24, 2012; John Michalczyk, interview by Joanne Wright, February 11, 2012, and Fr. Leo Manglaviti, interview by Joanne Wright, March 1, 2012.

7. Bishop Timothy McDonnell, interview by Joanne Wright, signed March 25, 2013.

8. Reprinted from *America* (March 28, 1964) with permission of America Press, Inc., 1964. All rights reserved. For subscription information, call 1-800-627-9533, or visit www.americamagazine.org.

9. Fr. Dominic Maruca, S.J., interview by John M. DeJak, January 24, 2012.

10. John Michalczyk, interview by Joanne Wright, February 11, 2012, and Leo Manglaviti, S.J., interview by Joanne Wright, March 1, 2012. John Michalczyk entered the Society of Jesus in 1961 and was a junior when Father Ciszek came to Wernersville. Leo Manglaviti, S.J., entered in 1963 and was a novice then.

11. Fr. Denis Como, S.J., interview by Joanne Wright, January 16, 2012. Fr. Como added some handwritten reflections to the text of the interview on March 3, 2012.

12. For what follows: Fr. Brian W. Van Hove, S.J., interview by John M. DeJak, April 11, 2012.

13. The interview conducted by Sr. Rosemary Stets, O.S.F., "What Was Father Ciszek Really Like? An Interview with a Jesuit Who Lived Closely with Him after His Return from the Soviet Union," was published in the newsletter of the Father Walter Ciszek Prayer League vol. 6, no. 4 (1994): 3–4.

14. John Courtney Murray, S.J., (1904–1967) was an American theologian (member of the New York Province) who was especially known for his efforts to reconcile the situation of a pluralistic society with Catholicism. After his priestly ordination in 1933 he pursued further studies at the Pontifical Gregorian University in Rome and completed a doctorate in theology in 1937.

15. Gustave Weigel, S.J. (1906–1964) entered the Maryland novitiate in 1922, six years before Walter Ciszek. They met first at Woodstock College, Woodstock, Maryland, in 1932–1934, when Ciszek was studying philosophy and Weigel, ordained a priest in 1933, was finishing his theology. In 1935–1937 they were together in Rome, the two years in which Weigel managed to complete a doctorate in theology at the Gregorian University. He became a leading voice in the ecumenical dialogue with American Protestantism.

16. Fr. Robert F. Taft, S.J., interview by Fr. Marc Lindeijer, S.J., revised and signed by the interviewee on October 10, 2011.

17. Maureen O'Brien, interview by Joanne Wright, signed on July 7, 2012.

18. Fr. Daniel Fitzpatrick, S.J., interview by Joanne Wright, October 17, 2012.

19. Br. Edward Niziolek, S.J., interview by Joanne Wright, October 15, 2011; Fr. George L. Drury, S.J., interview by Joanne Wright, October 30, 2011; Fr. Robert R. Dorin, S.J., interview by Joanne Wright, January 17, 2012; Fr. James W. Skehan, S.J. interview by Joanne Wright, signed April 9, 2012.

20. This paragraph is based on James T. Maier, interview by Joanne Wright February 27, 2013; Fr. William J. Sneck, S.J., associate director of novices 1980–1985, interview by Joanne Wright, May 5, 2012; Judith Roemer, the Spirituality Center's lay collaborator in that period, interview by Joanne Wright, signed January 21, 2013; and Fr. Paul McCarty, S.J., who happened to be at Wernersville that summer, interview by Joanne Wright, January 17, 2012.

21. Fr. Joseph Lingan, S.J., interview by Joanne Wright, signed May 15, 2013.

22. This surely must be understood in the sense of St. Paul's assertion that God made Jesus "who had no sin to be sin for us, so that in him we might become the righteousness of God" (2 Corinthians 5:21); that is, God imputed our sins to Jesus, the Lamb of God who takes away the sins of the world, so that we may be set free.

23. The text is rather sketchily written; hence, it has been edited more than usual, adding various words to make it easier to understand, and omitting two less-relevant phrases.

24. The title is taken from an earlier paragraph of the text.

25. Sister Rosemary Stets, O.S.F., "God's Continuing Providence in the Life of Father Walter Ciszek, S.J.," in the newsletter of the Father Walter Ciszek Prayer League, vol. 4, no. 5, 3–4.

26. The transcription of the manuscript comes from Lt. Col. William S. Lawton Jr., then vice president of Catholics United for the Faith. Father Ciszek was well-acquainted with him and with various other leading members of CUF. It is not clear, though, for whom—if anyone—the text was written. The six-page document is extremely important to understanding Father's spirituality. It is written in his usual Polish-American English, with less than the ordinary care for grammar

and punctuation, and often quite difficult to understand. Hence, substantial editing was necessary—naturally with maximum respect for the actual wording—to make the text accessible and let it convey as much as possible what Father Ciszek really wanted to say.

27. Bill and Daria Sockey, interview by John M. DeJak, December 15, 2011. When once asked how he could have seen the Blessed Trinity, Ciszek responded, "We have in our imagination physical images that we associate with spiritual things. And what God does is present those images to us when he wants us to physically see him." God appeared to him as he would expect to see the Trinity—with the images from his own imagination.

28. Here and in what follows, Father Ciszek repeatedly shifts from the first person to the second person; he still talks about his own experiences but ascribes to them a universal value: his "you" is everybody.

29. The original phrase was very obscure: "I cannot produce anything unless He gives it therefore, a patient waiting for Him to have, not for me to take condition, I did before, I always took condition of things." The current rephrasing certainly corresponds, at least in its meaning, with what follows.

30. The letters were written to Patricia Extance and are kept in the archives of the Father Walter Ciszek Prayer League at Shenandoah.

31. The following is based on Fr. Philaret Littlefield, interview by John M. DeJak, May 21, 2012.

32. What follows is a résumé of Fr. Francis Butler, S.S.J., interview by Joanne Wright, signed on February 25, 2013.

33. Maureen O'Brien, interview by Joanne Wright, signed on July 7, 2012.

34. The story is composed of an article published by Mother Marija of the Holy Spirit, O.C.D., in the newsletter of the Father Walter Ciszek Prayer League, no. 4 (1992): 7, and of an interview with her conducted by Joanne Wright, March 2012, and corrected in November of that year.

35. Based on the article "Community Vignettes" in the newsletter of the Walter Ciszek Prayer League, vol. 1, no. 1, (1985): 5–6; on the recollections of Sister Mary of Jesus, O.C.D., written February 19, 2013; and on Sister Andreja Vladia, O.C.D., interview by Joanne Wright, signed March 7, 2013.

36. "Dravest" is second person of the verb *to drive*. The meaning is, "You who drove Me away, drove love away from yourself."

37. Christ may indeed have accepted his suffering manfully. Ciszek probably meant to say "unemotionally," maybe thinking of his own bravado as a youth, when he did extreme physical exercises without showing pain or suffering.

38. The rhetoric that Father Ciszek is using here seems to exclude revealed truths as a proper object of faith. However, comparing these phrases with what he had said earlier, in the fourth and fifth paragraphs, it will be clear that he is merely (over)stressing a point. The *Catechism of the Catholic Church* (no. 150) teaches, "Faith is first of all a personal adherence to God. At the same time, and inseparably, it is a free assent to the whole truth that God has revealed."

39. That is, penetrates God's heart, touches him positively, for, of course, God can hear all songs.

40. "Wasted," where those are concerned who persevered in their rejection of Christ till the end. However, since we do not know their number, one cannot speak of "many" in an absolute sense.

41. The following is based on Fr. Philaret Littlefield, interview by John M. DeJak, May 21, 2011, and Carl and Marie Siriani, interviews by Joanne Wright, February 21, 2012, and by Fr. John Catoir, August 31, 2012.

42. Fr. Joseph Lingan, S.J., interview by Joanne Wright, signed May 15, 2013.

43. From Sr. Rosemary Stets, O.S.F., "Memories of Fr. Walter Ciszek," section A, 29–30.

44. Antoinette Rienzi, interview by Joanne Wright, signed September 26, 2013.

45. Bill and Daria Sockey, interview by John M. DeJak, December 15, 2011.

46. Bill and Daria Sockey, interview by John M. DeJak, December 15, 2011.

47. Marianne T. Breiter Bogunovich, interview by Joanne Wright, July 8, 2012.

48. Dolores Hartnett, interview by Joanne Wright, March 10, 2012.

49. From Carol Caraluzzi, "I Thank You, God, for Father Walter Ciszek," published in the newsletter of the Walter Ciszek Prayer League (Spring 2009).

50. On September 7, 1978, Walter Ciszek celebrated his fifty years as a Jesuit.

51. The letter has here a little drawing of an equilateral triangle, with on top faith and at the base prayer and humility.

52. The diagram in the letter shows two ovals with written in them, "outer circle is God's infinite love operating in vocation and experience in man"; "inner circle is our response of love to God's infinite love; faith-prayer-humility [the triangle] projects itself in service with obedience, with hope in God's infinite love—and gives gratitude and with assurance of salvation."

53. Cf. Note 3, *supra*.

54. Maureen O'Brien, interview by Joanne Wright, signed July 2, 2012.

55. Based on Dolores Hartnett, interview by Joanne Wright, March 10, 2012; Marianne T. Breiter Bogunovich, interview by Joanne Wright, July 8, 2012; and Sister Ruth Aubrey, A.S.C.J., signed April 20, 2013.

56. The following is taken from Dr. and Mrs. James Schaller, interview by John M. DeJak, February 2, 2012, and revised and signed April 17, 2012.

57. The following is based on notes from Carol Caraluzzi, published in the 2009 spring issue of the newsletter of the Father Walter Ciszek Prayer League, and on Patricia Extance, interview by Joanne Wright, April 16, 2012.

58. Gerald Lilore, interview by Joanne Wright, signed May 19, 2013, with added fragments from Gerald Lilore, "Apostle to Siberia: Walter Ciszek 1904–1984" in Jeanne Kun, *In the Land I Have Shown You: The Stories of 16 North American Saints and Christian Heroes* (Frederick, MD: The Word Among Us, 2002), 213–19.

59. Recollections of Sister Mary of Jesus, O.C.D., written February 19, 2013.

60. Sister Rosemary Stets, O.S.F., wrote down her memories of Father Walter Ciszek between January 1987 and June 1992 in two sections, A

and B. The three quotations are from section A, respectively June 7 and May 18, 1987.

61. The commentary on the first eighteen chapters of the Gospel of Matthew, presumably composed in the second half of 1977, is missing. Also nonexistent are Father Ciszek's reflections on the first fifteen chapters of John's Gospel, but maybe they were never, or not yet, written.

62. Given that the biblical reflections selected here were often mere drafts, meant to be revised thoroughly before publication, a greater liberty has been taken in editing them so as to make Father Ciszek's thoughts more intelligible and accessible, without betraying his characteristic style and vocabulary. No square brackets were used to indicate added or omitted words, because it would have made the reflections difficult to read.

63. Here Walter Ciszek, led by his great devotion to Our Lady, seems to exaggerate her privileges. There are actually no grounds for ascribing to her the beatific vision during her earthly life, as is proved by Luke 1:45: "Blessed art thou who has believed." On the other hand, it is consonant with the dignity of the Mother of God that to her are attributed a high degree of supernatural knowledge of faith and, after her conception of Christ, a special grace of mystical contemplation (cf. Thomas Aquinas, *Summa Theologiae*, III, 27, 5 ad 3). Only in that sense did Mary enjoy a (not "the") vision of God while living in this world. (Ludwig Ott, *Fundamentals of Catholic Dogma* [St. Louis, MO: B. Herder, 1957), 198.]

64. The following is based on recollections of Sr. Mary of Jesus, O.C.D., written on February 19, 2013, and on Sr. Andreja Vladia, O.C.D., interview by Joanne Wright, signed March 7, 2013, and Antoinette Rienzi, interview by Joanne Wright, signed September 26, 2013.

65. Joseph Barinas, interview by John M. DeJak, March 15, 2012.

66. This quote and the following are from Sr. Rosemary Stets's manuscript "Memories of Fr. Walter Ciszek," respectively from section A, pp. 1, 16, and 18; and from section B, p. 28.

67. From a letter written by Mary Zentkovich to Sister Evangeline Ciszek, O.S.F., dated September 27, 1985, and kept in the archives of the Father Walter Ciszek Prayer League.

68. The following is based on Sr. Lucille Cutrone, C.F.R., "My Experiences with Fr. Walter Ciszek, S.J.," published in the winter 2007 issue of the

newsletter of the Father Walter Ciszek Prayer League; on Antoinette
Rienzi, interview by Joanne Wright, signed September 26, 2013; on
Mary Zentkovich, interview by Joanne Wright, March 2012; and on
Sister Santa Priolo, M.P.F., interview by Joanne Wright, April 2012; as
well as on a letter written by Mary Zentkovich to Sister Evangeline
Ciszek, O.S.F., dated September 27, 1985; on memories of Sister Santa
Priolo published in the Prayer League newsletter, vol. 2, no. 3 (Summer
1987); and on a longer version of these memories kept in the Prayer
League archives.

69. Mother Marija Shields, O.C.D., interview by Joanne Wright, March
2012, and corrected on November 11 of that year.

70. Two days before his death he had made his confession with his superior,
Fr. John Long, S.J.

71. Fr. Dominic Maruca, S.J., interview by John M. DeJak,
January 24, 2012.

72. Father Kolvenbach's letter (composed by Fr. Daniel Flaherty, S.J.) can be
found in *National Jesuit News* (March 1985): 15.

73. The card is conserved in the *Archivum Romanum Societatis Iesu*, part of
the General Curia of the Society of Jesus in Rome.

74. Maureen O'Brien, interview by Joanne Wright, signed July 7, 2012.
Other sources confirm that on October 5, 1973, Walter Ciszek began
his annual retreat at Wernersville.

75. The following is from Sr. Rosemary Stets's manuscript "Memories of Fr.
Walter Ciszek," section A, 18–19.

76. It may have been inspired by the Morning Offering of the Apostleship
of Prayer: "O Jesus, through the Immaculate Heart of Mary, I offer you
my prayers, works, joys, and sufferings of this day, in union with the
Holy Sacrifice of the Mass throughout the world. I offer them for all
the intentions of your Sacred Heart: the salvation of souls, reparation
for sins, the reunion of all Christians. I offer them for the intentions of
your Bishops and of all Apostles of Prayer, and in particular for those
recommended by our Holy Father this month. Amen." In June—July
1979, Walter Ciszek wrote a series of conferences on Reparation in
which he commented upon this prayer.

77. Letter from Mary Zentkovich to Sister Evangeline Ciszek, O.S.F.,
September 27, 1985, kept in the Prayer League archives.

78. Sr. Rosemary Stets, "Memories of Father Walter Ciszek, S.J.," kept in the Father Walter Ciszek Prayer League archives.

79. This funeral homily by Fr. John Long, S.J., was published in *National Jesuit News* (March 1985): 15.

80. This paragraph is based on the homily given by Fr. Daniel Flaherty, S.J., on December 11, 1988, and published in the newsletter of the Father Walter Ciszek Prayer League, vol. 2, no. 7 (Spring 1989).

81. Statement of Fr. Daniel L. Flaherty, S.J., to Fr. Marc Lindeijer, S.J., September 17, 2010.

82. Predecessor to the Soviet KGB.

83. From the homily given by Fr. Daniel Flaherty, S.J., on December 11, 1988, and published in the newsletter of the Father Walter Ciszek Prayer League, vol. 2, no. 7 (Spring 1989).

84. In 1966 and 1970, Walter Ciszek overworked himself, but he had his (first) heart attack only in December 1972, i.e., shortly before finishing *He Leadeth Me*.

85. Fr. Philaret Littlefield, interview by John M. DeJak, May 21, 2012.

86. Mother Marija Shields, O.C.D., interview by Joanne Wright, March 2012, and corrected on November 11 of that year.

87. Marianne T. Breiter Bogunovich, interview by Joanne Wright, July 8, 2012.

88. The manuscript is kept in the archives of the Father Walter Ciszek Prayer League in Shenandoah.

About the Author

Walter J. Ciszek, S.J. (1904–1984), an American Jesuit and native of Shenandoah, PA, is currently under consideration for canonization in the Roman Catholic Church. He spent 23 years in the Soviet Union, first in Moscow's Lubianka Prison and then in various work camps in Siberia. In those brutal conditions, he remained true to his faith and his priesthood, serving his fellow prisoners and setting an example of Christ-like love. Upon his return to the United States in 1963, he was assigned to the John XXIII Ecumenical Center, Bronx, New York City, where, until his death, he was a much sought-after retreat master and spiritual director. He is the author of *With God in Russia* and *He Leadeth Me* and is arguably one of the preeminent spiritual writers of the latter half of the twentieth century.

About the Editors

Dutch Jesuit Father Marc Lindeijer (1966) worked as assistant to the Postulator General of the Society of Jesus from 2009 until 2016 and was responsible for the cause for canonization of Fr. Walter J. Ciszek, S.J. He has a doctorate in church history and is currently a member of the hagiographical Association of the Bollandists in Brussels and professor of church history at the Interdiocesan Seminary Bovendonk in the Netherlands. His most recent publications, among others in *Bibliotheca Sanctorum, La Civiltà Cattolica,* and *L'Osservatore Romano,* have been on (future) Jesuit saints José de Anchieta, Jacques Berthieu, Felice Maria Cappello, Pierre Favre, and John Hardon. He also writes movie reviews for the Dutch *Ignis Webmagazine.*

John M. DeJak, an attorney and Catholic educator, is a researcher for the Cause for Canonization of Fr. Walter J. Ciszek, S.J. He practiced law and served on active duty as an officer in the U.S. Army's 10th Mountain Division prior to being named the founding headmaster of two private high schools in the Twin Cities area: Chesterton Academy and Holy Spirit Academy. He has taught Latin, Greek, literature, government, and theology in high schools in Chicago, Cleveland, the Twin Cities, and Ann Arbor. His articles have appeared in *Chronicles, The Bellarmine Forum Magazine, Gilbert Magazine, The Distributist Review,* and *The St. Austin Review.* He and his wife, Ann, and their eight children live in Saline, Michigan.